THE
HOLY
VIBLE

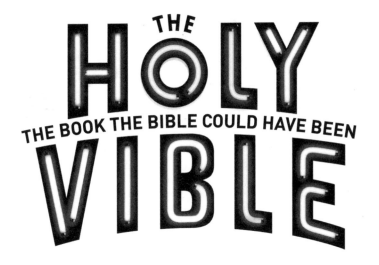

THE HOLY VIBLE

THE BOOK THE BIBLE COULD HAVE BEEN

ELIS JAMES AND JOHN ROBINS

TRAPEZE

First published in Great Britain in 2018 by Trapeze,
This paperback edition published in 2019
by Trapeze
an imprint of The Orion Publishing Group Ltd
Carmelite House, 50 Victoria Embankment,
London EC4Y 0DZ

An Hachette UK company

1 3 5 7 9 10 8 6 4 2

A CIP catalogue record for this book is
available from the British Library.

ISBN (Paperback): 978 1 4091 8238 2

Printed in Great Britain by Clays Ltd, Elcograf S.p.A.

www.orionbooks.co.uk

To John, the funniest man I know.

Firstly, to Brian May.
Your unique tone, perfectly pitched solos, and impeccable
guitar orchestration have been my constant companion,
through good times and bad.

Oh, come on!

Secondly, to John Deacon.
Whose subtle runs are the beating heart of the Queen sound.
You taught me that sometimes the smallest flourishes make the
biggest difference.

Are you serious?!

Thirdly, to Roger Taylor.
For so many triplets, fills and crescendos, I cannot thank you
enough. You were never fussy, always full-on.

We had a deal. I bumped Isy down for you! . . . And Beti!
My only child, for God's sake!

And finally, to Freddie.
Who shone so bright, and left so soon. Though you are gone,
your power, your passion, your drive, talent and charm
continue to illuminate the corners of our lives like no other.
Though we never met . . .

You never met any of them!

I've met Roger twice and Brian four times. You were there when
we interviewed him!

OK, fair enough, but you've never met John Deacon . . .

No, but I do know someone who knows where he lives, and I'm
perilously close to accessing his postcode . . .

God, you're weird . . .

. . . though we never met . . .

Are you honestly doing this?

All right, fine! . . . Jeez . . .

To Elis James, a capable broadcaster.

Contents

[Note for parents/underage legends. Though care was taken not to utter too many non-radio-friendly swears, the following chapters do contain language that if said on air would get us sacked or at the very least cause Vin to play *(What's the Story) Morning Glory?* in its entirety: A, J, L, O, P, S, T, V, W, X]

Introduction

In the beginning was the word, and the word was with Robins (because Elis was running late). And the word was 'Vibe'.

Hello, I'm John Robins, comedian, digital DJ and vibe-magnet. To my left is the man who, after adding it last minute to a poster advertising a Carmarthen drop-in centre for the over-60s, is the man responsible for the first recorded use of the word 'Vibe' in west Wales, Mr Elis James ...

Elis, what does 'Vibe' mean?

Well, it's a noun, a verb and a proper noun (if you live in a place called 'Vibe', or, indeed, if your name is Mr or Mrs Vibe).

Let's start with the noun. A vibe is a state of mind, a state of place or a state of atmosphere. 'This pub has a good vibe,' you might say. Or 'This pub is an excellent vibe-hub!' you might exclaim. Or 'My thoughts turn increasingly to a pub-vibe,' you might write in your memoirs.

Verb-wise, the word represents a fluid act of thought or expression. When the mics are five seconds from going live on your commercial digital indie radio show, and your producer is creating a seriously bad vibe ...

... noun ...

by chastising you for being distracted by Ronnie O'Sullivan's/Neil

1

Kinnock's Wikipedia page, you might say 'Chill out, Vin! We'll just vibe it! ...'

... verb ...

before stuttering over your words or creating a passable riff about how well suited a Cadbury's Creme Egg is for throwing.

The word can also be used in place of other, more boring words. 'How're things?' becomes 'What's the vibe?' And before you know it, your class of Year Nines know you just *get it.*

You're one of them, and can now stop risking serious groin strain by sitting on your chair the wrong way round.

The word can also be used to address a sensitive topic in a gentle manner. 'How's the vibe toilet-wise?' The Lovely Robin might text you, having just got the panicked 3am message you sent from the loo when he woke at eight for work. So then, Elis, what is *The Holy Vible*?

Well, John, it's a kind of A to Z of the vibe.

A 'Vibephabet,' if you will?

Exactly. In fact that was one of the many rejected titles.

Indeed it was. Shall we recap the others?

Good idea. Other titles proposed were *Paradise Revibed*, *Vibe and Prejudice*, *The Catcher in the Vibe*, *David Viberfield* and *The Canterbury Vibes*, but as we discussed, why not aim for top billing and take on the big one!

Quite right. And, even if I do say so myself, I think we've improved in a number of key areas. For example, although God created heaven and earth in a week, what he singularly failed to do was write at length about Ronnie O'Sullivan, Carmarthen Town Centre ...

And non-dairy milk alternatives ...

Quite. Though, in fairness, he did cover shame, grief and, to some extent, post-apocalyptic mind scenarios, AKA the Book of Revelation. However, I think it's fair to say that this is, quite literally, the book the Bible could have been. Over the next 370 or so pages we'll be laying down thought pieces . . .

Topic symposiums . . .

Opinion storms . . .

Chat islands . . .

And wisdom tablets, in an easily digestible format. Our two distinct voices of Welshness on the one hand, and learning on the other, will be laid out by the fonts you see here. Elis's stout pull-yoursocksupmanship is displayed in the hearty type of Gotham Narrow, and the lithe, dexterous, engaging prose of Robins, illuminated (and illuminating) in the stylish, authoritative type of Kepler.

It is worth pointing out that if you're reading this on a Kindle . . .

AKA 'Space Scroll' . . .

'Cyborg Sheet' . . .

'Matrix Tablet' . . .

Then firstly, what's the weather like in your futuristic space hub? Have Wales qualified for Euro 2098?

And secondly, please initiate the default font settings to get the full impact of our back and forth . . .

To and fro . . .

Hither and thither.

Initially you wanted your chapters in 28pt bold, underlined Impact font, didn't you, John?

Yes I did, and if I'm honest, I think the book suffers from its absence.

I think it was an issue of space in the end . . . And ink. Also, being able to distinguish which of us wrote what will hopefully go some way to exploding the myth – that John has been propagating for a few months now – that he has done all of the donkey work because I am bad with deadlines.

Well, that's as maybe, but if readers could imagine all my bits in 28pt Impact bold underlined, I think that's very much the tone in which a lot of my sections were conceived.

Like screaming on a billboard?

Exactly! Yes, when reading any excerpts from my chapters, please do scream them for the full effect.

You see, over the past four years there are many topics that we've referenced, hinted towards . . .

Given delicious tastes of . . .

Quite, and we thought it would be nice to have some space to expand on them, spend some time with them . . .

Make love to them . . .

Yes, because, remarkably, over 600 hours of commercial digital indie radio wasn't enough for us to really get to grips with the hot topics of Gorky's Zygotic Mynci . . .

Correct motorway lanesmanship[1] . . .

Carmarthen as a cultural hub . . .

And which of Frank Zappa's classical albums to prioritise . . .

If you are a listener to the show, we hope this book is something to treasure. If you are coming at this book from another one of our comedic endeavours (the numerous sitcoms and radio comedy shows I have appeared on, my appearances on sports programmes such as *The Premier League Show* or *Fighting Talk* or maybe you saw the YouTube clip of John's appearance at the 2011 Chortle Fast Fringe/the advert for BHS he was on as a kid in 1990) . . .

Or maybe you've read the Wikipedia page for the Edinburgh Comedy Awards[2] and wondered who the 2017 winner was . . .[3]

Well, whatever has brought you here, we think there is plenty for you to enjoy.

Also, there are some useful appendices to serve as definitive references on some topics, a few of which are based on research carried out by devoted, hard-working and, I can only assume, time-rich fans.

Yes, our PCD PhDs.

Students of the vibe.

BA Hons of Badinage.

So, we do hope you enjoy it . . .

1 See **N: Normal, How to Be.**
2 https://en.wikipedia.org/wiki/Edinburgh_Comedy_Awards
3 [EJ] (*One* of the winners.)

We really enjoyed writing it

You haven't finished it yet!

Not this again . . .

I should remind you that our advance is dependent on us handing in the completed book on time. Or, in layman's terms, *my* half of the advance is dependent on *you* handing *your* half of the book in on time. Because, as we both know, I was wrapped up, with a month to spare.

Yes, John, but I have a wife and child!

We all have our crosses to bear.

And your cross is an empty seat in front of an empty table in an empty house.

Or, you could say, an efficient chair, in front of a punctual table, in an organised house.

Yes, I'll give you that, the silence you live in is very well organised.

Oh God, I'd love to alphabetise silence.

Maybe that could be the sequel?

An *A to Z of Silence*?! It sounds like bliss!

Anyway, before John gets to work on *Peace, Quiet, Reticence* . . .

Just making a note of those . . .

We begin with 'A Day in the Life of Elis and John', where we each give a glimpse of what life is really like for the other, off air . . .[4]

---

4 [JR] My account of 'A Day in the Life of Elis James' comes first, for the simple reason that it was finished three months in advance of Elis's chapter.

A:

A Day in the Life of Elis and John by John Robins

Elis will probably be woken by his daughter jumping on his bed at 5am because he has made his choice and it's too late now.[5] After silencing his 'coal on coal' alarm clock (to him, the sound of a traditional hammer and bell alarm is 'the hunting cry of the capitalists'), he will race to a cold shower because it makes him feel alive/'like an athlete from the former USSR'. I, Robins, do not have cold showers because I am not serving time in borstal/ on a gap year. I prefer a warm shower because it makes me feel warm.

At 7am he will then eat (slowly) a bowl of Coco Pops or Special K, because he has the morning eating habits of a child/dieting menopausal woman. I must admit, since the Edinburgh Festival 2012,[6] I, too, no longer enjoy the lie-ins of my 20s. The potent mix

---

5 Ironically, he's made his bed, but *doesn't* lie in it.
6 'Fiercely intelligent, but also genuinely sympathetic' ***** *ThreeWeeks*.

of a Red Bull habit (four years clean) and a disabling infatuation with a girl (twenty-five years dirty[7]) meant I spent that month in 2012 waking up at 7am every day, heart pounding, mind racing, mid-scream. I wonder how the pen-and-ink sketch of that scene would fit into Red Bull's quaint marketing campaign. That said, I haven't a bad word to say against them; I've long been calling for pre-teens to be sold alarmingly high levels of caffeine. Like I said, you've made your choice and it's too late now. You wouldn't give a ten-year-old a double espresso with four sugars and wonder why they're experiencing unusual emotional peaks and troughs, so don't come crying to me when a can of Monster puts them in detention. That said, I know for a fact that Elis and Isy limit their three-year-old's caffeine intake to one cup of tea in the morning, a mocha with lunch and a flat white before bed. And I, for one, applaud them.

By 11am, he will be over halfway through his Coco Pops, and will leave the chocolaty dregs to soak until dinner, when he'll have another go for dessert. By midnight, the bowl will be well and truly three-quarters finished. My breakfast routine couldn't be more different. It's dynamic, efficient and compelling.

Depending on digestion issues/night terrors, I will wake almost exclusively at 7.46am, or one minute before my alarm is set.[8] I will then make for the toilet. *However*, before toileting I will go downstairs to put on the kettle, so that when I emerge from the toilet the water will be at the perfect temperature for my morning cup of tea.[9] This is an example of a timesaving device

---

7 This sounds more sexual than I had intended. It is simply a reference to the fact it has been twenty-five years since I was first disabled by infatuation.

8 A superpower I have yet to discover the advantage of.

9 One bag Earl Grey, one bag normal, three-quarters of a sugar. Brewed for a minimum of a minute, or thirty stirs, if time is pressing. Add (almond) milk until it is the colour of healthily tanned skin/RAL 8023 (Orange Brown). See **Appendix v: Non-Dairy Milk Notes** for more detail.

I call 'household efficiency'. It's a regime I have invented since being forced to live on my own, through circumstances beyond my control, and I love it! I would say that it helps pass the time, but that couldn't be further from the truth; quite the opposite, it helps *save* the time. And not just time, but resources and mess. For example, on the rare occasions I need to blow my nose, I may first use the tissue to wipe condensation from the window pane/ excess sunflower spread from a knife. This not only saves on tissues, but on rot damage to wooden window frames/crumbs in spread. Classic! Having saved valuable seconds through 'household efficiency', I will then return to bed to check the money markets, bitcoin charts, gold price and savings best-buy tables for an hour to an hour and a half. Though the money markets have a limited direct effect on my life, it's good to stay abreast, and if the FTSE drops I'm perfectly poised to make any necessary adjustments, like a financial jaguar ready to pounce.

For an hour to an hour and a half . . .   *EJ*

I often think of Elis in these moments, how unprepared he is to react instantly to nuanced changes in the price of gold. I couldn't tell you when the next crash is coming, but one thing I do know is that it will catch that man unawares as he plays with his daughter, embraces his partner or runs errands to maintain his family home. He's made his choice, and it's too late now. As Warren Buffett said: 'Only when the tide goes out, do you discover who's been swimming naked.'[10]

Following his first cereal tussle of the day, Elis will begin one of his thrice-daily YouTube sessions. After running through the directions to nursery with his three-year-old daughter, he will

10 Of finance, not the actual tide. Though it's true for both.

stand at the window to check she turns the right way out of the front door before loading up his favourite website. He will immediately become lost in a nostalgic realm of goals from the 90s, clothes from the 90s, music from the 90s and mines from the 90s. Though it's not just the 90s! No, Elis's interests are broad. He will also queue up countless videos of goals from the 60s, clothes from the 60s, music from the 60s and mines from the 60s. He'll spice things up with the odd speech from Neil Kinnock at a Labour Party conference in the 80s or footage of a rural Welsh community in the 50s. When he finally realises he has fifteen missed calls, the penny will drop that he needed to leave half an hour ago for an appointment/job/meeting/commercial digital indie radio show.

A period of intense activity will then commence in which, while uttering a string of expletives, Elis will attempt to complete several tasks in such a short period of time that he does not complete any to a satisfactory standard: showering, drying, brushing teeth, moisturising, dressing and, inexplicably, ironing. While any normal person would be able to complete all these activities in under twenty minutes, having given himself *minus thirty minutes*, we get to the beating heart of Elis James: poor household efficiency. He will then spend a further ten minutes looking for his phone/glasses/keys/wallet before leaving without his phone/glasses/keys/wallet. One day, I will secretly instal CCTV in his house to confirm that Elis's catchphrase 'Sorry I'm late, it was the trains' is, as I suspect, a complete fiction.[11]

My mid-mornings are far more dynamic. If the previous night

---

11 A quick note on lateness caused by trains: it is entirely possible for a train to be late and for you to still arrive at your destination early. It depends on what train you catch. For proof, see every time I've ever been delayed by a train.

[EJ] I've never had to broadcast from a train. See podcast episode 86 'Tick Tock Robins'.

[JR] A podcast that, if I'd had my way, would have been named 'Elis's Lost Wallet', the real scandal of that episode, which got lost in a social media storm in a teacup.

has been booze-free, I'll tick off the day on my 2018 Queen calendar in red pen, like in a film. The 2018 Queen calendar was a gift in the Radio X Secret Santa and whoever chose it couldn't have been more on the money. My 2017 booze-free days were ticked off on a joke office calendar made up of photos of a researcher called Tom that I stole from the writing room of Channel 4's *The Last Leg*. Little did that researcher know that amusing photos of him in a state of drunkenness, posing with false breasts or asleep on a minibus, would one day be adorned with the drinking record of the most challenging and award-winning[12] year of my life.[13]

I will then make a coffee. '*But hang on, John?! You've not eaten yet!*' Pah! Would Mervyn King 'eat breakfast'?! I think not! He'd be too busy engrossed in the financial matters of the day, the UK bullion reserves, the strength of the pound, interest rates, placating doves, encouraging bears, monitoring hawks and all kinds of animal husbandry that a former head of the Bank of England takes in his stride. It is with similar disregard for food that, like King (and Sherlock Holmes before him), I will approach the challenges of my day. That said, if I'm hungry I may have a vegan yoghurt.[14]

For Elis the challenges of the day may include acting in a BBC Three sitcom in which he plays a truant child, acting in a BBC Two sitcom in which he plays a sexual deviant or hosting a BBC Wales show in which he takes an English comedian friend around Wales. Having turned down—

(Not been offered)   *EJ*

---

12 See picture section.
13 Dry January got off to a fine start, but I must admit February was a car crash. (See picture section.)
14 Alpro: strawberry and banana or pear and passionfruit. Superb.

—parts in all of these projects, I'm absolutely fine with it. I love how Elis challenges himself in increasingly testing/implausible roles. And I'm more than happy to watch the first few minutes of the first episode of anything he turns his hand to, on iPlayer, if it's still up. Elis is comfortable with my refusing all opportunities to be a household name as he knows that A) my integrity can't be bought and B) there's only one role I was born to play: John Robins. And he respects that. And anyway, even if I *were* a commissioner at BBC Wales, I'd never have given the green light to *James and Robins*. It doesn't have the alliteration of *James and Jupp*, and, as BBC Wales knows all too well, alliteration in a title is half the job done. That said, if I *were* a commissioner at BBC Wales I would have responded to my own letters of complaint/grievance in a more timely fashion, or at least had the forethought to set up an E-Mail account.

When Elis isn't shaving thrice daily to convince the world he's fifteen years his own junior,[15] he's providing voiceovers for an array of companies through a voiceover agent I got him in with in the first place. From the Welsh Electoral Commission to the Ford Transit, Elis James has a voice you can trust/fulfil ethnic quotas with. He has the calming yet assertive timbre of a humble herdsman reassuring an errant ram. I prefer to pick and choose my projects, and the voiceover agent, which we share and which I got Elis in with in the first place, agrees. My voice is not a toy to be tossed hither and thither. It is more suited to signature events such as state funerals, coronations and the opening of Parliament. And, as we all know, those events don't come around every day! I, for one, would happily never record a voiceover again if it means we have another twenty years of HRH Queen Elizabeth II #YouGoLiz! That said, I am available

15 See BBC Three sitcom, *#Crimes*.
  [EJ] *CRIMS*, John! *CRIMS*! IT'S CALLED *CRIMS*!

for voiceovers and anyone interested should contact Sue Terry Voices.[16]

No, my afternoons are more erudite affairs. I will check my E-Mails, the BBC Sport website, Ronnie O'Sullivan's Wikipedia page and Martin Lewis's MoneySavingExpert website before updating my accounts. Once I have performed these tasks six or seven times, it's usually almost 4pm. At which time thoughts inevitably turn to the pub and/or my beer fridge. Or, if I'm doing Dry January, a low-level anxiety will slowly build to genuine physical discomfort before erupting into a furnace of fear that will keep me awake until 3am. On the rare occasions I have a gig, meeting or commercial digital indie radio show I will arrive an hour earlier than an hour before I need to be there. I do this by a simple system of catching the train before the train that, if it were late, would still bring me to my destination an hour early. A train I have, at time of going to press, yet to miss.

Apart from that one time . . .   *EJ*

At around 4pm I sometimes take a walk in rural Buckinghamshire and reflect on how the seasons mirror my mood: autumn (cruelty of passing time, nostalgia, loss of innocence), winter (bleak thoughts, loss [general], emotional wasteland), spring (rebirth [failed], potential [unfulfilled], awakening [early due to bad dreams]) and summer (too hot).

While I ponder the great questions of our time (perfect pub/perfect three drinks/perfect five drinks/if a teleporter by your front door opened on one pub, which would it be?/which three drinks would it contain?/which five drinks would it contain?),

---

16 Subject to fee and usage agreements. Will not advertise gambling products, companies or anyone, directly or indirectly, involved in the gambling industry.

[EJ] He's fine with fast-food restaurants, though.

Elis will be travelling home from filming to make sure his daughter made it back from nursery, before popping a lasagne in the microwave and settling down to watch *Match of the Day* (from 1994, again). He may pause, following a particularly baggy shirt or thunderous Andy Cole volley, to think about baggy shirts or how nothing in life is as satisfying as a baggy-shirted volley thunderer from the 90s. This is the Elis I know and love. It's where our interests converge – The Past. For me, it's my own past; for him, that of society. In the same way I can glance at a photo of my friend Chris drinking a pint of ale in The Star pub, Oxford, 2004[17] and be paralysed by nostalgic grief, so Elis can see a sketch of a trade unionist in *Punch* or the sponsor on the Sheffield Wednesday 1993 away kit[18] and wish, with every cell in his body, that it was back then. They were the best of times, they were the best of times.

It's at this point that Elis will then fulfil his duties as a father, which, I have to say, he does with aplomb. First, he will make sure she is fed, washed, clean-toothed and ready for bed at the appropriate time (remarkable when you consider how incapable he is of doing this for himself, a 39[ish]-year-old man), before reading her bedtime story, *A History of Welsh Communists*. I can see him now, beaming with pride as he reads tales of various battles won for miners – working hours, sick pay, compensation and safety – just loud enough so that she can hear from her room upstairs.

I, however, have some seven or eight hours to fill. Living alone with a mind as fertile as my own means that there is an ongoing conversation happening in my own head 24/7, 365. I'm sure fans of the show would pay literally billions to tune in, but there are times it can become arduous and impossible to escape from. Often in these moments I will involuntarily utter a phrase

17 See picture section.
18 [EJ] Sanderson.

out loud, giving insight into the ideas/inspirations/emotional tumult silently raging inside. In a typical day spent alone the entirety of my emitted speech may read something like this:

7.46am.	'Fuck's sake . . .'
7.46am.	'Always, always a minute before . . .'
7.47am.	'I'll just turn that off.'
8.56am.	'Could hit $1,300 an ounce, could do . . .'
10.21am.	'And then back-to-back Masters wins. Selby must be so jealous!'
10.24am.	'What no one mentions is how good he is into the middle pockets . . .'
10.26am.	'And left-handed!'
12.40pm.	'Hello to you, our old friend hummus . . .'
1.25pm.	'Thanks, Lynne . . .'
1.26pm.	'D'you fancy a curry?'
1.27pm.	'Help me out, mate . . .'
1.28pm.	'Probably me next . . .'
1.30pm.	'This is where the idiot lives . . .'
1.31pm.	'D'you fancy a curry? . . . D'you fancy a curry? . . . D'you fancy a curry?'[19]
2.04pm.	'. . . carry them in separately and then nothing gets spilled.'
2.05pm.	'. . . pop that in the bin on the way back, and that goes on the stairs to take up to the bathroom later . . . Classic household efficiency!'
2.10pm.	'Oh look, shredders are on offer at Robert Dyas.'
2.22pm.	'. . . argh, God . . .'
2.23pm.	'You can't drink now, you mad bastard!'
3.58pm.	'. . . and they weren't just a front man . . .'

---

19 A classic Partridge quote attack.

4.10pm.	'But you don't *need* a shredder . . .'
4.17pm.	'Hello . . . Hiya Chris . . . right . . . that sounds cool . . . what's the money? . . . Sure thing! . . . I can make any of those dates, what about El? . . . what do you mean he's filming?! What's he fucking filming now, for crying out loud?! . . . Fuck's sake . . . Yeah, will do.'
4.18pm.	'Hi, El, it's me. Give me a call back when you get this.'
4.40pm.	'Hey, did you get my message? Saw you liked Josh's tweet so you must have your phone. Call me back ASAP.'
5.26pm.	'Answer your fucking phone!'
5.27pm.	'Hi Miles, it's Robins. Is Elis with you? OK, can you get him to give me a ring when he's out?'
6.01pm.	'Pint of Tribute please.'
6.39pm.	'Yeah, same again.'
7.12pm.	'Yep . . . No, same glass is fine.'
7.45pm.	'What rums do you have? . . . with Diet Coke please . . . Yeah, Pepsi's fine.'
9.00pm.	'But you can't peel the fucking film lid off cos when you do the fucking edges comes off and you're left with the fucking middle bit so you have to use a fucking knife! Fuck's sake, Quorn!'
10.40pm.	'I work all day and get half drunk at night, waking at four to soundless dark I stare, in time the curtain edges will grow light, till then I see what's really always there, unresting death a whole day nearer now.'
10.42pm.	'. . . asks what the maximum break prize was before a ball was potted! Then made one! The audacity! Who else could do that? Who else?! Tell me!'
10.43pm.	'Selby wouldn't have the balls . . . literally . . . God, you're good.'

And by then, I'm more than ready to lie awake for a couple of hours before bed. Bliss.

Elis's evenings will be much less eventful affairs. With his daughter tucked up in bed, he might have half a bottle of Doom Bar in front of a programme in which George Monbiot makes an appearance as a talking head, before he has to switch over to some godawful dancing programme, reluctantly watched by new dads across the country who just can't be arsed to argue anymore. By which time, he'll have lost interest in the Doom Bar. Thus, as I'm sure we can all agree, I win.

1–0 Robins!

A:

A Day in the Life of Elis and John by Elis James

7.01am. John wakes with a start. He immediately leans over to give his Edinburgh Comedy Award a gentle kiss and this calms him[20] – he can already feel the anxiety of his dream subside. John shakes his head dismissively at the memory of it. As if dream-John would forget that Ronnie O'Sullivan's fifth 147 break was against Drew Henry during the 2001 LG Cup! Of course, being held at gunpoint is stressful, but not stressful enough to forget something like that! It's almost as if his subconscious is taunting him. John puts the Edinburgh Comedy Award down next to his sleeping bag and the Queen hoodie he uses for a pillow, and ponders. It was definitely the right decision to have the word 'Perrier' engraved onto it. He just wishes he'd told the engraver that the word 'Perrier' has three r's in it. Oh well. The prospect of letting

---

20 Before he won the Edinburgh Comedy Award (formerly known as the Perrier) in August 2017, John would calm himself after a bad dream by kissing his Bronze Duke of Edinburgh Award.

off some steam by writing a scathing online review of T&S Quality Engraving Chesham prompts him to get out of bed.

8.06am. In south London, Elis's[21] house is a finely oiled machine. It's difficult to imagine anyone making toast for a three-year-old and reading an online article about the best stretches to avoid shin splints at the same time, but years of lateness and worrying about medial tibial stress syndrome have actually made Elis[22] quite efficient in the mornings. And, if the article about shin splints requires Elis[23] to sit and think for a moment, Isy can always take over.

7.51am. Having written the online review of his local engravers and posted it under the pseudonym 'Back Chat',[24] John is beginning to get thirsty, so he walks into the bathroom and drinks straight from the tap. In a minute, he'll wash up his cup and plate from the previous night to make his breakfast, but that can wait – he needs to check on his investments. The drift mine, an hour north of Phoenix, Arizona, he has invested in has had a bad night on the Dow Jones, and he is financially down on his luck. Within seconds, he is on the phone to his elderly neighbour, Olive, apologising profusely for the piercing scream. He considers texting Elis about it before remembering that Elis won't understand any of the words he's using, so he walks back to his bedroom to give the award another calming kiss. John sets his alarm for 8am and decides to treat himself to an award cuddle in the

---

21 [JR] Elis, you've accidentally gone 'third person' here.

22 [JR] And again!

23 [JR] Oh I see, it's intentional. Nice touch!

24 'Back Chat' is a reference to the John Deacon-penned single from the 1982 Queen album *Hot Space*. The single stalled at number 40 in the UK single charts and John Deacon has made it clear that he loathes the accompanying video. It's one of two Queen-inspired pseudonyms John uses for online reviews; the other is 'The Loser in the End', Roger Taylor's sole songwriting contribution to 1974's *Queen II*, and the pseudonym John uses when writing bad TripAdvisor reviews of restaurants or service station hotels he has stayed in.

sleeping bag for a few minutes before checking his E-Mails. Being this busy is tiring!

8.38am. Elis is on the way to a voice-over. He's actually slightly late because he was reading Tough Mudder testimonials on Facebook, but the people at Saatchi & Saatchi can wait. He's halfway through writing 'remind them about John' on his hand before he starts smiling. How curious that the accident of birth that is having a Welsh accent could be so advantageous over John in the notoriously competitive voiceover game. Elis considers telling the team at Saatchi & Saatchi about the Scottish accent John does to infuriate Gordon Smart, before thinking better of it.

9.04am. Having been staring at his cup and plate drying slowly on the drainer for over 25 minutes, John decides it's time to start drafting letters of apology to some of the people he thinks he upset at primary school. Through a combination of skills gleaned from reading Sherlock Holmes books and the fact The Lovely Robin's mother still lives in the area, John has access to all of the addresses he needs. He sits down, has a quick check of the price of gold, makes sure the award is safely tucked into his sleeping bag and begins to type. This morning, he is typing a letter of apology to a girl whose rubber he borrowed without asking in February 1990. After furnishing the letter with a few Philip Larkin quotes, a Dark Star brewery T-shirt and a Frank Zappa mix CD, he decides that actually posting it would be insane, and so he places it in the drawer with all the others. This has been John's morning routine for over fifteen years. Feelings of historic guilt now momentarily assuaged, he crosses himself in front of his Freddie Mercury altar before going for a piss.

12.07pm. The voice-over was a success! As a treat, Elis goes to browse the football boots in his local Sports Direct, which somehow takes over two hours.

2.12pm. Some local Brownies named Polly and Emily arrive to check on John. They are accompanied by group leader Brown Owl. There is no badge for checking on digital DJs, although Brown Owl has said 'she will look into it'. Polly and Emily ask if he'd like any washing hung out, but John replies that he is wearing his Queen T-shirt and the other one is on the back seat of his car in case of emergencies. Brown Owl accepts John's offer of a cup of tea and, after she's finished drinking it, John gives the cup a quick rinse and has a coffee. As Brown Owl drank her tea, John ate a vegan biscuit from the plate but there aren't enough to go round. As it's now Brown Owl's turn with the plate, she has a slice of unbuttered toast, which she eats at a pace that annoys John. Brown Owl spots the NHS-grade invalid overbed table[25] John uses to rest his computer on when he checks his E-Mails, and asks if he has been ill. When he replies 'No', she tells the girls to leave.

3.01pm. After twenty-two minutes of sweet solitude, Chris Heggs, a local Lib Dem councillor, pops in to check on John. Having seen the state of John's Skoda Fabia and noticed his love of Queen T-shirts, Chris is hopeful that, as a fellow rock fan, politically, he and John are birds of a feather. They live in a Tory heartland, but Chris sees himself as a slight radical and is looking for like-minded people to potentially go canvassing with. John wearily answers the door – he hasn't checked gold prices for over an hour and is tense at the thought of fluctuations in the market. They stand in the doorway talking about broadband speeds in the village until Chris drops into the conversation that he once went for a curry with Tim Farron, upon which John slams the door in his face.[26]

2.36pm. As Elis is leaving Sports Direct with some new shin pads, he bumps into Rex Dronfield, one of the top TV commissioners at the BBC.

---

25 [JR] £28.90 from NRSHealthcare.co.uk.

26 For details, see *Celebrity Mastermind*, Series 16, Episode 6.

Rex and Elis share a mutual love of the same shin-pad brand (Sondico), and talk effortlessly and convivially about shin pads through the ages. Having both laughed at the primitive shin pads on display at the National Football Museum in Manchester, and agreed that ankle protectors are for dweebs, Rex says, 'We really should meet for a coffee' and writes down his personal E-Mail address for Elis. Despite being stunned that a person could be important enough to warrant *two* E-Mail addresses (work and personal), Elis politely thanks Rex before promptly losing the bit of paper. Still, he's had a nice chat about shin pads and nothing can dampen his mood as he cycles back to south London with a huge grin on his face.

3.13pm. Physically shattered by having to make two unanswered phone calls to his agent about a spelling mistake in an E-Mail, and mentally drained by having to make sure his Queen CDs were still in alphabetical order (the Brownies were in the room alone for the ten minutes or so that John was on the toilet, and he is suspicious they might have been touching them for something to do), it's time for a well-earned nap. Naps used to be an emotional lottery, a gauntlet John was wary of running, but not anymore. Through a combination of visualisation techniques and controlled hyperventilation, John is now able to control his dreams. In an ideal world, John will wake up refreshed after dreaming he is being given the Perrier Award by Freddie Mercury in front of all of his bullies from school, before accepting Brian May's offer to support Queen in the past and waking up refreshed. John's dream-control technique isn't foolproof, however, and on this occasion, he wakes up having dreamed that footage of him having sex with a farthing on the set of *Celebrity Mastermind* was broadcast on BBC One.

6pm. Elis's house is a hive of activity as he makes his daughter's favourite meal: fish fingers, beans, a raw carrot and, improbably, quinoa. He hilariously puts the shin pads on his arms and pretends to be a robot in an example of really top parenting. As he removes the fish fingers from the oven, he notices the 88 text messages and 16 missed calls from John, but he is too busy to call him back. It must be the price of gold again.

6.01pm. Refreshed from his nap, it's time to celebrate another successful day by going to the pub. John tries to decide which of the six pubs in his village he will go to. John has very prescriptive tastes when it comes to the pub, and some of his ideal criteria are difficult to achieve. Pubs should:

• Be in Oxford
• Be in the past
• Contain The Lovely Robin
• Be totally empty but not in financial difficulty because that would be depressing
• Have a roaring fire that's kept well under control
• Have a jukebox that only plays Queen, Frank Zappa, Meat Loaf, Chris de Burgh and Bonnie 'Prince' Billy
• Have a nice selection of ales. Neckoil for John, something quite malty that tastes of Shreddies for Elis (although Elis is showing worrying signs of drinking less and probably doing a Tough Mudder because he is 37) and, incredibly, Stella on draught for the usually mild-mannered Lovely Robin.
• No dogs
• No karaoke. No big screens, small screens, live bands, contact with the outside world apart from phones that are on silent with the keyboard clicks off. Quiz nights are acceptable as long as John wins and they can be cancelled at short notice at John's behest. No talkative regulars unless they were roadies for Queen.

Frustratingly, although very good, none of the six pubs near John match all of his criteria, so he decides to just go to them all before having a curry.

8.06pm. Their daughter bathed and in bed, Isy and Elis settle down to watch some TV. After a slight disagreement, the following things are vetoed by Elis: *Stranger Things* (too far-fetched), *The Handmaid's Tale* ('bit full on, it's quite late to start watching that now, isn't it, I mean it's almost 9 o'clock, I will watch it I promise, I promise, no I definitely will, I will . . .') and *The Voice* (no, definitely not. Absolutely not . . .). Great relationships are built on compromise, however, so eventually Isy watches *Married at First Sight* on catch-up as Elis reads the Wikipedia entries of 90s' footballers on his phone. It's domestic bliss!

8.46pm. John leaves the final pub in search of a curry, but as it's a Monday night his local Indian restaurant is closed, so John leaves a message with his accountant. He's checking to see if a taxi to another town to pick up a takeaway curry is tax deductible, under the pro-viso he pitches a programme about it to Dave or, at a push, E4. If not, he'll just eat crisps. After a few minutes he takes the risk, know-ing if he keeps the receipt, he's covering both bases. The programme idea he will pitch to potentially tax-deductify his taxi journey starts to take shape. 'John Goes to Another Town to Pick Up a Curry in a Taxi Possibly with Elis James if He Answers the Phone. On DAVE'. The taxi driver asks him why he's smiling so much, so to avoid small talk John says, 'Historic murders'. He then realises he might need some details about hiring a taxi for the show to beef up the pitch. An incredibly confusing conversation follows.

9.23pm. At the curry house, and the takeaway is now six minutes and twelve seconds later than the 'half an hour' the takeaway said on the phone. John checks his recent call log on his phone to confirm this. Yes, 36m 14s since they said, 'Ready in half an hour'. John is so angry he has to go for a short walk.

10.06pm. John returns home. Having misplaced his fork (John is suspicious Brown Owl might have borrowed it), John is using all of his bushcraft skills to eat a takeaway curry with a knife. He left his spoon at his old flat in Bristol, one of only two things in his life he has ever misplaced,[27] and as someone who doesn't like breakfast cereal he has seen no reason to replace it. You'd think being forkless would pose a problem for the late-night curry eater, but nothing is a problem when you are blessed with John's initiative. John has removed the strap from an old Queen fan club digital watch (don't worry, he has a duplicate) and he is using the natural curve in the plastic to scoop curry into his mouth over the sink. Once the main body of curry has been eaten, he uses the pencil he used to write the notes for his award-winning Edinburgh show to skewer rogue pieces of onion, tomato, etc. The rice he simply pours into his mouth, using the malleable foil box to create a funnel. Within three minutes, the entire meal has been finished. If anything, Brown Owl borrowing his fork without asking has saved on washing up, as he didn't need to use his plate. It's all coming up Robins!

---

27 The other was a pair of Oakley sunglasses he left in a phone box in 1998.

B:

Body, Shock Your[28]

As I have got older, I have become more and more interested in natural highs. Hanging out with Robins causes me to occasionally worry that I don't 'feel' enough, and so I've given spicy food,[29] poetry and headstands a go. I enjoyed them all, until John pointed out that being upside down and eating curry are not emotions. However, one natural high that is better than all of those things put together is running.

I am not particularly athletic, have no flair for sport, and have not been blessed with any genetic advantages that allow me to enjoy exercise.[30] But, all this aside, going for a run on a cold, still day must be one of life's great pleasures.

---

28 [JR] Once you've read this, re-read but replace the word 'running' with 'drinking', 'run' with 'drink' and 'mile' with 'pint', and it turns into an essay that could have been written by me/someone who is a laugh.

29 See **S: Spice, Project**.

30 Welshman's Thigh – the lifelong condition I suffer from that means I have embarrassingly short, powerful legs and a disproportionately big bum – is actually a curse rather than a blessing. Inherited from my dad, other sufferers include Kelly Jones from The Stereophonics, 1970s rugby player Gareth Edwards, and Rob Brydon. It makes buying trousers off-the-peg absolutely impossible.

Have you never been to a pub?   *JR*

If you are not a runner, like me you probably had a bad experience with running at school. At age 11, I was introduced to cross-country during PE lessons, when we were told to run through town up to Carmarthen reservoir ('Please don't fall in and drown Year Seven, because I hate doing the paperwork that will entail'), through some muddy fields and back to school, a distance of about two and a half miles. Inevitably, being west Wales, this was in the pissing rain and straight after my typical school dinner of turkey burger, beans and chips, chocolate sponge with white custard and a can of Diet Coke.[31]

Being told to 'get on with it' meant that everyone in my class got a stitch, apart from talented runners Luke, James and Nerys – and for a long time I thought I was physically unable to run for distances longer than a short sprint, in the way that I'm unable to lift up a car or bite through concrete. I was actually fine with this, and so knuckled down to the important business of GCSEs, checking my underarms for hair and feeling sexually anonymous at parties.

Having gone through university doing nothing more strenuous than walking to lectures or carrying cans back from the little shop,

Now this is a regime I could really get on board with ...   *JR*

I became aware that I was probably not the fittest wannabe historian in academia. Spurred into action after taking part in an impromptu kickabout and being sick on the pitch in front of a girl I liked, I decided to take advantage of being at my physical peak and do some exercise. I challenged myself to run a mile, to see how that felt. It felt awful. After a positive first fifty metres or so, it soon became unpleasant and the shakes began at around the halfway stage. Showing the kind of grit

---

31 [JR] Clearly a case of false memory syndrome here. Diet Coke was not introduced to Wales until 2004 and has still yet to be rolled out to some areas of rural Powys.

Cockneys were so famous for during the Blitz, I soldiered on and was sick at the finish line.[32] At this stage, although delirious with fatigue, I realised that I had made a rudimentary error. Instead of running for half a mile and then turning round, thus enabling me to finish at home, I had instead run for a full mile in a straight line. I was now a mile away from my house – and with sick on my hand. Like a Formula 1 driver, who, instead of completing 52 laps of Silverstone, has just driven the 190 miles in a straight line away from the track all the way up the M1 to Darlington, the prospect of the trudge back to the podium was a lonely one. This was pre-mobile phones, so I knocked on the door of a nearby house and was surprised to discover that it belonged to our family GP. I explained my situation with quiet dignity, before asking for a glass of water, a flannel to wash my face and use of his phone so I could call my mum to pick me up.

Mam said 'Well done' in the car, but I wasn't sure I deserved praise. I was 21, had run for 12 minutes, had been sick and had to use my GP's landline to call for a lift. Muhammad Ali was the boxing World Champion at 22, Michael Owen had scored for England in the World Cup at 18. I had a better set of A-levels than Michael Owen, but surely three A-levels and running a mile without being sick weren't mutually exclusive? Unusually for me, despite finding something initially difficult, I decided to stick at it.

I didn't vomit the second time, which was an improvement. After a few weeks I was able to pace myself properly, which meant I could run a mile fairly comfortably, despite being very slow. This was hugely gratifying, as I was still amazed I could run that far without stopping. Within a few months I could run three miles in about 25 minutes, was grouchy if I couldn't go, and was boring people in the pub about PBs (personal bests) and whether Saucony running shoes were worth the money.

---

32 Top tip: do not hydrate with three pints of Ribena before going for the first run of your life.

Having just googled them, I can assure readers that they are not, being as they are equivalent in price to a secondhand sofa or four months' car insurance (fully comp, 12 years no claims). *JR*

I will never run a marathon because I simply can't be bothered. It is too far and the training is too time consuming. But the runs I go for are a massively important part of my week. Before I did any exercise (and I did absolutely nothing for 7 years, from training with Carmarthen Town Under-14s to the age of 21), I didn't believe that exercise could be pleasant, in any way addictive or that the endorphin rush people talked about could exist. I thought it was a chore that middle-aged people did because they were scared of getting heart attacks, a chore like cleaning the garage or knowing where your passport was.

I'm getting an endorphin rush from knowing where my passport is right now . . . I even know where the expired one is, corner cut off, of course . . . *JR*

But, after a 25-minute run I feel fantastic. My sleep will improve and I'm a happier and more patient person.

Less of a laugh/more of a lightweight. *JR*

A run will give me a healthier sense of perspective on everything, from my often-poor performances on TV panel shows[33] to Brexit. It is an elixir that I would recommend to anyone.

Just enjoy how clear your head feels after a little run, and how chilled you feel about the edit of BBC Three's *Sweat the Small Stuff*

---

33 [JR] For details, see YouTube.

from 2012. And if you've only got ten minutes, go for ten minutes. No one has ever regretted doing something worthwhile for ten minutes.

> **Amazingly, this is almost a direct quote from 'Just For Today', from the Twelve Step programme used by Alcoholics Anonymous and similar groups. 'Just for today I will try to live through this day only and not tackle my whole life problem at once. I can do something for twelve hours that would appal me if I felt I had to keep it up for a lifetime'**

Running isn't for everyone, but there will be some kind of exercise that suits you, whether it's my mum who loves Zumba and 'funky pump' (two kinds of dance-based aerobics) or the Bristolian trip-hop musician Tricky who loves cycling and Panantukan (a kind of Filipino boxing). I am a very weak swimmer, because I was taught very badly as a kid and also am of the opinion that being in the water is unnatural. But if that's your thing, then great. Keep looking for the right exercise for you, as you won't regret it.

STAGE ONE

A few tips:

1. If you haven't done any exercise before, it won't be easy to begin with, although everyone tells me the NHS Couch to 5K app is fantastic for beginners. What I would say is that once you become a runner (or a cyclist or whatever), if you have time off and go back to it, starting again is never, ever as hard as the first time. I had a year off running because of stand-up in my late 20s, but I only had to use my GP's landline to phone my parents once. And – I cannot emphasise this enough – once your body is used to exercise, it is genuinely enjoyable.

2. Listening to music makes running much easier. I tend not to do this, for two reasons: I enjoy romantic notions of being in open dialogue with my pain and the boxers I like from the past didn't have iPods (Jimmy Wilde, born in Tylorstown, Wales, in 1892, and Howard Winstone, born in Merthyr Tydfil, Wales, in 1939). Plenty of studies show that people find it easier, though, so do yourself a favour and download some Royal Blood to your phone.

> Ronnie O'Sullivan, an example of a runner who is a laugh, also runs without music as he likes how the sounds of nature clear his head of thoughts. *JR*

3. Having read Alan Sillitoe's wonderful *The Loneliness of the Long-Distance Runner,* during runs I often imagine that I'm a working-class boy at borstal, using long-distance running to emotionally escape my desperate situation. The 1962 film version, starring Tom Courtenay, is also great. However, the Sillitoe method occasionally makes my conversation quite weird when I get back to the house, something to bear in mind if you're tempted by this.

> If you're re-reading in my **Running** = **Drinking/Run** = **Pub/Mile** = **Pint** translation, I'd recommend Hans Fallada's *The Drinker*, Patrick Hamilton's *Hangover Square*, Kingsley Amis's *The Old Fools*, Charles Jackson's *The Lost Weekend*, Olivia Laing's *The Trip To Echo Spring*, and John Cheever and Raymond Carver's short stories. And especially the latter's poem 'Luck'. *JR*

4. I sometimes imagine that I'm playing football for Wales when I'm running (you can choose any team you like). After Euro 2016, I was on the treadmill at the gym, imagining that I'd scored the winner in the semi-final against Portugal. I replayed the goal from

all angles, gave an interview to Jason Mohammad at pitchside and also watched the goal from the stands in my mind. It was only when I got off the treadmill that I realised I was crying.

5. Don't eat for 90 minutes to two hours before you go for a run, or you'll get a stitch like a six-year-old at a birthday party.

STAGE TWO

Once you've been exercising for a while, you may find that it becomes harder to lose weight and increase tone. This is because your body has got used to the exercises you're doing, your excess weight is no longer there to burn additional calories and the muscles involved in what you've been doing have become toned.

It is now time to 'shock your body.' You could incorporate sprints, hill running, maybe longer distances. But unless you are training for something, or are desperate to improve, feel free to leave it.

> I love how, within a sentence of getting to the point of this chapter, you've just said 'feel free to leave it'. I'm really laughing here.

To supplement my running and cycling, and shock my body even further, I have started to take cold showers. I initially gave them a go after reading one of those 'New Year's Resolution Ideas that Have Benefits You Won't Have Thought Of!!!' articles in the paper, and guessed they might be fun. Within ten seconds I noticed that cold water woke me up more efficiently than caffeine and gave me an endorphin rush that lasted until midday. Like lots of endorphin rushes, it became addictive and, as my tolerance for cold water grew, I began to push things further. I stayed in a hotel a few weeks ago and gave myself a headache as I rinsed my hair, and it was absolutely exhilarating. The cold water causes you to breathe deeply, which fills the body with oxygen; it also increases your circulation, which improves your heart health. Aside from making you feel more alert, cold showers improve your immune system, personally cheer me up and apparently stimulate weight loss. What I really like about them, though, is that they are less pleasant than being warm. After a very hard day, I might treat myself to a hot shower, and I feel like a decadent monarch whose debased behaviour is bringing the country to the brink of a revolution. As I stand there, breathing at a normal rate and applying Radox without wincing, I think, 'This is what Henry VIII's life must have been like,' and I instantly feel disgusted but special.

Being cold also makes me feel like an athlete. The Welsh rugby team sit in cryogenic chambers to recover more quickly from injury, and extreme cold has been proven to help athletes train harder. I am not an athlete, I am a digital DJ, but if I could swap my ability for intro-ducing James Bay songs to being good at the long jump, I would do it in a heartbeat. A cold shower in the morning makes me think I've been chosen to represent Wales in the Commonwealth Games, and I am getting my training off to the very best start. In reality, I am having a cold shower before I go to finish the voiceover on a programme about movie blunders, but I tend not to dwell on my actual life.

Emil Zatopek, the 1950s Czechoslovakian distance runner (and arguably the greatest runner of all time), used to push his body to extreme limits in the name of success – my favourite being he would run laps in training with his wife on his shoulders, in order to make the actual race feel easy. Zatopek refused to allow his real life commit-ments to get in the way of this training – as a soldier he would jog on the spot during sentry duty, and when forced indoors to do laundry, he would jog on top of the washing in the bath. Washing my hair with Herbal Essences Hello Hydration, as my teeth chatter, is my nod to one of the greatest athletes the world has ever produced. In reality, I am a lazy daydreamer who doesn't answer his E-Mails, but being chilly for a few minutes before I eat a bowl of Special K and have a coffee allows me to think that real change is just round the corner.

Taking a cold shower is easier[34] than you think. Start off as normal, and then increase the cold water gradually to allow your body to get used to it. Try to relax your shoulders, and only give ten seconds of really cold water a go the first time. You might make noises like a cow giving birth, but that is to be welcomed. It's real. You are experiencing real life.[35] Starting slowly like this makes it more likely to be enjoyable, and I'd be surprised if you don't leave the bathroom with a spring in your step and a brain that's ready to face the day. One can only imagine the kind of radio I might have made, the games of Betabet™ I might have won, if I'd been following this regime as a younger man. As I get older, I worry that I'm not the mentally agile person I used to be, but through a combination of exercise and cold water I am convinced I have found a dental floss for the mind.[36]

I was told something that really stayed with me recently: 'The inspirational people at the gym aren't the sculpted body builders, but the overweight or unfit people who are giving it a go for the first time.' I couldn't agree with this more. Whenever I see someone struggle round the park, it fills my heart with joy and I want to shout a show of support from my car. I mentioned this on the radio show and received E-Mails from listeners who would welcome that kind of vocal encouragement, although I'm not so sure and I'd hate for any new runners to think I was taking the mickey. Rest assured, however – if you are new to exercise, I am with you every step of the way.[37] Go forth, shock your body, turn that dial down to freezing and change your life. You won't regret it!

---

34 [JR] /stupider/more pointless.

35 [JR] in the 1700s/Hannah Hauxwell's house.

36 [JR] The only possible advantage I can see to any of this is a small reduction in the cost of your gas bill. And, as a man who frequently sleeps in a woolly hat to avoid whacking on the radiator, it's a searing indictment of the cold-shower philosophy that I have not been tempted to try it.

37 Metaphorically.

C:

Carmarthen

Matthew Stevens, the snooker player. John Nash, the architect who designed Regent Street, The Mall and Buckingham Palace. Nicky Stevens of Brotherhood of Man (still the only Welsh winner of the Eurovision Song Contest). Comedian Rhod Gilbert. Rugby player Ieuan Evans. Wynne Evans, the opera singer from the Go Compare adverts. The inventor of the ball bearing. These people are all blessed. They are charmed. They have won life's lottery. They are from Carmarthen.[38]

Architecturally Carmarthen is the perfect blend of nineteeth-century streets and big high-street names. What's the point in enjoying an old building if you can't open a 1/2/3 account at a nearby branch of Santander?

> The exact reason I find the failure of my petition to have a Jessops within Durham Cathedral so frustrating. The place is just asking to be photographed, and that market needs catering for!

JR

---

38 To be honest, John Nash is not from Carmarthen, but according to his Wikipedia he did live there for a bit.

According to the sign on the A48, Carmarthen is Wales's oldest town, and in my opinion it knocks Pontypridd, Merthyr Tydfil, Aberteifi and the North Walian ones into a cocked hat. Those places simply cannot compete with the tapestry of experience you get in Carmarthen, or as Carmarthen's residents refer to it – 'town'.

Whether you're an asthmatic walking to Furnace House Surgery to get your annual flu jab, a music fan making a pilgrimage to Slipped Discs in the market to buy the latest Fleetwood Mac CD or simply taking a gentle stroll to Siop Y Pentan to enquire about getting the name of your house engraved on some slate, you'll notice that everyone is smiling at you.

> So that's what they were doing! I had assumed it was a kind of snarl/sideeffect of the drugs pandemic that has blighted Wales post-Thatcher.

This is because Carmarthenites are aware that in a concept symposium like Carmarthen, positivity breeds creativity, and there is no such thing as a bad idea.[39] This unique way of seeing the world frees us to riff and think imaginatively, unfettered by the staid conventions of a town like Llanelli or New York. Notts Square, home to the British Heart Foundation charity shop and the statue of General Nott (which has Grade II-listed status), has now been designated a 'break-out zone' by Carmarthenshire County Council, where the town's artists meet on beanbags (drizzle permitting) to discuss which conventions they're going to smash next. So, it's home to some free thinkers, but what's a day in the 'Welsh Greenwich Village' actually like?

No need to set your alarm early to maximise your time in the European Rio de Janeiro, as you'll probably be woken by seagulls or

---

39 Apart from the numerous Australian-themed bars that have mysteriously sprung up and then failed in the town.

people who find the place name 'Abergwili'[40] as funny as John does.[41] In terms of breakfast, I'd probably stick to cereal, but lunch is a different matter. From fish and chips (1900 to the present) to the takeaway-baguette boom of the early 2000s, Carmarthen has always embraced culinary change. It is served by a Morrisons and a frankly *massive* Tesco (as my mum once said, 'a Tesco so big, people from Swansea have driven down just to look at it'), so, whether it's cauliflower or milk you like, Carmarthen has plenty to offer. If African safari parks can boast the 'Big Five' of lion, leopard, rhino, elephant and giraffe, Carmarthen offers the big five culinary experiences:

CHINESE
INDIAN
PIZZA
SCAMPI
COOKING AT HOME

Scampi, eh? Sounds delicious, great choice! One plate of competitively priced scampi, chips and peas at the Old Priory Guesthouse later and you're sated. Satisfied. But what if you're naked? Well, whether you're the victim of a stag-do prank or an alien that's taken on human form and landed in the phone box by where Wimpy used to be on Guildhall Square, you needn't worry. As long as it's not after 5pm, you can kit yourself out in the latest catwalk trends, as Debenhams, River Island and Next vie for the attention of the fashion-conscious shopper,

---

40 [JR] For English speakers, this is pronounced [əbɪgˈwɪli]/'A big willy'.

41 Abergwili is an electoral ward on the outskirts of Carmarthen. Both my sisters were taught piano in Abergwili, my friend Gareth lived there and, as the literal English translation of Abergwili is 'Mouth of the River Gwili', I have no idea why John finds it so funny and I think he should grow up.

[JR] Hey, don't get me wrong. I'd love to have grown up in Abergwili! Imagine growing up in Abergwili! Big posters of Abergwili everywhere! In a way, we all come from a kind of 'wili' anyway, so probably best to come from Abergwili!

all within comfortable distance of a car park and the office on Barn Road where my dad used to work.

So, dressed well, and stomach lined, what's a night out like in Carmarthen? After trying a 'proper coffee' at Costa, browsing the fixed-TV mounting brackets at B&Q or visiting one of the town's many love spoon[42] emporiums in a bid to rescue a dying relationship by buying one of those really massive ones, you might pop into Innovation Lounge Wales (my friend Simon's house). Having changed the name of his house from 'number 14' to 'Innovation Lounge Wales' on account of having broadband, Simon will put on the kettle or get cans from the fridge as you browse the internet's latest memes at your leisure. And at speeds of up to 0.7 Mbps, according to Speedtest.net, this puts Simon in the top ten percentile for urban Wales. Having discussed for hours whether that dress was white and gold or blue and black, and enjoyed several 'Gangnam Style'-related gifs, it's time to put on your dancing shoes. Every night is party night in Carmarthen, although realistically, most debauchery tends to happen on a Saturday.

Sure, you could play it safe and stick to the tried-and-tested pub and club scene, but as long as you're willing to go through the pain barrier you can 'do a Dylan' on your night out. Legendary poet Dylan Thomas once broke his arm in the Boar's Head on Lammas Street (Carmarthen's oldest pub), but was too drunk to realise and so went to watch a film at the Lyric Theatre. Although the Lyric no longer shows films, you could mimic Thomas's growing realisation that his arm was bending the wrong way in front of a pantomime, a Bee Gees tribute band or the monthly comedy club. Welsh people know, however, that the Lyric was no small-town fleapit cinema. In 1993, it became the first cinema in Wales to show *Jurassic Park*, after the mayor got hold of Stephen Spielberg's personal fax[43] number and contacted him direct, warning of a 'crisis'

---

42 [JR] Is this a Welsh thing/sex toy?

43 A form of correspondence that was simultaneously paper and electric, which bridged the eras of letter and E-Mail.

if the film was not shown in town. Spielberg assented, and the British premiere was jointly held in Carmarthen and Leicester Square. The foyer was decked out in inflatable dinosaurs, the bar sold 'Jurassic Cocktails' (vodka, port and Cointreau), and the staff wore black tie, but I couldn't get a ticket because unfortunately my dad was not a Freemason.

As you make your way from the Lyric Theatre, I would suggest stopping in at the Plume of Feathers (Wales's smallest pub[44]), the Ivy Bush Hotel (tantalisingly only a swimming pool away from four-star status – apparently Napoleon once stayed there[45]) and Morgan's Fish and Chip Shop, widely regarded as 'superb'. These places are all a short amble from Savannah's, a nightclub dedicated to the over-25s and a widely renowned cathedral of decadence, where everyone from divorcees to dairy farmers can cut loose. I had my 18th birthday party there, as the over-25s rule is relaxed for private functions. I'm proud to say I reached adulthood in a setting that comfortably competes with the Hacienda, Studio 54 and New York's Paradise Garage for depravity. From Blue Curaçao to Fosters, it has everything a reveller could need, apart from an adequate outdoor smoking area. As one of the lucky few deemed fit to work in Savannah's, I often reminisce with fellow alumni. Who could forget my first shift where, as an 18-year-old, 'RINGO! RINGO!' was chanted at me as I pulled pints and I watched a man in a wheelchair break up a fight, before finding a discarded catheter in the toilet as I cleaned up. Having danced the night away, and probably flirted with someone who works for the Castell Howell Frozen Food Company, it's traditional to film a scuffle on your phone outside Chick-King before calling your mum for a lift home.

Carmarthen is not all dancing till you drop, eating chips and

---

44 Annoyingly, the Plume now has a bit of competition for the title of 'Wales's smallest pub', but having checked these places out online, I can confirm that they are not pubs but dog kennels that serve Carling.
45 I must admit, I need to check this. The swimming pool thing is true, according to my mate who used to work there.

catwalk styles at high-street prices, however. According to some variants of the Arthurian legend, Merlin the wizard was born in a cave outside Carmarthen. Legend has it that if a particular tree called Merlin's Oak[46] fell, the town would be flooded. To prevent this, and mindful of what the downfall of Carmarthen would do to the West Walian economy (Carmarthen has one of only two branches of River Island west of Swansea), the quick-thinking council dug up the tree when it died and pieces of it remain in the town museum, providing a slightly disappointing if very quick tourist experience for the rest of time. Growing up in a town that creates famous wizards has an interesting effect on the psyche of its inhabitants. From insurance-comparison celebrities to ball-bearing aficionados, its former residents provide proof of the kind of person Carmarthen creates. It creates winners. Carmarthen is more than a town, it is a state of mind, and I feel proud to strut with the confidence a Carmarthen upbringing gave me. From medieval plague pits to a leisure centre, from a cattle market to a Halfords, Carmarthen really has it all.

CARMARTHEN, A TIMELINE

AD 74   The Romans build the fort at Moridunum, on the outskirts of the town. The amphitheatre is still there, the most westerly amphitheatre in Britain and one of only seven that remain in the UK. As an amphitheatre, it pre-dates Carmarthen's current six-screen Vue Cinema by almost 2,000 years, but teenagers now use the former to drink cider and get off with each other.[47]

1349   The Black Death arrives in Carmarthen, generally regarded as a negative.

---

46 Now a roundabout.
47 And the rest.

1360   John Andrew Spilman becomes Carmarthen's first recorded mayor. There is now a street and hotel named after him, and the hotel bar is very popular with farmers at the weekend.

1818   There are cheese riots at the Quay, a mere 180 years before Boursin is made available at the local Tesco. #Victory

1876   The remains of Sir Richard Steele, the playwright and co-founder of *Tatler* and *The Spectator*, are found in Carmarthen. He married a Carmarthen woman named Mary Scurlock and apparently, when found, Steele's skull was in an excellent condition.

1968   My mum's friend Yvette gets done for underage drinking at The Coffee Pot, a cool coffee bar-cum-beat club, now a branch of Nationwide.

1974   The National Eisteddfod, the celebration of language and culture in Wales, is held in the town. It hasn't been held there since. This injustice is one of the reasons I have stopped drinking. I never thought I'd say this, but the National Eisteddfod has angered me sober.

1976   Mam and Dad get married in Carmarthen. My father is sent by my grandmother to get his shoulder-length hair cut by a barber in nearby Cross Hands. When Dad comes back, having only given his blunt fringe a small trim, she cries. Otherwise, the day passes without incident.

1980   Still riding high from the staging of the National Eisteddfod just six years previously, my parents celebrate with my conception.

1982   Carmarthen is twinned with Lesneven in Brittany. This leads to a fruitful cultural exchange between the two towns, culminating in 1996, when my French exchange partner Christophe becomes the first person I have ever seen smoke and use a urinal at the same time.

1992   I start secondary school at Ysgol Gyfun Bro Myrddin, a Welsh-medium comprehensive routinely rated as 'Outstanding' by Estyn (the Welsh version of Ofsted). Despite the school's very good academic record, the grief I get for having a calligraphy pen in my pencil case on the first day scars me for the next 15 years.

1993   Because of a dearth of entertainment in the town, I spend all of my spare time in 1993 looking at football boots in Owen Sports, a sports shop at the bottom of Cambrian Way. I don't buy any, because I haven't grown out of my old ones.

1994   Most of my friends start to learn the guitar. We are encouraged by John James, the owner of Y Stiwdio Gerdd (a music shop in the town), who lets us play the expensive guitars in his shop for hours under the proviso that we are looking to buy one. This kindness is tested to its limits when I see my friend Matthew try to play a goldtop Gibson Les Paul, while eating a kebab.

1995   The coat my mother bought me for school mysteriously finds itself in the bin, after the hard kids, who hang out by the phone box next to the steps of Carmarthen Magistrates' Court, keep shouting that I look like Rodney from *Only Fools and Horses* as I walk to Woolworths.

1996   My first piss-up, which actually happens in the nearby market town of Llandeilo, because I somehow managed to get served Fosters Ice in their rugby club. In a bid to look older I wear one of dad's ties from when he was a civil servant in the 70s, and I end up looking like an extra from the BBC's supernatural cop show *Life on Mars*.

1997   In order to beef up my UCAS form, I accept the brickbats and catcalls of my peers and take a place on the Carmarthen Youth Council. I am instrumental in setting up a Youth Centre that allows truants to smoke. I also do work experience at the nearby *Llanelli Star*, and am in the office when the sub-editor comes up with the headline 'LLANELLI MAN ON BENEFITS FINDS £10 IN CRISP PACKET'.

1998   My 18th birthday party at Savannah's. A fancy-dress theme, and I wear a gold catsuit. The catsuit isn't as attractive to girls as I had hoped, although my friend Gareth gives me a big lovebite as a joke, which makes the family party I have the next day slightly awkward.

I've seen a photo of you in that catsuit and if it's not put in the picture section I will burn down your house.   *JR*

1999   Back in Llandeilo Rugby Club, my band, Jenny and the Bodybags, perform their first gig. As the singer and guitarist, I decide to make a statement by performing in my mum's wedding dress, although sadly there are no photos of this event. The audience is left bemused, while Llandeilo Rugby Club is frustratingly short of A&R representatives from major record companies, despite being a mere four-hour drive from London. Before the first song, I emerge from a bodybag, actually a big holdall I got from a friend who had a part-time job in a bike shop.

2007   My parents get Sky.

2010   Carmarthen welcomes PizzaExpress, Costa, Debenhams and River Island. Sadly, the revamping of the market means that 'Semen World', the bull-hire equipment shop my aunty and uncle ran for many years, has to move premises.[48]

2017   Carmarthen is named one of the best places to live in Wales by the *Sunday Times*, a far more reputable publication than the *Rough Guide* (who even reads that anymore?), which has in the past described Carmarthen as 'stodgy'. Despite Carmarthen's post-2010 resurgence, the *Rough Guide* currently describes the town as 'the unquestioned regional capital but one that fails to live up to the promise of its status', which, I promise you, is utter, utter BS.

---

48 [JR] Please tell me it moved to Abergwili . . .

potato!

D:

Diaries, Elis's Gig

I started doing stand-up around January 2005. I was 24 years old and working part-time as an administrator for a homelessness charity, having previously done some sterling data-entry work at not one but *two* gas pipe companies.[49] I'd been obsessed with comedy since I was a child and, at the risk of sounding like a tiresome idiot you'd want to avoid at all costs, I had used humour to navigate almost all social situations for as long as I remembered. It was only in the new world of office work that I'd realised this personality trait has its downsides. For instance, the head of finance at the London office almost certainly doesn't want to hear your impressions.[50] He wants to wearily explain to you that the Staples invoice won't be paid until next month's cheque run because you were late in submitting it, before going home to his wife and kids.

I didn't grow up loving stand-up. It was sitcoms, particularly the ones shown on BBC Two on a Friday night throughout the 1990s, that I loved

---

49 I'll never forget the phone call from my temp agency boss, where she said, 'Having talked to Paul in the office about it, I see pipes as your future.'
50 That said, I stand by my 'Ian Paisley calculating VAT on computer paper' as one of the all-time great examples of DUP mimicry.

as a teenager. *Red Dwarf*, *Blackadder*, *I'm Alan Partridge*, I loved them all, I loved them unconditionally. Given the ubiquity of stand-up comics on television nowadays, it's difficult to imagine how underground and alternative stand-up was when I was growing up. There were very few stand-up shows on television: ITV's *Live at Jongleurs* and the BBC's *The Stand-Up Show* are the only ones I remember. Both were on very late and were seen by critics as a poor representation of how exciting stand-up could be. Stand-up was generally regarded as being impossible to transfer to television and, barring a few notable, famous exceptions such as Victoria Wood, Dave Allen, Billy Connolly and Eddie Izzard, British comics in particular were seen as curious oddballs more suited to the Edinburgh Festival than mainstream success.

The trouble with wanting to write and be in a sitcom was that I had no idea how the process worked. All comedy seemed to be made in London, a place I had only ever been to on holiday[51] or on school trips. I had also never met any actors who did comedy – being in Cardiff, of course, I had met people who'd been on *Pobl y Cwm* and serious dramas on S4C about abortion and slate quarries, but no comedians. I was working in a pub and met a TV gag writer who told me I should do stand-up as a way of being seen by TV producers. In a welcome piece of serendipity, within days of this meeting an open-mic stand-up night started in Cardiff, and I put my name down. Bearing in mind that I was 24 years old, old enough for an eight-year career in the army, no longer eligible to win the PFA Young Player of Year Award and old enough to drive abroad, the naivety I showed after my first gig was incredible. I did my allotted five minutes and got a couple of laughs – one laugh, incredibly, for a sentence I hadn't realised was a joke. As a helpful introduction

---

51 [JR] Didn't your mum have to cut short your first trip because you found Regent Street 'too loud'? Not only is that one of the sweetest things I've ever heard, but it also remains a very valid point – it's one of the real failings of London as a tourist destination/place for a 36-year-old man to have to navigate on foot.

[EJ] Yes, that's true. Our family holiday in the summer of 1985 was cut short because I couldn't cope with the noise.

to the world of open-mic comedy, a ladies' hockey team wandered into the pub[52] halfway through my set, unaware there was anything on. Amazingly, one or two of *them* laughed, thus convincing me I was able to play to audiences as diverse as people who did and didn't like hockey. I stayed for a few pints after the show, glassy-eyed and lightheaded with adrenaline. When I eventually got home that night, my eyeballs were burning with excitement and I didn't sleep at all before having to get up for work the next day. As I lay in bed, the same thought kept whirling round my head. 'They were strangers! Actual strangers! I didn't know any of those people! I can make strangers laugh!' I made a mental note of all the comedians I was suddenly in competition with:

- Simon Pegg
- Jo Brand
- Eddie Izzard (but I wasn't sure if he still did stand-up)
- Jeff Green (or did he just do panel shows?)
- Frank Skinner
- David Baddiel (did he just write books now?)
- The four I had seen at the Cardiff Glee Club on New Year's Eve
- Bernard Manning/Roy Chubby Brown (but wasn't that a different circuit to the one I was on?)
- The other two who had been on at my gig that night
- Jack Dee
- The guy who had hosted the amateur film night I had been to in Swansea and who was quite funny (did he count?)
- Lee Evans
- Peter Kay
- Bill Bailey[53]

---

52 The venue was the Mochyn Du pub in Cardiff. At time of writing (June 2018), there is no blue plaque to commemorate this, and the pub is now known as Bragdy a Chegin.
53 I hadn't realised Sean Hughes and Phil Jupitus had started as stand-ups. I don't think I realised Dylan Moran had done stand-up, as I knew him as the guy from *Black Books*.

I loved the sitcom *Spaced* but had read that Simon Pegg had retired from stand-up, so discounting him, Bernard Manning, Roy Chubby Brown and a few of the other tenuous ones such as the amateur film-night guy from Swansea, that meant there were only 13 stand-up comedians![54] Surely there was room for a 14th? Was I just incredibly lucky that the stars had aligned, and that the opening for the 14th comedian had been in Cardiff, where I lived? I realised at about 4am that there were only British stand-ups on the list, but breaking America could come later – I didn't want to live in America anyway – my skin is too fair for hot weather and we'd just signed another 12-month tenancy agreement on the house. Yes, being a national treasure in the UK would suit me just fine: rich enough to get a foot on the property ladder, but retaining my anonymity for holidays abroad.

Suddenly, going into work that day felt very pointless, even unfair on my colleagues. As the 14th comedian, I would surely have a DVD deal very soon. As the five-minute set I had done at the pub the night before was obviously bulletproof, I should just write another 10 to 15 of those. I was due back at the same open-mic night a few weeks later, and it is difficult to describe the enthusiasm I felt for that gig. When you are unhappy in your job (and I don't want to denigrate the good people who work for gas pipe companies up and down the country), you view everything through the prism of how unhappy you are at work. Suddenly all the things I have always loved – football, music,[55] – had a kind of greyness to them, but somehow being amazing at stand-up the first time I tried it offered a way out.[56] Who'd have thought that doing impressions of the coach on the way to play for

---

54 When Frank Skinner moved to London in 1990, he estimates that there were around 45 stand-up comics populating what was then known as the 'alternative circuit'. There were still comics doing the 'mainstream' working-men's club/social club circuit back then.

55 [JR] movie blunders.

56 I remember doing a gig with Jon Richardson a few years ago, and he told me that he still had his 'real-life' CV on his desktop, to remind him that if comedy ever went wrong he'd be back working in kitchens.

Carmarthen Town Under-12s could pay such dividends? In fact . . . was there anything in that? I should probably write that down. Always nice to add 'impressionist' to your CV.[57]

I turned up at the next open-mic night with some new vibes written in my notebook, and of course my bulletproof five minutes from the previous gig. I got one or two laughs, but there was a detectable awkward squirming in seats at my new, more challenging material about the round-robin E-Mails[58] people send when they're travelling. 'That's OK,' I thought. 'I'm challenging. Bill Hicks was challenging.' At the end, a Brummie open-mic act came up to chat. He had got laughs, his routine about Müller Crunch Corner yoghurts had definitely been the high point of the night.[59] I was mentally adding him to my list as the 15th comic working in Britain, when he shattered my world. 'That was great. Do you work for Mirth Control?'[60]

'No . . . ' I replied, thinking *but there's only this gig, the Cardiff Glee where I went on New Year's Eve, the Comedy Store in London, which had a documentary made about it, and the room in Edinburgh where the festival happens.*

'Oh, Mirth Control are great,' he said. 'I'll have a word with Geoff on your behalf. He runs about 80 gigs up and down the country.'

Suddenly, my burgeoning comedy career went from inevitable success to statistical unlikelihood in the space of one helpful conversation. As the Brummie Crunch Corner man kindly wrote out the E-Mail addresses (he was an early adopter) and phone numbers of gigs in

---

57 I can do the coach at Carmarthen Town Under-12s, Ian Paisley, a passable John Peel and an impression of people doing impressions of ex-Labour Deputy Leader Roy Hattersley.

58 [JR] No wonder, in 2005 they'd have had absolutely no idea what you were talking about!

59 [JR] If this is the guy I'm thinking of, his nauseating, misogynistic routine about vaginas inspired me to write my first motivational note in my diary. It was something along the lines of 'never write a nauseating, misogynistic routine about vaginas'. And, though one can never know what the future holds, as of 2018, I've kept that pledge.

60 Mirth Control is a company run by a comedian named Geoff Whiting. They are famous on the circuit for giving most comedians their first paid gigs, which is true for both John and me.

Bristol, Birmingham, London and Northampton, I did some punishing mental arithmetic. This Geoff guy ran 80+ gigs, so unless stand-up had somehow been nationalised, there must be other promoters. Even if 'Geoff' was improbably the only promoter, that still meant four comics a night at his 80+ gigs . . . Oh God. There must be hundreds of us. I was the 400th stand-up. I was the 400th stand-up and my new, edgy material about the people who send those round-robin E-Mails when travelling was a failure.

After moping through a pint of Erdinger with the promoter (the Brummie guy was incredibly travelling to do another gig, which felt like a right kick in the nads), I resolved to improve. Knowing that I was the 400th stand-up meant I would have to be good, but the 80+ comedy clubs that apparently existed also meant doing enough gigs to leave my real job was suddenly possible.

The initial spurt of enthusiasm you get on discovering something new and all-encompassing is one of my favourite feelings. It's the way I felt after discovering cold showers. It's the way I briefly felt about learning to juggle.[61] Ignoring all of the obligatory press talk about 'creative revival' and 'new-found inspiration,' there is no way an established band feel the same enthusiasm for their 12th album that they did for their first, when they were 18, newly signed and had no idea what some of the buttons on the mixing desk did. I understand that some people are in love with the process of songwriting, or pottery, or designing Formula 1 cars, but that first opportunity . . . when you feel like someone has left the door open and you're in there by mistake? Nothing beats that.

It was around this time that I started keeping my gig diaries.

---

61 My other favourite feelings are as follows:

   1. Finding something it would be a massive ballache to lose (e.g. your passport, the night before you go on holiday).

   2. Being late but being told the person you are meeting is going to be later than you (2005–to date, this still hasn't happened with John).

   3. Being told you can knock off anything an hour early.

Performing stand-up comedy becomes addictive very quickly, and I was desperate to improve. Gigs as an amateur, open-spot comedian are actually quite hard to come by, and so writing a no-holds-barred account of my evening was my way of making those gigs count. In theory, I would make a note of where I could improve, and which successful things from my set I should keep doing. Looking back, it is hideously embarrassing. As an exercise, scroll back a few years through your sent items[62] and read an E-Mail at random.[63] Even if it's only a few years ago, chances are you won't recognise the person who has written it. There might be jokes or references in there you don't remember (Subject – Re: The Crazy Frog), or on a basic tonal level you will probably view yourself with horror. A blog or diary entry (unless the diary is so old it becomes charming) will be even worse. That is how I feel about the material I wrote, and the self-flagellating advice I wrote to myself. I am exceptionally harsh on myself because I wanted to improve, and this is an aspect of my personality I am actually quite proud of. However, my scattergun approach to writing material led to some comedy that makes me want to cringe my spine into dust, and although almost nobody gets it right first time, I am in the rare situation of having a record of almost all of my early failings.

One of the few pieces of advice I will give to budding comedians is that I am no more naturally funny or at all cleverer now than I was in 2005,[64] but I have done thousands of gigs. I am not wittier in social situations, but stand-up is a craft that can be learned. Not everyone who sticks at stand-up will become good enough to go full-time,

---

62 'Sent items' – an electronic, permanent record of all the E-Mails you send, is one of my favourite features of modern E-Mail. So useful.

63 [JR] As someone who does this regularly, I urge extreme caution. If you are in any way predisposed to regret, crippling nostalgia or self-reproach, then I would advise against opening up this can of worms.

64 [JR] If anything I'd say it's been a steady decline since the legendary 'scissors' routine I saw you do when we first met in 2005. 'I think those scissors are too sharp' still makes me laugh!

but almost everyone will improve. However, I hope that some of the extracts I have included below serve as proof that even a competent stand-up like myself will usually get off to a very rocky start. The other thing I will say is that stand-up is how I met John. Who would have thought that when Robins crops up in those early entries, that nascent talent I am writing about, that pre-smoking-ban-fag-in-hand-vibe-surfing-Daewoo-Lanos-driving-compere the south-west comedy scene was so desperate for, would go on to become such a competent digital DJ.

19th of June 2005, Bristol Jesters, score 5/10

The shape of the room is hard. I couldn't connect with people. Ironic impressions just sound like I can't do the impression. Head teachers drinking from a cafetiere is too easy a target. Also the joke about Kofi Annan doing a speech at the UN Christmas do was confusing and very few people got the reference.

WRITE JOKES ABOUT RADIATION AS EVERYONE HAS HEARD OF IT

7th of August 2005, Wharf Pub, Cardiff, score 6/10

Opened by mentioning the death of Robin Cook, the former foreign secretary, at tonight's show. A lady in the front row asked who he was, the joke tanked and I never recovered. I think that's the end for me and topical. Tried to get them back with Geordie Financial Year[65] but by then the lady who hadn't heard of Robin Cook was ordering food. Tonight was tough.

13th of August 2005, Yellow Kangaroo, Cardiff, score 7/10

As we are now over four months into it, I have to accept that Geordie Financial Year is no longer topical enough to be funny.

---

65 See **Y: Year, Geordie Financial**.

That said, my impression of the man who mixed-up Bargoed and London and couldn't remember where his son worked got a round of applause – it never gets anything in England, but the two Matts said there was nothing wrong with having a specific Welsh set. Rang Robins —

'Hello, comedy wisdom line . . . '[66]   *JR*

— who told me that not having my details on comedycv.co.uk was a disgrace and was costing me work. He's right. He said that his £60 gig in Tamworth came directly from the site – but there's no way I'm ready for that.

26th of January 2006, Jesters, Bristol, score 6.5/10

YOU'RE BETTER THAN DOING JOKES ABOUT ALLOY WHEELS. Also the Cockney impression didn't get a laugh because I opened with it and at that stage the audience didn't know I wasn't actually a Cockney (re-jig this for Stroud).

4th of March 2006, Plymouth, score 6/10

I don't seem to be able to write new material that's as good as the stuff I came up with in my very first set – I am at a creative impasse and I don't know why. Time and time again I find myself in a sticky situation and I revert to my default setting of 'Cornish one-night stand', 'Geordie Financial Year' and 'Alloy wheel'. Of the new stuff, 'Crimean War alcopops' is too niche, 'Student bin observation' is too age specific and 'Pesto pasta routine' makes me appear arrogant.

---

66 [JR] I probably actually said that.

16th of June 2006, St Ives, Cambridgeshire, score 4.5/10. £75 cash.
Imagine Savannnah's[67] but bigger, with scarier bouncers and in the middle of an industrial estate, and named after an electronics firm (Lawton Electronics Ltd). There are 24 people here.

Mistake number 1: I went straight into banter. That is the compere's job. BANTER SHOULD BE RELEVANT. Stick to the set – only include banter where necessary and if it adds to the joke. By trying to do ten minutes of material after ten minutes of mediocre chat meant that I lost the buzz John had created.

> I do like the sound of this mysterious buzz-creator . . .

Mistake number 2: John *had* created a buzz —

> You're welcome!

— but I completely failed to ride this. I completely misread the room and even asked the same questions John had asked ten minutes previously.

Mistake number 3: COME INTO THE LIGHT. How can an audience laugh when I look so disinterested and scared? Show my face, for God's sake.

Mistake number 4: WHERE HAVE MY ASIDES GONE? Material about Barrymore, you idiot? That is as hack as you can get.

Mistake number 5: GIG MORE GIG MORE GIG MORE. You only improve by learning to read bad rooms. Getting a 5/10 out of a bad room means you can get 11/10 out of a good room. I am beginning to see the logic of running my own stand-up night in order to work with bad crowds.

---

67 The nightclub in Carmarthen where I had my 18th birthday party (see **C: Carmarthen**).

MUST TRY HARDER.[68]

25th of March 2007, Poncho Comedy Club, Cardiff, score 8/10
Arrived late – Robins was actually sat on a table, just improvising with the crowd –

I'm sorry, did somebody order a RULEBREAKER?!   *JR*

— it was superb. Neil from Newport talked about a child being tied to a dog and the audience lapped it up, his is a very authentic voice. During the interval, Robins showed me his Sat Nav and told me that when you consider how much petrol you save in not getting lost looking for a venue it actually pays for itself, but he gigs more than me. Night over-ran thank God – too many of the audience have seen my alloy wheel and Geordie Financial Year stuff. So I did the new story about being sick after running for a mile which did well – I think the audience could tell how fresh this story is, and that I was enjoying myself.

and it's still paying dividends some 12 years later.[69]   *JR*

28th of March 2007, 13.37pm (*this was written on office headed note-paper, shortly before I was made redundant*)
'Catacombe. Sterile. Banquet. Vagabond. Grocer.'
Remember these – because these are funny words. (What about pipe?)

---

68 [JR] I remember this gig and, in fairness to Elis, the room was ABSOLUTE DS and it's much easier to create buzz as the compere, where you can chat, reference how bad the room is, essentially just be a pleasant presence, than it is to do stand-up. I probably should have told him this, but I'll bet I rode the wave of my buzz-creating genius and let him stew for three and a half hours on the journey home.
69 [JR] See **B: Body, Shock Your.**

29th of March 2007, Poncho Comedy Club, Cardiff, score 5/10

Tonight was tough. I don't think I'll ever forget the looks on the audience's faces as I said the word 'vagabond' over and over again to silence. People were confused because nobody really says the word 'vagabond' anymore – sure, the word is funny, but only in the context of a joke that's actually about vagabonds. Low point was when people arrived halfway through my set, had to ask if 'this was comedy' and when Sian the promoter said, 'Yes, isn't Elis great,' they all left. I saved the set by doing my default northerner impressions at the last minute – I have to move on from these. The new stuff isn't working and I'm stuck in a dangerous rut.

11th of August 2007, So You Think You're Funny Semi-Final, score 8.2/10

Set list: Geordie Financial Year, Leeds train station baguette impression, Cornish one-night stand, CD cases.

I performed this at the Hawaiian on Sunday and it came in at ten and a half mins – more than two mins over my allotted time. Dan Atkinson told me that I would be marked down for overrunning, but the Hawaiian in Cardiff is home turf – I have to expect the gig in Edinburgh to be tough. Geordie Financial Year no longer feels relevant but Robins told me that I must have faith in my best stuff. Got an E-Mail from Julia Chamberlain, the organiser – she seems to really want us all to succeed – her E-Mail suggested that we don't go on stage with loose change in our pockets and other bits of great advice.

8th of February 2008, Theatr Hafren, Newtown supporting Rhod Gilbert, score 6.8/10

Classic theatre gig in a town where the nearest comedy club is 85 miles away. They enjoyed it, they were respectful, but a bit quiet. The only time the gig really caught hold was when I took the mickey out of a woman in the front row who had never been to Leeds. I should have realised that this was the way to go, but due to nerves I stuck rigidly to my material. Taking the mickey out of the woman who had never been to Leeds established that I had funny bones – coming out of this banter early was a missed opportunity.

23rd of July 2008, Shore Pebbles, Womanby Street, Cardiff, score 7/10

Tough gig, as the microphone was in Pontypridd. Difficult to motivate myself, as the doors were open because the room was so hot, but the venue is directly opposite a nightclub that was playing drum and bass. Only did 18 mins of my allotted 20, as I literally couldn't be bothered to do 'Boiled-sweet observation', but the bouncer sarcastically shouting 'More' at the end convinced the drunk bar owner to pay me an extra tenner, thus topping up my fee to £60.

27th of February 2009, Southampton Uni, score 6.5/10

Despite trying it again (in front of Steve Bennett[70] as well), Kitchen scissors didn't provide quite the reveal Robins thought it would, even though the preamble is promising. That said, Naked man at Carmarthen leisure centre got a great response – maybe this is one for the Edinburgh show? I think my kitchen scissors and razor blade stuff should be combined into one five-minute routine about sharp things.

---

70 Editor of Chortle.co.uk, the comedy industry bible/tabloid/website.

E:

E-Mail, Are You On?

INT. JOHN'S LIVING ROOM. DAY

Two men, JOHN Robins (handsome, lithe, award-winning[71]) and
ELIS James (dishevelled, mouse-like, semi-retired[72]) sit at a
table. They sip weak ale and flick through copies of Horace's *Ars
Poetica* (Robins) and *Shoot Annual 1996* (James).

> JOHN
>
> Elis, I'm off to send a letter.

> ELIS
>
> Hmmm, but you've not got your coat on and it's
> freezing outside.

> JOHN
>
> But I'm not going outside!

> ELIS
>
> Have the Royal Mail installed a post box in your

---

71 See picture section.

72 [EJ] OK, I get it, we were meant to be writing this chapter together but I'm late so you've
taken it upon yourself to begin and are pursuing an anti-Elis agenda. It's fine, John, because
I'm a relaxed surfer dude and I know for a fact you will have typed this through gritted teeth
because you are Not. Chilled. Out.

house? I know you've petitioned them to but I thought your demands had fallen on deaf ears.

JOHN

Elis, the letter I'm sending needs no post box!

ELIS

What?! Is this some top-secret military weapon test letter? Is it the Heat Seeking A4 Manila I've heard whispers about on Usernet discussion groups?

JOHN

Oh no, this is a letter literally anyone can send.

ELIS

From your house?! You'll be telling me you don't even need a stamp next.

JOHN

But Elis, you don't.

Elis gasps, John turns to camera and smiles a beautiful smile.

JOHN

E-Mail, the unstamped letter you can send from your house without a postbox.

THE END

Ah, Elis, so glad you could make it.

Sorry I'm late, it was the trains.

Of course it was. I was just sharing the script for our most recent advert with the readers.

Oh great, the Compuserve E-Mail advert?

That's the one!

But isn't that kind of throwing them in at the deep end a bit? Shouldn't we give them a bit of grounding first? We want to get as many people involved as possible, don't we?

Good point. Want to start us off?

Sure. Now, John, if I'd told you in 2004 that you could post a letter that didn't exist, and it would arrive at its destination in under ten minutes, what would you have done?

I would have called your local GP and arranged for him to make an emergency house call. Elis, I'd have had you sectioned.

Quite right too, at the time, discussion of instantaneous letters and envelopes with no stamp would have been one of the first things any health practitioner would have looked for in patients suspected of suffering from mania, paranoid delusions or nervous collapse. But not any longer!

Elis is bang right. As recently as 2009 the possibility of messages travelling almost as fast as the speed of a slow plane/very fast car would have been the stuff of science fiction. But thanks to research and development spearheaded by the likes of Alta Vista, Encarta and PC World, it is now commonplace.

Yes, as of 2018, 'E-Mail' (short for 'Electronically Delivered Mail Without a Stamp) has broken into the mainstream. No longer the hobby of basement-dwelling desktop dweebs, this year the medium passed a major milestone. As of February 1st, research shows that over FIFTY PER CENT of people have access to E-Mail, either at home, through a relative, or at their local library.

That's right, and over a third of businesses now accept incoming E-Mail and over a quarter are able to send replies. Ladies and gentlemen, the future is here.

But what exactly is an E-Mail, John?

Well, imagine a letter, just like the ones you type on your word processor, but a letter with no paper, ink or even, increasingly, the sender and receiver's full name and address typed at the top right and left of the page respectively.

But how can people decipher who the message is to or from, without the respective addresses included in full?

Well, imagine being able to combine your name and address, likewise those of your recipient, in just one line . . .

What? ElisJamesFlat4a131HighfieldRoadCrystalPalaceLondonSE4TRJ UnitedKingdom.[73]

Exactly. What you've just imagined is an E-Mail address. And sometimes they are even more concise than that. My E-Mail address, for example, is JohnRobinsQueenFanBristol1982@ blueyonder.net.

What's that bit of graffiti in the middle? Is that a 'street' thing?

Ah, that symbol is called an 'at' symbol, short for 'I'm "at" the address of blueyonder.net'. It connects your name with the company who handle your incoming and outgoing E-Mails, a bit like a postcode, but more accurately, which form of privatised delivery service/courier you use.

And what readers should bear in mind, is that once you have an E-Mail address, and you have the E-Mail address of the person you want to

---

73 This address has been falsified to protect the whereabouts of Elis's actual house, which was bought for him by his 'CRP' (see **Appendix i: Glossary of Terms**).

contact, as well as a desktop PC and an internet connection of 28–56 Kbps, you really are good to go. You write your message . . .

Is there a limit to the length of message, El?

No, that's another big plus of E-Mail. The message you send can be of any length and, indeed, cover any topic.

And once you've sent that message, how long until it appears?

Currently well under an hour, and most of the time less than fifteen minutes. There are companies in Silicon Valley working day and night to send the first sub-minute E-Mail. It's some time off, but the race, dubbed 'Project E Sub 60', is well and truly on.

Incredible, but the possibilities don't stop there. Since 2012 it has also been possible to add attachments such as ClipArt, company slogans and small photos to E-Mails. An attachment is very much like a parcel, but one flattened down to fit in the 'envelope' of the E-Mail.

And John doesn't mean flattened like parcels sent by our old friend the Royal Mail!

Quite. Elis is being light-hearted, but he's highlighted another huge advantage of E-Mail: they cannot get damaged in transit.

Not even torn?

No.

Can they get wet?

Absolutely not. In a way, E-Mails are waterproof. They're the letter that doesn't exist, which you don't need a stamp for, that you can send from your own home without a postbox, that cannot get wet.

And if you want to send the same letter to more than one person, E-Mail has a clever solution. Say, for example, a message about a situation at work, perhaps concerning the state of the kitchenette and/or communal toilet, needs to be sent to everyone in the department. Well, after writing the E-Mail, you simply add more addresses to the recipient box and hey presto, the whole office knows that anything left in the fridge come 3pm Friday is headed for the bin/what Keith did in the toilet. At time of going to press, you can send the same E-Mail to 12 people, which for a department of 50 is only four-and-a-bit E-Mails, but in theory, one day, recipients could be endless.

It's mind-boggling stuff! Another advantage to E-Mail is you no longer have to be at a desktop PC to send them. As long as you are connected to the internet or Ethernet you can send them on an iPad,[74] iPhone[75] or laptop.[76]

But it's not all good news, is it?

I'm afraid not. Just as your letterbox was liable to be stuffed with leaflets and chain letters, so your E-Mail inbox can fill with unwanted advertising and scam messages known as 'SPAM', which stands for Suspicious Promotional and Annoying Mail. Simply turn on your inbox filter . . .

Like a filter in a vacuum or car air vent?

Exactly, and you'll be hoovering up unwanted E-Mail in no time. The odd vital E-Mail will sometimes get put in the wrong box, causing you to be offish with a comedy promoter for seven years, but when you eventually find that they did try to book you once for a gig in 2011, at least you'll know it wasn't anything to do with your act.

---

74 Like a large iPhone.
75 Like a tiny laptop without a keyboard.
76 Big iPad.

Quite. As you can see, the possibilities for E-Mail are literally endless. And we'd encourage everyone reading this to find out more. If you go to your local WH Smiths and look in the computing section, many magazines will have free CD-ROMs attached to the front, which can get you started. Simply boot it up, follow the instructions and away you go. Then, the next time someone asks, 'Are you on E-Mail?,' you'll be able to reply . . .

'Of course. You simply have to be these days!'

E-MAIL: A TIMELINE FOR THE TECHNOLOGY THAT CHANGED A GENERATION

1951   Sci-fi novelist Arthur C. Clarke is told to remove a reference to a 'space letter' from one of his novels by his editor, who describes it as 'too far-fetched'. Clarke protests that sci-fi shouldn't be constrained by contemporary ideas of the possible, to which his editor replies: 'A space letter? No need for a stamp or the Royal Mail? Grow up, man.'

1967   The Summer of Love. Around 11.4 billion letters are delivered by the Royal Mail (excluding packages). There just can't be a more convenient way of communicating with someone than taking the time to write a letter, find an envelope and a stamp, and walking to your nearest post box to send it. Can there?

1976   Steve Jobs realises that he's quite interested in computers. Sends a letter to his mum about it.

1980   The Golden Age of the Fax (GAF) begins. A fax is a primitive, paper-based version of an E-Mail, and was widely regarded as unimprovable.

1987   Elis James's father sends his first fax. It simply reads 'HELLO TESTING FROM WALES' and is sent to the other fax machine in his office. As it arrives successfully, the entire office takes the afternoon off to drink Guinness at a nearby pub, but things at the civil service were different in the 1980s.

1994 The BBC's *Tomorrow's World* runs a feature on E-Mail. It is roundly mocked by the British public. E-Mail is expected to go the same way as other inventions premiered on the show, such as the inflatable dialysis machine and the genetically modified fish that comes with its own chips.

2001 George W. Bush is shown E-Mail for the first time. He finds the whole process so terrifying he declares war on Afghanistan. He refuses to make the technology available to the public for fear of stoking a revolution.

2009 Barack Obama gives the go-ahead and E-Mail is made available to the public. It is initially only used by small numbers of the metropolitan elite.

2010 The 50th E-Mail is sent. The sender receives phone calls from both Bill Gates and the Queen.

2012 John Robins gets an E-Mail address. After six months of pestering, he eventually sets one up for Elis, for a modest fee of £3,000quid.

2015 Manchester Utd goalkeeper David de Gea fails to complete a dream move to Real Madrid after the fax machine at Old Trafford breaks on transfer-deadline day. This is grist to the mill of E-Mail advocates everywhere. Is fax fallible?

2018 FIFTY PER CENT OF BUSINESSES HAVE AN E-MAIL ADDRESS. Elis and John are commended by the CBI for their efforts in spreading the word about E-Mail.

F:

Football, and Why It Matters

About a year ago, I was in a taxi in north London. Naturally, I asked the taxi driver which team he supported, to which he replied, 'Tottenham Hotspur, mate, man and boy.' As the driver was in his late 60s, I asked him if he remembered Cliff Jones, the Swansea-born winger who was part of the great Spurs double-winning team of 1961. 'Cliff Jones? He is my favourite player of all time. How do you know about him? I must have watched every home game he played for Tottenham. No one's talked to me about him in this cab for years.' I genuinely thought he was going to cry. It was as if I, a total stranger, had gone up to him and told him how every person he'd gone to school with in the 1950s was getting on. Football leads to conversations like this every day, and this is why football matters.

I have given up trying to persuade people who don't like football that it has any value. Many years ago, I would take on the naysayers, convinced I could force them to see the light, that they could feel what I feel, that I was one persuasive argument away from discussing *Match of the Day* with them, or whether Yeovil's ground still has an uncovered away end. But, in the same way that I can't be persuaded to like pears and will always think children performing musical theatre is a complete waste of everyone's time, I have never succeeded. That said, if you are one of those rare football agnostics, this chapter will serve as my final attempt to persuade you and I would like it to be read at my funeral.

Will do! *JR*

Football is more popular globally than rock music, democracy and capitalism.[77] It is played everywhere. The 2006 World Cup Final was watched by over 3 billion people, the first time that over half the world's population was definitely doing the same thing at the same time.

Apart from sleeping *JR*

Nothing has united the world like football. Obviously, it's not stopping the arms trade or curing cancer or ending child slavery, but I would say it is definitely the most important of the least important things,[78] and if you are interested in popular culture, it is impossible to ignore. If you haven't already noticed, I absolutely bloody love it, so I'll try to explain why.

Before we get to what football means to the millions of people who watch it, let's discuss how great a game football is. Some sports such as cricket or rugby revolve around the accumulation of runs or points, but goals in football have a rarity value that is uncommon. This can lead to entire games, tournaments or even careers changing on the

---

77 As David Goldblatt points out in his incredible book *The Ball Is Round: A Global History of Football*.

[JR] Which I bought you, didn't I! What a lovely guy!

78 This quote has been attributed to both the Pope and Carlo Ancelotti.

basis of a 90th-minute winner, often against the run of play. An unexpected goal, or a goal in an otherwise tightly contested match, has an explosive element that is difficult to beat (a knock-out in boxing is the closest comparison I can think of). Plenty of football matches are painfully dull, which is why these moments mean so much. No rugby match between top-level Test sides has ended 0–0 since 1964; even the most dreary cricket match will have a few boundaries to applaud, but every goal is special. One thing that often seems to be forgotten by football critics[79] is that playing football is difficult. I am 37 and have been playing football regularly since I was about six. This 30-odd-year dedication to playing the sport is very common. What is also very common is that I am absolutely rubbish. If by some horrendous quirk of fate I was forced to play in a Premier League fixture, even if I were as physically fit as the 21 super-athletes I was sharing a pitch with, my lack of skill would become apparent within about 15 seconds.[80]

---

79 [JR] For fear of derailing this chapter, I've decided to keep my interjections to the footnotes. Safe to say I think this is where I begin to disagree with you, Elis. Who are these 'football critics'? I'm not sure I know who you're arguing with! Some demon rugby-obsessed PE teacher who banned football at school, no doubt.

[EJ] Yes, John. You have to remember I grew up in a country where liking football was regarded as somehow unpatriotic and even effeminate. I have had these arguments for my entire life. And when the Premier League began to inflate footballers' wages to hitherto unimagined levels, debates about whether they were 'worth it' were conducted in the national press for about ten years.

[JR] Fair point. I do like how you've managed to argue that football's allure is that it's mainly uneventful. Interesting point.

80 In November 1996, the Senegalese footballer Ali Dia somehow persuaded Southampton manager Graeme Souness that he was FIFA World Player of the Year George Weah's cousin, in an attempt to get a trial at the club. The person who contacted the club purported to be George Weah calling on behalf of Dia, whereas it was in reality Dia's friend from university. After lying about Dia having played for Paris Saint-Germain and the Senegal national team, Souness was convinced enough to give him a one-month contract. Despite appearing out of his depth in training, he was brought on as a sub in a game against Leeds Utd, but was so bad he was then substituted for someone else. He is the best example of the gulf in talent between a normal person and a Premier League footballer I can think of. Southampton player Matt Le Tissier said: 'He ran around the pitch like Bambi on ice, it was very embarrassing to watch.' Dia was named number 1 in a list of the 50 worst footballers of all time in *The Times*.

Throughout my life I have heard football deniers claim that it 'just 22 men kicking a ball around',[81] when this could not be further from the truth. If it were just '22 men kicking a ball around', then I would be doing it, and earning £150,000quid a week.[82] The amount of skill, dedication and relentless application it takes to become a top-class footballer is beyond the imagination of a normal person.[83]

David Beckham took free-kicks hundreds of times a day, many thousands of times a week, from when he was a child to when he retired at the age of 38. Naturally this applies to all the top exponents of any

---

81 [JR] I have never heard anyone actually say this!

[EJ] Then you have had a charmed life, and for the first time in history, I am jealous of you. Try growing up in a country where football is sometimes referred to as 'Wendyball'.

[JR] Wow. I mean that's insane. I've just only ever heard that line as a parody of the sort of people who might say it. I guess growing up in England has given me a very different outlook on football. That said, I still maintain that most football fans actually hate it most of the time.

82 John and I would pre-record the show, working around the Premier League fixture list. Something I am not allowed to do as a fan, but a luxury afforded to the former England international Peter Crouch when he was briefly on the station.

83 [JR] I think most sane people can appreciate that professional football, like the highest level of any sport, takes skill, dedication and application, and is something beyond the majority of people. Like with any sport you don't get better by playing, but by practising, and I'm assuming you don't go to football training three times a week? Wouldn't you be just as out of your depth if you had to run a marathon with Mo Farah? Or play in the England hockey team? Or darts against Phil Taylor? I wonder if growing up in a country full of rugby fans has exposed you to more criticism/dismissal of football than most?

[EJ] I agree with you that most people accept there is some skill involved, although this is not the case across the board. I once had an argument with the novelist Sarah Dunant (patron of the Women's Prize for Fiction) about this on Radio 4. She accepted the value of rock music, but seemed amazed when I told her that I could play most Beatles' songs on guitar (like most guitarists I know), but that the knuckleball kind of free-kick Gareth Bale is so good at was totally beyond me. I think football's sheer ubiquity causes people to assume it's easier than other sports.

[JR] I also think, conversely, that the fun of playing it is that maybe once in a while you can pull off something truly incredible, and then spend months and months trying to replicate it. I remember at comedians' football when Danny Bhoy screamed 'Get iiiiiii-in!' before scoring from the halfway line into one of those six-a-side goals. For maybe five seconds he was Matt Le Tissier. I'm not that great at golf, but twice in my life I've chipped in from maybe twenty yards. I remember each time vividly.

sport (Martina Navratilova's attacking serve–volley game wasn't pre-destined in the womb; and had Shane Warne thrown all of his energies into quantity surveying, he couldn't have become the greatest spin bowler cricket has ever seen in his spare time). But in my experience, the skill needed to become a footballer tends to be dismissed more easily than other sports.[84] What are the other sporting equivalents of 'it's just 22 men kicking a ball about?'[85] No one ever says, 'It's just some bloke executing a series of swings, balances and releases on a set of parallel bars' about gymnastics, even if they think gymnastics is a boring waste of time. People never dismiss the commitment and flair it takes to become a top-level athlete in other sports (with the exception of dressage, which must be the most mocked sport in history). I have my suspicions as to why, and I think there's an element of class-based prejudice. Paul Gascoigne and Wayne Rooney are two of the most talented footballers England has produced over the last 30 years, but they are routinely sneered at, and I think it's because they are men from working-class backgrounds who have been made unimaginably rich for kicking a football. I don't remember Tim Henman[86] (according to Google, net worth £17m) ever getting the same treatment. But Tim Henman didn't have tattoos, a huge Rolex watch or a chandelier in his kitchen like Jamie Vardy does.[87]

As a schoolboy I was lucky enough to play against ex-Spurs, Everton, Fulham and Wales footballer Simon Davies, and the gulf in

---

84 [JR] Elis, who has done this to you? Who hurt you? If someone was mean to a seven-year-old Elis who just wanted to play football, I swear to God I will hunt them down . . .

85 [JR] Mate, how many people dismiss cricket as boring? 'Like watching paint dry.' Also, the rubbish people come out with when I refer to snooker as a sport! Utter, utter nutters.

[EJ] True. And I disagree with those people. Although cricket doesn't permeate into popular culture in the same way, and so cricket critics (cricktics?) are never as angry.

86 Or Nick Faldo, or Rory McIlroy or Nigel Mansell . . .

87 [JR] I think this is a very, very interesting point, and I totally agree. The attitude towards them is often reminiscent to the contempt you might get from aristocracy to 'new money'.

talent between Simon and the other hopefuls on the pitch was gargantuan. He was playing for Solva Under-12s against Haverfordwest County Under-12s, and it was like competing against someone from another planet. Haverfordwest is the biggest town in the county, and we were used to winning, but after an hour Solva were 15–0 up and Simon had a hand in all the goals. We were chasing shadows and, as the rain hammered down and we were buffeted by wind from the Irish Sea, it quickly became hugely demoralising. On the minibus home, we discussed whether he was older than us, and playing for a younger age group to make up the numbers. We raged bitterly about how unfair that was, until my dad said, 'I don't think it's that. I think he's going to play for Manchester United.' And Dad was almost right. Even at the tender age of 11, Simon's huge talent separated him from the mere mortals he was sharing a pitch with.[88]

As most football fans have at least had a kickaround, they are able to appreciate the sheer talent that is being shown by players at the highest level.[89] Before anyone claims that it is Neanderthal or uncultured[90] to appreciate what people can do with a football, allow me to quote from one of the 20th century's greatest historians, Eric Hobsbawm:

---

88 [JR] I remember the same playing cricket in my teens. There were two brothers who went on to play for Gloucester, and not even for the first team, and they would regularly make centuries at 13 years old. CENTURIES!

89 [JR] But aren't many of the shots in top-level football exactly like the sort of thing you or I would do in a kickabout: arrogant, optimistic strikes from 30 yards that end up in Row Z? That happens multiple times a game. You're somehow arguing at the same time that the rarity of excitement and quality in football sets it apart from other sports and also that the players are somehow superhuman in their talent, way beyond the imagination of the general public. See me after class.

90 This is from page 80 of Nick Hornby's *Fever Pitch*: 'A feminist colleague of mine literally refused to believe that I watched Arsenal, a disbelief that apparently had its roots in the fact we once had a conversation about a feminist novel. How could I possibly have read that book *and* been to Highbury? I admit that discourse has moved on since *Fever Pitch* was published, but I definitely grew up at a time when being into football was seen as slightly thuggish and uncultured. Like lots of people I know, I had a sabbatical from football from 1997 to 2000 to try and appear more sensitive in front of girls.

' . . . who, having seen the Brazilian team in its days of glory, will deny it the claim to art?'[91]

Being small isn't a particular disadvantage in playing football. Lionel Messi (in my opinion the greatest player ever) stands at around 5´7˝. Lionel Messi can do things with a football that will bring me to tears, and he routinely makes much bigger men who are trying their best to kick him look stupid. This modern-day David vs Goliath morality tale is no exception – he formed part of the greatest Barcelona team of all time alongside Xavi and Iniesta, neither of whom is taller than 5´7˝. Although it is true that all sports benefit from certain physical characteristics, there are all sorts of sizes playing top-level football, whereas rugby seems to be played exclusively by physical freaks, and I can't think of many professional basketball players who struggle to fit a light bulb. Alongside its inherent simplicity (you just need a ball to play football and, as *The Fast Show*'s Ron Manager pointed out, you can use jumpers for goalposts), not having to be 6´5˝ makes football a very accessible game to play. And, as my old primary school proved, the pitch doesn't even need to be flat.

However, even in this age of sports science and nutritionists, where footballers train in GPS vests that are worth £10,000quid and their every move is watched by cameras from 50 angles and pored over by analysts, coaches and pundits, it still has the capacity to surprise. As I write this (17 June 2018), Iceland have just drawn with Argentina at the World Cup. Argentina have won the World Cup twice (1978, 1986), are regarded as one of football's powerhouses, and in Lionel Messi have the world's best player.[92] Iceland has the same population as Coventry, and their right-back had to take annual leave from his job as a salt packer in a warehouse to play in the tournament. One of the game's great countries is conducting a national post-mortem because they've

---

91 Eric Hobsbawm, *Age of Extremes: The Short Twentieth Century 1914–91* (1994), p. 198.
92 OK, OK, I accept that some of you think it's Ronaldo. Let's chat about this at one of the book tour shows.

drawn with a team whose goalkeeper is a film director and is from a place where it's practically impossible to play football outside because of the weather. You never know what is going to happen in football, which is what keeps people coming back for more. It could be rubbish, it could be magical, you just don't know.[93]

I often think that the match is secondary to the day itself. For instance, one of the things I loved about going to watch Swansea play at the Vetch Field was the sense of place – the ground had been there since 1912, and you could really tell. Some of the graffiti at the back of the North Bank venerated men who'd played for the club before I was born. The pubs around the ground had been a part of people's matchgoing routine for generations. However, what I really love about attending football matches is the sense of being at an event that really matters – knowing that you have a hot ticket, and the eyes of the world are on you. The first major sporting event I attended was actually a rugby match, the Llanelli v Neath Schweppes Cup Final, on 7 May 1988. The game attracted a world-record crowd for a domestic club rugby match (around 56,000), and the sheer scale of it is one of the things I vividly remember – that over five times more people were there than lived in my home town, and we were all walking to the same place to do the same thing at the same time. The other thing that struck me was the smell, oh, that wonderful smell – fags, fried onions, lager, urine. If Isy was willing to swap her shower gel and perfume for this 'Big Four', I would be in heaven. There is nothing else like it.

I like being part of a crowd. I went to watch Swansea play Watford a few months ago and, as predicted, the Swans played very badly.

---

93 [JR] And the last thing you'd want was for something to be consistently magical, eh?

[EJ] What is consistently magical? You can say Queen if you like, but I would reply with the lyric 'It's bytes and mega-chips for tea' from their 1984 misstep 'Machines (Or "Back to Humans")'.

[JR] Fair point, though I'd say that the Ryder Cup is consistently magical. But I don't think football is unique in being unpredictable and having the potential for upsets. Surely that's the joy of all sport?

However, with around 20 minutes to go, something changed. The team began to play with more verve and desire, and the supporters responded, urging them on. It felt like we were feeding off each other. As soon as Swansea equalised, I knew we would get another, and the other 1,500 or so Swansea fans all thought the same thing. As I watched wave after wave of Swansea attacks, I looked around and the supporters in our end were literally bouncing up and down in expectation, and when the goal eventually came, it felt like uncorking a bottle of shaken champagne. I took a friend and his 13-year-old son, and for the first 70 minutes we bemoaned the poor performance, the lack of application from our players, how cold it was, whether we should have stayed at home and done something worthwhile, like learned a foreign language or defrosted the freezer. But as soon as the winner went in, attending became the best decision any of us had made for a long time.[94]

I practically floated back to the car, and it was socially acceptable to accept hugs from strangers and slap people on the back that I will never see again. I have had some of the greatest moments of my life at music gigs but, by and large, it's quite predictable what will happen – plenty of bands don't change the set list throughout a whole tour.[95] Even those great nights where something magical is in the air (I saw Radiohead on the *OK Computer* tour in 1997, a gig I think about quite regularly), I could have repeated the experience by going to watch them the following night in London. You cannot predict what will happen at a football match, and the frisson that gives me is addictive.

At its heart, however, what raises football above the general

---

94 [JR] This is understandable, coming from a man who, as yet, does not have a cash ISA. And, I now suspect, has a freezer that needs defrosting. A freezer with ice-covered elements is very inefficient. So he's probably losing the cost of a match-day ticket a year in higher electricity bills.

95 Any jazzers reading this: don't worry, I know – your lot are the exception.

appreciation I have for almost all sporting prowess (how can your pulse not quicken when Serena Williams effortlessly brushes her rivals aside or when Mo Farah runs his way into the record books), is the tribal devotion you are encouraged to have for your team. I completely accept that there are thousands of armchair fans who feel the triumphs and disappointments of their chosen side as keenly as the ones who bother to travel up and down the country to support at the ground. But it's the second group I'm interested in, and it's that group I feel a part of. If you are the type of person who will take an afternoon off to go and watch your side play on the other side of the country, especially if your team isn't very good but you simply can't countenance not being there, I am like you and I understand you. Let's go for a drink.[96]

Football teams are named after places. Not animals, businesses, industries or people. Back when I used to watch a lot of Swansea away games (2002–2008, before stand-up comedy got in the way), I was addicted to going to places I had never been before to stand for 90 minutes with people who had probably heard of my secondary school.[97]

I once went to Carlisle on a Tuesday night (a round trip of 600 miles) to watch the Swans battle out a 0–0 draw. The game was largely uneventful (I think we hit the crossbar a couple of times), but I felt a kinship with every one of the 500 people in the Swansea end who had bothered to show up. I once went to Torquay on a Tuesday night to watch Swansea play in the LDV Vans Trophy First Round (South),

---

96 [JR] I, however, am not like you, I do not understand you, so please don't come and chant songs in my pub or on my train. It's intimidating and anti-social. If, however, you want to hold a child's hand on the way to a stadium in a calm and peaceful manner, wearing some form of scarf, or talk to an old man at the bar about the past, in front of a sepia photo of someone in big shorts, that I do admire. In summary, keep the noise down.

97 [JR] It's interesting that this could easily be a description of the life of a stand-up. (Apart from the school thing.)

and the 88 Swansea fans who made the trip were rewarded with free chips as the burger van at Torquay Utd's Plainmoor ground had made too many: 'To be honest, mate, we were expecting more of you. If you don't eat them, they're going in the bin.' These people are often mocked and their contribution is occasionally downplayed, but they are what makes football great. Jonathan Wilson, the journalist who has written the undisputed bible of football tactics,[98] has disagreed with this, especially the assertion that 'without the fans, football is nothing'.

> The idea that 'there'd be no game without the fans' is commonplace. There would; it's just it would be small-scale, played out on parks with nobody on the touchlines but the subs and a couple of bored players' girlfriends like most Sunday football. Sport doesn't need crowds to thrive; the likes of hockey, angling and rock climbing get by perfectly well without thousands of people roaring encouragement or abuse at the participants.[99]

But I think Jonathan is wrong.[100] Not only do football fans make the game a spectacle. They *are* the spectacle. They are the reason countless people will describe Cup Final days or league title wins as the *best day of their lives*. Playing football without a crowd 'behind closed doors' (a punishment meted out by the authorities for a variety of different reasons) does more than affect match-day revenue. It reduces football to its most basic form, and it becomes just another sport. A technical exercise. Plenty of people aren't there to watch Lionel Messi. They are there to watch people watch Lionel Messi.[101]

Ultimately, like any sport, football is about stories. It's not about

---

98 Jonathan Wilson's *Inverting the Pyramid: The History of Football Tactics* is a quite extraordinary piece of work. I met him a few months ago, and the man knows more about Hungarian football in the 50s than John knows about farthings, shame and Queen combined.
99 From 'The Essential Backdrop' by Jonathan Wilson in *The Blizzard*, September 2012.
100 [JR] Let's be honest, he's talking out of his arse. Is rock climbing 'thriving'?!
101 [JR] That is a fantastic sentence.

tactics, or formation, or team shape, it's about defying expectations, and people becoming heroes. With an obvious bias to my teams, here are some of my favourite moments:

Wales at the 2016 European Championships

Prior to 2016, the last time Wales had qualified for a major international tournament was 1958. To put that into some perspective, the satirists of the time were still making jokes about the Suez Crisis and Paul McCartney had known John Lennon for about 12 months. Since that World Cup in Sweden, Wales had come within one game of qualifying for a major tournament a staggering 11 times, always to fail at the last hurdle, and it had become an albatross for the fans and the team.

We had failed in a myriad of different ways – missed penalties, dodgy refereeing decisions, losing to teams we should have beaten – but my personal favourite is when we were beating Iceland at the Vetch Field in Swansea in 1981 and the floodlights failed. After a 43-minute delay, where supporters stood in the dark, the game resumed but the Welsh players were shaken by the hold-up and unable to retain their composure. An Iceland team comprised largely of amateurs came back to equalise and knocked us out of the 1982 World Cup. Two of the greatest failures in our canon of disappointments (losing to Romania, thus failing to qualify for the 1994 World Cup, and losing to Russia, thus failing to qualify for the 2004 European Championships) were games I had attended, and like most Welsh football fans I assumed we were cursed or jinxed and it would never happen. I had watched Northern Ireland, Latvia and New Zealand play on the biggest stage, but I had accepted that for Wales it wasn't to be. We even sang songs about it. I still went to the games to be crushingly disappointed, because that is what football fans do. I had wanted qualification since I was ten, and now I was in my 30s, I accepted that supernatural forces were at play – every two years there was a huge football party, and my country were never invited. I felt sorry for the genuinely breathtaking talent that missed out (Ian Rush, Ryan Giggs, Neville Southall), but mostly I felt sorry for myself.

Fast forward to 2016. Wales had a truly phenomenal player in Gareth Bale. With him as the talisman, a squad that was mourning the tragic suicide of manager Gary Speed qualified for the European Championships in France. At this point, I was happy as I had achieved my ambition of seeing Wales qualify in my lifetime. By the time the tournament arrived, the only thing I needed to be delirious was to hear the anthem being sung at the first game, and to hopefully see us score a goal. But during that summer, Wales exceeded all expectations by becoming the smallest country to ever reach the semi-final of a major championships, beating tournament favourites Belgium in the quarter-final with an unforgettable goal from Hal Robson-Kanu, a man who at the time didn't even have a club. The bond between players and fans felt very real, every fantastic second felt like a party, and the fact that the Welsh supporters were so well behaved makes it one of the most magical times of my life.[102] For a team I could relate to so much (Gareth Bale went to the same school as my friend Nathan, Aaron Ramsey went to the same school as my friend the lovely Rhodri, and Joe Allen went to the same school as my friend Andrew) to perform so well, for a country whose football team had

---

102 [JR] I would argue the reason that Euro 2016 was so incredible was because it was such an outlier in the history of international football in the UK. Everyone loved Wales's story because it was such a contrast to decades of moaning, anger, frustration and negativity that is the overwhelming feature of football, in my opinion. The reason I have started to dislike football over the past couple of years is because it dawned on me that most football fans dislike football most of the time. They dislike everything about it: the wages, the manager, the ticket prices, the board, the owner, the players not putting the effort in, the new ground, the old ground, renaming the ground, the time the match starts. It's a swamp of endless bile. And then I was watching the cricket and the opposing fans and *opposing players* applauded a *rival* batsman making a century, and I thought, 'YES! This is a sport people love!' They love the sport. As much, if not more so, than the team. And that breeds respect and joy for the game. In a way that, I would argue, your tribalism in football doesn't.

been a punchline for so long to be a global feel-good story, gave me a feeling of joy that will stay forever.

Denmark win the European Championships of 1992

Denmark hadn't actually qualified for the 1992 European Championships, but were given less than a week to get a squad together to replace Yugoslavia, who had just been barred from playing because of the outbreak of war in the Balkans. In one of the greatest shocks in the history of the game, they went on to beat World Champions Germany in the final, despite being without their best player Michael Laudrup, who had chosen to go on holiday after an argument with the manager. Denmark won a thrilling match 2–1 as Laudrup, the greatest footballer the country has ever produced, listened to the game over a payphone from the bar of his hotel, because he couldn't find a place that was showing it in New York.

Wrexham beat Arsenal in the FA Cup 3rd round, 1992

Arsenal were reigning English Champions in January 1992, and were drawn against Wrexham in the FA Cup. At the time Wrexham was the smallest town to have a team in the Football League, and had finished bottom of the entire thing the previous season, only being spared relegation to the Conference because the Football League was being restructured. Arsenal went one nil up in the first half, before a 37-year-old Mickey Thomas scored the equaliser and local lad Steve Watkin scored the winner with eight minutes to go. Hero of the hour Steve Watkin now works as an accountant, but his goal is shown every year as part of the BBC's FA Cup coverage, and I never tire of seeing it.

Swansea City retain Football League status, 2003

After the club's fans had battled to remove owners seemingly hell-bent on destroying the club, Swansea City FC were in administration, unable to buy players, without a bank account and with a playing squad that was hugely out of its depth. Local boy Brian Flynn was brought in to manage the side and prevent the Swans from being the first team to have played in the First Division to be relegated from the entire Football League. With a few weeks to go the club looked doomed, but a succession of heroic performances meant that victory on the final day of the season against Hull would be enough. Swansea were 2–1 down at half-time, but local lad James Thomas, a boyhood fan of the side, scored an audacious hat-trick to win the game for Swansea 4–2. Thomas is now an emergency medical technician for the Welsh Ambulance Service, and if I ever meet him I will hold him until I am asked to stop. This game was the starting point for the club's rise through the divisions, culminating in winning the League Cup at Wembley and qualifying for Europe. From no bank account to play-ing in the Premier League and Europe within the space of ten years. Football, bloody hell.[103]

---

103 Alex Ferguson's reaction when Man Utd won
the Champions League in 1999. I think it is perfect.

G:

Gorky's Zygotic Mynci[104]

I am a very different person to how I was in 1996. I no longer lie about how often I shave, I no longer think I deserve credit for putting cereal back in the cupboard and I'm now a total, unashamed convert to flossing. However, one thing I am as sure of now as I was then is that Gorky's Zygotic Mynci (1991–2006) are the best band of all time.[105]

Over the years I have awarded this accolade to a few other groups. The Gorky's didn't change the planet like The Beatles, they never had the commercial success or even the patronage of the music press like the Super Furry Animals,[106] and calling it a day after five short

---

104 I'm aware the main difference between me writing about the Gorky's and John writing about Queen is that most readers won't be familiar with the Gorky's' work. If what you are about to read inspires you to listen to the band, I have suggested records to get started with at the end of this piece.

105 [JR] I mean, you know what I'm thinking here. Feel free to fill in this footnote yourselves_____

106 [JR] Neither did they perform the best set at Live Aid, invent the music video as we know it, produce the bestselling album of all time in the UK, record the soundtrack to *Highlander*, have all members write a Top 10 single, use any home-made guitars, six-pences as plectrums . . . I COULD GO ON!

years means The Smiths left us with an impeccable, faultless back catalogue.

> **Luckily Morrissey remains to diminish their reputation with every passing interview.**

But, as much as I love these bands, whether it's the 16-year-old me who should be taking his GCSEs more seriously, or the 37-year-old me who should be taking commercial digital indie radio more seriously, none of those other bands distil my personality into music like the Gorky's do. The sheer popularity of The Beatles or The Smiths also means those groups will never feel 'mine' like the Gorky's did. Gorky's Zygotic Mynci were brilliant, they were different, and they were mine.

> **I'm not sure you can own a band in the same way you can own a lead singer's GCSE art coursework.**[107]

The Gorky's were formed at my school in Carmarthen in 1991, which was clearly hugely significant for me. In 1996, after a torrid period of work experience at the Crown Prosecution Service, where I fell asleep with boredom during a GBH trial at Swansea Crown Court and was reprimanded in front of everyone by the Judge . . .

> **ORDER! ORDER! God, I wish I'd been there, gavel in hand! I'd have absolutely torn you to shreds. In fact, I'd have sent you to prison.**

---

107 [EJ] Spoiler alert, but if you listen to the episode of Richard Herring's Leicester Square Theatre podcast where John and I are guests, you will discover that I bought Euros Childs's GCSE art coursework from a bigger boy who found it in the art room at school and sold it to me at an exorbitant rate. I regret nothing.

I was beginning to suspect that traditional office work like my parents did was not for me. As I gazed reproachfully at my pathetically small hands and weak arms, I was also becoming aware that physical work, like my cousins or grandfathers had done, was probably not an option either. With my football career having stalled at Carmarthen Town Under-14s level, I was beginning to feel justifiable concern at where my future lay. It was around this time that I discovered the Gorky's. Although I loved comedy, it was a completely inaccessible art form to attempt – the nearest comedy club to where I lived was over 100 miles away in Bristol,[108] and I had never met anyone who had ever met anyone who had ever met a comedian. Comedy seemed a completely alien world of people who'd either been discovered at the Edinburgh Festival (in Scotland! Two countries away!) or Cambridge, which meant I needed decent A-levels, as well as a sense of humour.[109]

Like most teenagers, music was my other obsession, along with comedy and football, but that also seemed a remote world of confident Mancunians with drug[110] habits, assassinated icons or boy bands. Just as I was beginning to worry that going to a small school in a small town meant that doing something creative for a living was something that happened to other people, the Gorky's appeared on the front cover of *Melody Maker*.

---

108 The Cardiff Glee Club opened in 2001, although there were apparently gigs happening in Cardiff's Wharf Pub before that. The closest I came to live comedy was my mum's friend Helen going to watch Phil Cool and Jasper Carrott's 'Carrott and Cool' tour at Carmarthen's Lyric Theatre in 1992.

109 Before anyone thinks that I am Billy Elliot, I went to a very good state school that sent one or maybe two pupils to Oxbridge every year. Oxbridge certainly wasn't out of the question—

[JR] Hmmm, let's not get ahead of ourselves

—but by 17 I had written off the idea, mainly I think because I was lazy and was scared of the work it would entail but also out of a slightly misplaced sense of class loyalty, as I thought Oxbridge would be full of dicks who liked rowing and rugby and the Conservative Party.

[JR] And one bona fide legend.

110 [JR] /discount toastie.

The Gorky's! On the front cover of a proper music paper! They had gone to my school! My mum worked with the singer's mum! They used to go to Slipped Discs, the record shop in Carmarthen market where I went on a Saturday and that was next to the carpet shop where my friend Gavin worked![111] And they had achieved this success by singing in Welsh, and not fitting in, and playing their first gigs in Carmarthen, and it suddenly felt like having my brain turned off and turned back on again. I would like to bottle the feeling of seeing someone with your background succeed at something you would like to do, and give it to every worried, discomfited teenager on the planet.[112]

> This is a genuinely lovely sentiment. Though if you'd given me that bottled feeling I'd have been/was/am crippled by jealousy and bitterness. That said, I do wish Joel Dommett well.

Who knows, maybe if they hadn't existed I would have affected an Essex accent and formed a Blur tribute band? But it's more likely I would have become the world's worst clerical assistant at an office in Llanelli and got a stomach ulcer from stress. Maybe, and I know I wasn't capable of this, I would have done what fellow Carmarthenshire boy John Cale had done in the 1960s and bought a one-way ticket to New York to prove myself on the other side of the Atlantic, but I knew John Lennon had been refused a Green Card under the Nixon administration and I was very keen to do things by the book.[113] Maybe if the Gorky's hadn't existed, I would have joined the merchant navy and had experiences, or become a club promoter in Ibiza and never looked back, but they did exist, and that gave me a huge shot of confidence

---

111 [JR] You own their GCSE art coursework!

112 I love the phrase people use about diversity in the media: 'You can't be what you can't see.'

113 In this analogy, I think that John, embarrassingly, is my Lou Reed.

[JR] I think this is the greatest compliment I've ever been paid. Can we recreate the cover of *Songs for Drella* for our debut album?

– it allowed a 16-year-old dreamer to dream a bit more, and feel less of a wanker for doing it.

Supergrass used to sell a badge at gigs that said, 'Supergrass: Everyone's Second Favourite Band', which I think is creditably self-aware.[114] There is an alchemy to a band working their way into your soul, and it doesn't begin and end at the songs. One of the first things you'd notice about the Gorky's' releases in the mid-90s was the brilliant record covers, which were great to look at, beautiful enough for you to want to put on your wall, totally different to anything else in the record shop and told you exactly what the music would sound like. Even the font[115] the band's name was written in was perfect visual shorthand for 'We are a quirky offbeat band and if you like us, you'll become obsessed with us. If you meet someone else who likes us, you will bond in a way that normally only happens in 1980s' Coming of Age movies.'

When I discovered them in the mid-90s, the Gorky's were making music that was very melodic and catchy, but playful, psychedelic and unpredictable.[116] The band also weren't afraid of the odd wigout in the middle of a single, or including a late-night argument about a teabag on their early records. This was unbelievably charming and made me love them even more. The early records were notable for the snippets of rehearsals that were often at the beginning or end of songs – being told off by parents after neighbours had complained about the noise ('What have I told you? BASS SOUNDS TRAVEL'), or just telling the dog to sit. I was in a band at the time and we tape recorded our rehearsals – and five boys from west Wales larking about in a garage in 1991 sounded the same as five boys larking about in a garage in 1996, the difference being that the five boys in a garage in 1991 had a record deal and Japanese

---

114 [JR] Though inaccurate, as we all know, everyone's second-favourite band is The Cross, Roger Taylor's solo outfit.

115 Sadly changed in 1998.

116 This sounds like I'm punting out for work at *Classic Rock* magazine.

fans camped in their garden.[117] But it was those little glimpses into the personality of the band that I loved so much, in an era before social media, and when musicians seemed completely elusive.[118]

Each Gorky's record is different, and I, The Lovely Robin and my friend, The Lovely Rhodri, all agree that the best thing they did was 1995's *Llanfwrog* EP. The record is very melodic, gently psychedelic folk sung in a mixture of Welsh and English. As I sit here trying to work out why I like it so much, I'm realising how pivotal the Gorky's were to forging my identity – either by pointing me in the direction of things that were cool, or by reassuring me that being a beta-teenager was actually fine. But on a simpler, more prosaic level, I think blending catchy melodies with listenable experimentalism is an irresistible combination.[119] It's Rush and Dalglish, it's ham and mustard, it's an iPhone and a trip to the toilet.[120] When you blend this with their humour, whether it's the pretend radio jingles on their third album *Bwyd Time*, the band doing photoshoots for the serious music press dressed as druids (when everyone else was wearing Fred Perry or dressing like it was 1973) or how much of a laugh they seemed to be having in their early videos, I was totally smitten.

---

117 I was in two bands as a teenager. The first was called Pysgod Sobr (Sober Fish), a fairly conventional grunge band like all teenage bands seemed to be in 1996. We rehearsed in my parents' garage, and during one gig in Carmarthen's Riviera nightclub I went to buy a can of Sprite during a guitar solo in an attempt to display an air of disaffected nonchalance. Frustratingly it had to be Sprite because the bar had already refused to serve me lager for being underage. Following the band's split ('musical differences'), I licked my wounds for a couple of years before forming Jenny and the Bodybags. Influenced by the 60s' Situationists, anti-authoritarian Marxism and the more extreme end of Sonic Youth, we split up after a gig at Ferryside Rugby Club forced us to realise the audience for that kind of thing in west Wales was very, very small.

118 If you work at *Classic Rock* and want to offer me a position, do contact me through my agent, Chris Lander, at Phil McIntyre Entertainment.

[JR] Same contact for positions at the Official International Queen Fan Club.

119 As well as *Classic Rock*, I would be happy to contribute to *Q*, *Mojo*, *Uncut* and *Total Guitar*.

120 [JR] I laughed for over 45 seconds at this, but I fear you've just lost your job at *Classic Rock*.

It's difficult to imagine how remote a town could feel in the pre-internet age.[121] Carmarthen only had one proper video shop, so watching any of the films I had read about was practically impossible unless they were on TV or available to buy from HMV in Cardiff or Swansea. We had two record shops, but nowhere to buy clothes unless you were happy to dress like you worked for a building society. Euros Childs, the lead singer, and John Lawrence, the guitarist, were actually from hippified south Pembrokeshire[122] and made the 30-mile commute to my school every morning. Growing up in Pembrokeshire meant the band's songwriters were mainly influenced by the second-hand vinyl they bought from local charity shops, which created the curious situation of a bunch of 16-year-olds in the 90s being influenced by Caravan, Kevin Ayers and The Incredible String Band. They were the teenage outliers you had to take seriously, but the mix of unfashionable influences, their youth (they had a record deal when they were still in school) and the fact that they were about as laddy as a probiotic yoghurt meant their intermittent appearances on ITV's *The Chart Show* or *Jools Holland* felt brilliantly subversive.

To write this piece I went back and watched a lot of the band's early interviews, which I'd taped from the TV and watched again and again. The band were hugely bashful and shy in interviews, and in the context of the time felt like they came from another planet. The band became more conventional as they got older, but I found it hugely comforting as a teenager that a group with such a normal background were capable of making such idiosyncratic music. They didn't dress like prog rock musicians . . .

---

121 [JR] To get an idea, why not visit modern-day Carmarthen?

122 [JR] Genuinely thought 'hippified' was a place name the first few times I read this. Even googled it.

> **Apart from when they dressed like druids? Sounds pretty prog rock to me, El ... [123]**

... there were no capes or wings or pretentious stage outfits – in fact, they didn't even look like the cool indie bands of the time, simply dressing like a bunch of west Walians with long hair. But they made records that still sound as fresh to me now as they did then, and had the Gorky's not existed I'm sure I'd be a very different person. The Gorky's taught me it was fine to stick out a bit, that there were cool things around if only you looked for them, and that being born in Pembrokeshire instead of New York or London isn't a hindrance if you're good enough at something. No music can move you like that first band you fall in love with. And I'm glad it was them.

Some places to start:

With nine albums and fifteen singles, there's a lot to get through.[124] Each album is pleasingly different, so this list reflects my own personal tastes.

Llanfwrog (EP, 1995)

I think this is peak Gorky's – all of my favourite things about the band combined into one flawless, four-track EP. Melodies that will stick in your brain, they're quirky without being alienating. I would suggest you watch the video for 'Miss Trudy' on YouTube, in which Euros does a wink to camera so perfect it should be put on the UNESCO World Heritage List.

'Patio Song' (single, 1996)

Their most famous song. It was Radio 1 single of the week when Mark and Lard hosted the breakfast show, and this got the band on *Jools*

---

123 They were being tongue in cheek, you div.

124 [JR] Nine albums 'a lot to get through'?! Are you high?! See **Z: Zappa, Where to Start With.**

Holland. It is absolutely lovely, and every time someone tells me they walked down the aisle to it (which happens more often than you'd imagine), I think, 'Yes! Of course!'

'Her Hair Hangs Long' (*How I Long to Feel That Summer in My Heart*, 2001)

By now the band were less explicitly experimental, and were pouring their energies into writing brilliant pop songs. This is the high point on a great album, and as an added treat my friend, the lovely Rhodri, contributes guitar on this track.

'Fresher Than the Sweetness in Water' (*The Blue Trees*, 2000)

That rare example of a cover being far superior to the original, this version of the Honeybus song from the late 1960s is so catchy you will find it difficult to remember how your life felt before hearing this song for the first time. I've included it as a palate cleanser for the slightly weirder stuff below.

Introducing Gorky's Zygotic Mynci (Compilation album, 1996)

This was initially very hard to get hold of (a friend of mine won the Japanese version in a competition on Radio Cymru), and so I obsessed over it. It's a very good introduction to the first two albums and the five EPs they released on Ankst (1994–96), and because the internet has changed everything this compilation is now about as accessible as bread.[125] It serves as a greatest hits for their early period, and is predictably excellent. I remember reading an interview with Jon Bon Jovi in *Q* magazine around the time this was released, and the journalist remarked that he had a copy lying next to the hi-fi in his hotel room.

---

125 [JR] Ironically one of the few things it's genuinely hard to get hold of on the internet.

God knows what he thought of it. As an experiment, try listening to 'The Game of Eyes' (one of my favourite songs ever) and imagine that Bon Jovi is in the room with you.

Tatay (LP, 1994)

My favourite album, but not the one I would suggest you start with (that would be *How I Long to Feel That Summer in My Heart* or *Barafundle*). It's their weirdest release, but what filled me with awe was their ability to derail songs like 'Y Ffordd Oren' and 'Naw E Pimp' with backwards keyboards and still come up with something I would be humming as I walked to school. This record deserves a special mention for the recorded snippets of the band rehearsing. My favourite example is a late-night argument at what sounds like a sleepover, when Steffan, the then violin player, replies to pleas to be quiet with an indignant 'Oh sorry, owner of the house'. Ah, the past.

Isy's favourite song is 'Let's Get Together (In Our Minds)' from *Gorky 5* (1998). How this wasn't a huge hit is beyond me – the string arrangement makes me want to try to jump into the music. A triumph. It's also worth noting that in their early videos they made being young look absolutely brilliant. If you're going on a YouTube binge, I would pay special attention to 'Merched Yn Neud Gwallt Eu Gilydd' (Girls Doing Each Other's Hair), 'Pentref Wrth Y Mor' (Village by the Sea), 'If Fingers Were Xylophones' and 'Iechyd Da' (Good Health).

H:

Humblebrag

John, what's that stain on your trousers?

Oh God, I hoped no one would notice. Someone threw up champagne on my Dolce & Gabbana jeans. Note to self: next time Martin Amis specifically requests you to host his Q&A at a drinks reception with free Dom Perignon, bring a poncho! Damn you, English Literature PhD!

John, have you gone insane?

No, but you'd think I had, wouldn't you? If I spoke like that for a second in real life what would you do?[126]

I'd have you committed, I think. If I had the time . . .

Oh, have you been busy recently?

---

126 [EJ] One tragedy of modern life is that people actually do speak like this. I have heard people saying 'lol', instead of actually laughing out loud. The sensible thing to say at this point is that language always develops, and I'm sure bishops and MPs wrote letters to *The Times* in the 1960s about words like 'cool' or 'groovy', but I'm afraid I draw the line here. I draw the line at the way people spoke in 1998.

Well, hubby came home yesterday evening and asked if I'd enjoyed my 'day off'. Erm 7.30am Spin class and cleansing shake @UKFITSLAM, 8.45am Drop Charlie and Florence off at #megatots with homework on Spanish Armada done (they've been given projects from the 5–7-year-old class! So much for watching *Shrek*!), 9.30am Begin writing pitch for @Nutrition4Health, 10.45am get told pitch is too advanced so rework. Midday resend amended pitch and Dan refuses to believe I did it in only an hour! (um, this bitch can type!). 2pm Begin redecorating the second guest room (why on earth we thought THREE GUEST ROOMS was a good idea when we bought this place I'll never know FML 😭😭😭. Jess arrived at 3pm to refresh the flowers and said I should be an interior designer! (Erm been there, done that!) 4pm Pick up Florence and Charlie and have just about enough time to pick up the plans for the extension while hearing about the As they both received. So, erm, yeah, I spose I did enjoy my 'day off?!' HAHAHAHAH! Remember when you see your better half sat with a glass of red looking her best at 6.30pm it might have taken every ounce of energy for her to look so relaxed! 🐵 🐵 🐵 #ProseccoPlease #Fitness4Life #BringGin #PitchBitch #HiddenTalents

Elis, have you had a breakdown, are you out of your tinyhighmouthmind?[127]

No, John, I'm not, but what would you do if that's how I spoke to actual people I knew?

I would shoot you in the face six times.

And rightly so. When you say a humblebrag out loud to actual people it sounds completely and utterly bonkers. And this is why it's not really a form of speech that exists in the spoken world. But increasingly that is exactly how people are talking online to all sorts of people: friends,

---

127 [EJ] This insult crops up a lot. Take a moment to put the kettle on, stare at the front cover of this book and marvel at how tiny and high my mouth really is.

neighbours, strangers, old classmates, a local printers you used in 2009. Welcome to the world of the humblebrag.

Log on to Twitter, LinkedIn or Facebook and you will find it spreading like a virus throughout your timelines, feeds and friends. We've done our best to raise awareness, we've been high-lighting some of the nation's worst humblebrags since 2014, and yet if anything, it's getting worse. So, using our expertise, we've concocted our very own humblebrags to help you to spot those of others, and more importantly, your own.

1 – The Classic
Something bad happened to my nice thing

Basic: 'Suntan lotion leaked in my Louis Vuitton handbag! FML!'

Moderate: 'Just spilled a £35 glass of brandy all over my Jimmy Choos! And they're suede! FML!'

Advanced: 'If only Theo were as good at looking after his paints as he is at using them! Three years old and he can already paint accurate human faces, animals and landscapes, but can he do it without spilling bright green paint all over my Axminster carpet?!!! 😡 😡 😡 Maybe I'll save the £6,500 bill for his 18th?! FML!'

2 – When Rich and Rich Collide
My two expensive items caused me a problem

Basic: 'Nice one, Apple. No headphone jack on the iPhoneX, now what do I do with my brand new Bose Quiet Comfort 20s?! £200 wasted!'

Moderate: '£62,000 for the Convertible and £25 cab to get the shopping home in an Uber 😩 Maybe thinking I could fit a 72-inch plasma in the BMW was a bit optimistic after all?!'

Advanced: 'Note to self: next time you're planning on install-ing a hot tub maybe remember that wood and water don't mix! Yes, turns out my beautiful mahogany inlay has started to warp so looks like it'll be another trip to the showroom! Honestly, they must think I'm addicted to buying wooden floors! Well, not again, it's marble this time, which I'm reliably informed WILL NOT WARP! Lol.'

3 – I Have a Degree

I have a degree

Basic: 'Yes, I have a degree in engineering, but no I can't set the clock on my cooker!'

Moderate: 'Lydia: "Mum, why are so many people sad?"

You'd have thought with a PhD in Psychotherapy, an MA in Philosophy and winner of not one but two scholarships to study the impact of the internet on the human psyche, I might be able to do a bit better than just welling up at how emotionally sensi-tive my little darling has become!'

Advanced: 'FYI, yes I do have a degree in Surgery (MMBS). I also have a doctorate in Surgery (DSurg), twelve years' clinical experience, an award for Teaching Excellence from St Bart's and I've had four research papers published in the *British Journal of Surgery*. I'm also a Member of the Royal College of Surgeons and Visiting Professor at the American College of Surgeons. BUT NO I DO NOT KNOW WHAT THE WEIRD LUMP ON YOUR NECK IS, SO MAYBE LET ME ENJOY THE BIRTHDAY PARTY/LEAVING DRINKS/CHRISTMAS DO/FIVE-A-SIDE/CHARITY 10K/TRIP TO THE SHOPS/HOLIDAY IN PEACE!!!! 😫'

4 – Being Famous, Rich or Successful is Weird and/or Annoying!

My life is different to yours but I'll act like it's a shared experience

Basic: 'Virgin Business Lounge sucks, can't even get to the buffet without getting hassle. I swear to God if another person asks for a photo I'm flying first next time!!! 😫'

Moderate: 'That feeling when you kinda like the track iTunes recommends, so you buy it without really paying attention. Then realise you just spent £9.99 on your own album! Yeah that 🎧'

Advanced: 'OK, so this just happened:

Guy at gym: Hey, you really look like the girl in that Powerhouse Fitness Poster.

Me: I am the girl in that Powerhouse Fitness Poster.

Guy: No way. I don't believe you.

Me: Why?

Guy: Cos you're way hotter than the girl in that poster.

[Finds invoice for photoshoot on phone]

Guy: Holy s**t, you earn that much all the time?

Me: Sometimes ;)

So yeah, now I'm going on a date with a guy who didn't believe I'm me? #FML #AdventuresOfSadie #JustAnotherDayInTheOffice #HopeHesNotACreep!'

5 – Busy Brag

I'm very busy doing things

Basic: [Opens application form] 'Question 1: "Have you been abroad in the last 24 months. If so where?" Um, this might take a while!'

Moderate: 'You'd have thought I'd have arranged both of my Naples photoshoots to be in the same week? Erm, I spose not! Guess who's going back to Naples for the second time in a month?! #AdminFail! #NeedP.A. #OhWellGotTheAirMiles

Advanced: 6am wake up, 6.20am 3k run, 7am make brekkie for the kids, 8.30am babysitter comes, 8.31am start work on decking outside the summer house (yes I am paying for a baby sitter when I'm at home, #InTheDeckingZone), 11.25am complete decking in record time, 11.26am make cup of tea, 11.28am realise babysitter is paid til 4pm, 11.35am book Amanda a weekend away in Paris (yes, her third holiday of the year and yes she deserves it), 12.10pm finally dig out the BBQ and get the old girl fired up for a test run, 12.50pm so many sausages!!!!! 2.15pm dishwasher loaded, washing in, ironing done. 2.30pm FINALLY FIND REPLACEMENT WHEEL FOR THE MK II ON EBAY 2.33pm DRIVE TO HIGH WYCOMBE PUNCHING THE AIR IN CELEBRATION, 3.15pm arrive home, 3.55pm new wheel on, babysitter paid, babysitter leaves, 4pm lose to kiddies at scrabble AGAIN (I really need to outlaw made-up words!), 4.45pm put dinner on, 5.10pm Amanda home.

Amanda: 'Did you get the pictures framed?'

Me: 'DO'H!'

Sets alarm for 6am That's tomorrow sorted then! 😂😂😂😂😂😂😂😂😂😂😂😂😂😂😂

6 – Disaster Bragging

A terrible thing happened but never mind that I'm amazing

Basic: 'Terrible, terrible news about the attacks outside Parliament. Was there just two weeks ago picking up a gong for Best Campaign at the Music Design Awards. Makes you think . . .'[128]

---

128 [EJ] Over the last few years, I cannot think of a horrific tragedy that hasn't had a humblebrag attached to it. It was genuinely jawdropping how the attacks at the Bataclan reminded so many people of the holiday they had to Paris that was paid for by their end-of-quarter sales bonus.

Moderate:

My heart goes out to all the victims.

Advanced: 'To all those who criticised me for posting that photo of myself. It was actually taken on the beach where the tragedy occurred. I'd been there for a photoshoot two months before and it could have been me! You shame those poor people with your cruel comments. I won't be bullied into not expressing my sadness for all who lost their lives.'

7 – The LinkedIn[129] Madnessfest

I run my own business! Running a business is hard! I'm great at it! I speak in a language no one can understand! And I'm so full of wisdom! Even though I'm working really hard! And being a success!

Basic: 'Woah, 1,500 notifications? LinkedIn is becoming un-usable, sorry everyone but won't be able to respond to all your birthday wishes individually, I've got a bell to ring!'[130]

Moderate: 'Hmmm, just got told I was overqualified for a position today. Interesting. This was based on my having a Business BTEC Level 3 diploma (Distinction) and over four

---

129 [EJ] It might be because it doesn't really apply to me, but I think LinkedIn must be the most irritating website of all time. What started off as an innocent way of networking with people you share an industry with has become a cesspit of boasting and, more irritatingly, business-speak that I find difficult to understand but I fear is how we will all talk in the future, unless you are one of those people who daydream about moving to the Centre for Alternative Technology in Machynlleth and living off the land.

130 [JR] I'm pretty sure this is business-speak for making money/making the most money/signalling that you're a complete tool.

years' experience as a sales manager above the level this job was advertised as. Yes, maybe I am overqualified on paper, but does that mean I'm overqualified in other ways? Maybe I want to experience the freedom of a risk-taker rewarded on his gut instincts rather than the hours he punches in, maybe I'm tired of banging my head on the ceiling and want to start lower in order to fly higher? Or maybe I think I can better inspire others around me in a shirt in the desk pool rather than in a suit in his own office. They're right, I am overqualified, and all I needed to come to realise that was a second alone with my own thoughts.'

Advanced: 'Just got told, "You can't do that" as I handed in my notice as Head Strategist at Millennium Media Sales. Naturally I asked why?

'"You're the best salesman we have."

'I replied: "Firstly, it's sales*person*. And yes, I have been the best for the last ten months. But now I'm just in the way of the next best salesperson. If you truly want this company to thrive, you have to keep renewing your talent pool. If I stay here, then there are four candidates in this team who will never fulfil their potential. What else?"

'"We can't afford it, you bring in so much money."

'"Aren't you listening to me? Yes, I brought in £675,000 group profit from £1.7 million gross sales last year, but how many people are performing beneath themselves because they look at me and think, 'He'll never go, I'll never do as well as him.' I'm about to triple your earning potential by walking out of this door. Anything else?"

'"Well, I'm sure gonna miss having someone so wise and eloquent around the place. I don't think anyone else on the team would say what you've just said."

'"Maybe you're right, and maybe, just maybe, they'll surprise you."

'Takeaways: sometimes, when others see you at your most successful, that is when you need to take stock and start again. If you only live on the praise of others, who will you go to for hard lessons? Never let your success get in the way of less able candidates' progression. Sometimes, the best way you can help a company is let them try to do it without you. You can fly further alone than carrying others.'

So there you have it, some templates for spotting common humblebrags. Do let us know when you find one in the wild, or witness new ways people have found to disguise their boasts with moans. The genre is constantly evolving, after all. Though do be careful not to engage the perpetrator. One thing social media needs even less than humblebrags is more arguments or negativity. Maybe enjoy screengrabs with like-minded friends over a session ale, before E-Mailing them to Elis and me!

I:

It's Just a Body[131]

When Elis and I first discussed the process of writing a book, I had a very specific fantasy about how this might work. I imagined taking long walks through the Buckinghamshire countryside, stopping at gates, follies and streams, a pencil between my teeth, notebook in hand, capturing the quintessential British landscape in vaunting prose. Then I would head back home via a pub where I would meet Elis, we would talk through pint after pint, moving from the beer garden to a snug, a dictaphone capturing every second of our riff collage. Later I would stumble back to my house, pour a mug of red wine and smoke 20 roll-ups as I transcribed our recordings onto endless sheets of that yellow A4 paper American lawyers use.[132]

I'm sure Elis's vision was similarly rose-tinted. He probably saw himself at press conferences for Swansea City reserve-team coaches, using shorthand to capture the thoughts of their youth scouts, pressing senior board members for comments on rumoured takeovers, before sitting in empty terraces with a polystyrene cup of strong tea, ruminating on his top fifty away

---

131 The original recording of this conversation is featured in the audiobook, which is available for download now.

132 And, fun fact, comedian Ed Byrne. Apparently they cost £9quid each.

games and his guide to the ultimate matchday schedule.

As I'm sure you can imagine, the reality is slightly less relaxed. During the composition of this book we both had other commitments. While I was completing a 68-date UK tour over the course of 14 weeks, driving over 13,000 miles in a 2005 Skoda Fabia with no central locking, Elis had to spend an afternoon in March recording a clip show about the greatest-ever movie blunders for a digital TV channel I cannot remember the name of.

So it transpired that the all-night 'riff symposiums' weren't quite as frequent as we had imagined. That was until Friday 11 May when, just three days before the deadline, we realised we hadn't written a chapter for the letter 'I'. As we were both at the offices of our publishers making a last-minute plea for them to reconsider our 'Tops Off' cover idea, we decided, quite literally, to improvise it, to riff, to jam, to nod and wink our way to completion. What follows is a complete transcription of that recording. As to whether the whole book should have been written in this style, we'll leave it to the public/Booker Prize panel/Will Gompertz to decide.

Transcription Begins
Orion Publishing, Monday 11 May 2018, 2.54pm. 'I: It's Just a Body'

Nudity . . .

Skin . . .

Engorgement . . .

Lumps, both good and bad . . .

Play . . .

[Laughter] Nature's lukewarm pleasure . . .

The realm of the senses . . .

God's Gift . . .

Flirting . . .

Yeah . . . Sensations . . .

The Mons Pubis . . .

[Laughter] Variety . . .

Birth marks . . .

Confidence . . .

Sadness . . .

Pride . . .

Spots . . .

Pleasure . . .

Goosebumps . . .

Orgasm . . .

[Laughter] Natural lubrication . . .

Leeches . . .

Oil . . .

Perspiration . . .

Scent . . .

Hair . . .

Solid . . .

Sinew . . .

Liquid . . .

We could go on . . .

. . . gas . . .

[Laughter] The main message is, we're all different . . .

. . . All bodies are all things to all people . . .

Yeah, we're like the raggy dolls. As a population, we're just a big, big bunch of lumpy bumpy big small soft hard absolute legends . . .

And it's that kind of relaxed, open-minded attitude to the human body that has seen Elis James appear on both *Loose Women* and *The Wright Stuff.*

Exactly.

Give us a potted history of the James torso.

Embarrassingly small and thin until the age of 28. Twenty-eight to 30, with your encouragement, got into the real-ale-and-pork-pie-at-midnight regime . . .

Slash scene?

Slash scene. Yeah . . .

That was after a trip to The Victoria pub in Bristol where I introduced you to pork pie with mustard as a pub snack.

Yeah, I'd never had that before.

You'd never had a pork pie?!

No, I'd had other pies, but the pork pie was something I associated with the Famous Five or the Secret Seven . . .

Is the pork pie not a Welsh thing?

Well, Welsh people eat them, but it's not something my mum made, or would buy. But I had a pork pie with you, that was great, back in the days when you were still eating meat. And after that I use to unwind after gigs by drinking London Pride and eating pork pies *in bed*!

Nice!

So then that's when I'd say I was at my heaviest, and I decided to address this with a regime of running and cycling. And now to be honest I've realised that you can't change your body . . . well, you *can* change your body . . .

[Laughter] You absolutely can.

[Laughter] You absolutely can, but you're working with what you've got.

Yes, but I think the phrase 'It's just a body' is to try to alleviate shame around the natural give and take, to and fro, of the body and its relationship with other bodies.

Yes, absolutely. Do you ever have body shame, John?

No, cos I said in my . . .

Award-winning . . . [133]

. . . Edinburgh show, I didn't have body shame because I've got bigger fish to fry shame-wise, so it's quite low down on the pri-list.[134] I have come to terms with getting, not just grey, but *white* hairs.

---

133 [JR] See picture section. Also, Elis did actually say this and whether he pre-empted me saying it myself we will never know.

134 [JR] I did actually say this. I can only assume I meant it as a funky shorthand for 'priority list', but when I listened back to it I was immediately sick.

On your head? I've got a few white hairs in my beard.

Yeah, it's the first time I've ever felt genuinely vain. Cos I did worry and look into how to cover them up.

And have you, cos I can't see any?

No. I thought about it and then was like, 'Oh, sod it. I just can't be arsed.'

I remember asking you at Edinburgh 2009 or 10 if you felt stiffness or ageing in any way, and you said, 'Absolutely not'—

[Laughter]

—you'd have been about 28 or 29 at the time. So is that the first thing about ageing that's bothered you?

Um, yeah, I think so, but it bothered me for about three days. And then I realised that, like when someone you know mentions their spots, and you're like, 'You don't have spots!' and then you notice for the first time that maybe they do have one or two spots, but you'd never have noticed them, or associated that person with spots, just like all the people I know with prematurely grey and white hair, I'd never actually thought about them as people with prematurely grey and white hair, it hadn't even crossed my mind. So I realised, we're all . . . none of us . . .

It's like my mum used to say – 'We've all got something, no one cares about your spots as much as you do.' Um. I haven't noticed your grey hairs. Personally, if you went grey I'd have thought it would look distinguished.

Yeah, that's the thing . . .

You're not Robert Kilroy-Silk, are you?

. . . But then sometimes people don't look distinguished, they just look older than they are, but then that's fine. I don't really . . . I don't . . . I just can't be arsed . . . I don't care . . . I can't care . . .

[Laughter]

I think the first time your body genuinely starts to age is quite a shock . . . cos I was kind of skinny as a rake until about thirty. And then it's kind of terrifying when your body . . . you know, people say like, 'Oh wait till you hit 30', and then it is quite genuinely terrifying, when, as someone who could eat and drink whatever they liked throughout their 20s, which I'm aware is a luxury,

Yeah.

but I think getting to the age where your body starts to do things you're not expecting is quite scary . . .

Yeah, I wake up at night for a wee. Whereas when I was 29, I reckon I could have had eight pints of Guinness, well, I often did, gone to sleep at midnight and woken up 14 hours later. Whereas now if I have a drink after 10 o'clock I'll wake up at like 3am.

I'll wake up to go to the loo sometimes twice!

I've never woken up twice, but it's one of those things that is associated with older people. I'm 37; if middle age means you're half of the way through your life, and 74 isn't considered particularly young to die, I guess we are middle-aged, but we are dealing with this in just a traditional, laid-back way, where your acceptance is just a laid-back, chilled thing . . . As John fills his vape with . . . Tabasco?

TOBACCO! I've just started using nicotine-free liquid, which is why I'm probably six milligrams grumpier than usual.

Right.

Cos I've gone a week without nicotine for the first time in 22 years.

Oh wow, well done!

Thanks, man.

Do you miss the fa . . .?

YEAH!

[There follows a discussion that has had elements redacted for fear they may compromise the terms of Elis James's critical-illness insurance]

██████████████████████████████████

Did you?!

Yeah.

WHY?!

Because we were aping the opening titles of an early 80s Welsh chat show where it was just lots of soft-focus footage of the chat-show host, so we thought it would be funny to copy them and have my hair done in the same . . .

Oh right, for the programme!

Yeah.

Not as like a parlour game?

No, no no. And we thought the first five pictures we'll copy exactly, and for the last one I ██████████████████████████

A ██████?!

Yeah

What sort ▮▮▮?

▮▮▮▮▮▮▮▮▮

Eurgh.

But it was lovely.

[Laughter]

But I haven't ▮▮▮▮▮▮▮▮▮ for years.

Mmmmmm.

And it was absolutely lovely.

Mmmmm [vapes].

And I thought, 'I could get into this . . . '

Well, you've never ▮▮▮▮▮▮▮▮▮ have you?

No.

Well, you could probably ▮▮▮▮▮▮ and be fine.

Yeah, no, I only ever ▮▮▮▮▮▮ when I was drunk.

[Vapes furiously] I think maybe I could start again when I'm 60 or 70.

It's like, as teenagers, we used to say, 'When we're in an old people's home we'll just take loads of drugs.' In a way that our grandparents' generation never did. But I suppose that we are approaching that time.

But will that be what old-people's homes are like when we're in them? Full of old ravers and Generation X?

It'll be full of old ravers and we'll be having our bums wiped by an iPad.

But I don't wanna have to be asked to be moved out of an old-people's home because there's too many drugs there!

Cos the old bloke next to you is on ecstasy at 79 . . . I . . . would . . . like . . . to die in my sleep.

Oh no. I want to die, fully aware, surrounded by loved ones . . . and then just 10,000 pipers playing 'Who Wants to Live Forever' . . .

. . . At the O2?

Yeah . . . That's all I want.

I, fingers crossed, will bottle out of reading at your funeral because I'd get too emotional, so might just text everyone. I'll send everyone in your phone book a text . . . I'll do a tweet . . . but one of the 280-character ones

And screengrab it for anyone who isn't on Twitter.

Yeah.

But Elis, back to 'It's Just a Body'.

When did your body start to change, John?

[Laughter]

[Laughter]

I guess 12 and then again at 33?

[Quoting Partridge] Oh, so one of the 'first in your class'?

I'd say the mid-point, maybe the second quartile.

I was a very late developer. Voice didn't break until the summer between GCSEs and sixth form.

That's a long time.

YEAH!

Tinyhighmouthtinyhighvoice . . .

Yeah. People said that, and crueller things. I didn't have any underarm hair until I was 21, gutted.

WOW, when was your first girlfriend?

Eighteen, yeah I think she assumed the lack of underarm hair was a choice, whereas in reality I'd go to bed every night begging for it to happen.

So, Elis, you're in the realm of the senses . . .

It's a bank holiday . . .

Lovemaking 101 . . . Communication . . .

[Laughter] Ideally I like to shake hands before . . .

[Laughter]

It's about communication.

Gotta get the paperwork out of the way.

Absolutely, and I welcome the paperwork, cos contracts don't lie, do they?

They don't.

It's about communication, it's about seeing it as an adventure you're going on together . . .

. . . Back and forth . . .

. . . Back and forth . . .

... Give and take ...

... Vis-à-vis ...

... To me, to you ...

[Laughter]

I think everyone has got a narrative to talk about in the bedroom.

Yes, and my narrative is 'total silence, lights off' ...

Everyone's got a bedroom narrative, and ...

[Laughter] What's your 'bedroom narrative'?!

... and the trick to successful lovemaking is to turn those two narratives into a duologue, a successful duologue.

Yes, one big story that, fingers crossed, doesn't have a twist at the end.

No sting in the tail. We don't want M. Night Shyamalan.

No, we want Angela Lansbury, Dave Eggers ... Dan Brown. You want lovemaking to be like a kind of physical *Digital Fortress*.

Yes ... Listen to your partner's eyes? Discuss ...

[Laughter] Yes, because the eyes are the window to the soul.

And the mouth is the ...?

... window to desire ...

[Laughter] And the tongue is the ...?

...

The rudder of shame ...

If my experience is anything to go by.

What's hair?

What is it? It comes from a follicle and is designed to keep us clean and disease-free.

I was thinking more euphemistically . . .

. . . At least your intimate hair is . . .

Yes, that's true, don't get rid of it.

Don't get rid of it?

Unless that's your choice? . . . Hard to know what to say these days . . .

Yeah.

But you are at greater risk from thrush if you remove your intimate hair. That is a fact, it's not a political statement.

That is not a political statement. And, as a consequence, I look like Geoff Capes down there. But people are under increasing pressure to try and meet physical requirements that are unachievable.

Who polices the police? . . .

Well . . . there's an ombudsman.

The Independent Office for Police Conduct . . . The IOPC.

Yeah, and then White Papers by the government, should they really put their foot in it . . .

[Here commenced a five-minute discussion about trends in pornography that has been removed for decency and to maintain high editorial standards.]

What advice would you give someone, asking for a friend, who's concerned that they might not have reached the heights of love-making that they thought they were capable of back when they were watching *Eurotrash* in the mid-90s?

Any interaction between a woman and a man . . . a man and a man . . . a woman and a woman . . . that's it . . .

All the options . . . A man and a man, a woman and a woman, a woman and a man and a man and a woman in the same room with the lights on . . .

. . . is a constant vibe negotiation . . . the vibe is always up for negotiation . . . unless you've been told it's not/to drop the vibe . . .

. . . and put it back in the drawer . . .

No vibe is set in concrete . . . no vibe is carved into slate . . . on the door of a Welsh bungalow . . .

. . . no vibe is out of bounds unless it definitely is . . . in which case . . . that's it . . .

A vibe isn't like getting a damp-proof reading . . . you're not taking one reading and saying you have got damp . . . or you haven't got damp . . . you're taking multiple readings, multiple times . . .

Over the course of a lifetime . . .

[Laughs] OVER THE COURSE OF A LIFETIME! . . . Over the course of an evening . . . an afternoon . . . a bank holiday . . .

Saturday morning . . .

Listen to your partner . . . Not just their body but the words that they're saying, the instructions they're giving you.

Yes, I would say that is sacrosanct.

And don't be afraid to instruct your partner, your loved one . . .

But never raise your voice . . .

Never raise your voice, unless you need to be heard over road-works . . .

[Laughter] the sound of a football match . . .

Or repairs next door . . . the finale of a marathon . . .

[Laughter]

Don't be afraid to voice instructions . . . your own fears . . . your own reservations . . . your own fantasies . . . but in a safe space where judgement is not knocking on the door . . .

Yea, yeah, yeah, yeah . . .

While everyone has it within their powers to accept or decline requests . . . let's leave judgement at the door . . . but leave consent standing right next to us at all times.

Absolutely . . . I would say if you're voicing fantasies and you're concerned that they might be slightly left field, more alternative underground fantasies, give 'em a quick google first, and you'll be surprised what's on the internet.

OR . . . do what Tony Blair did, and try to attract those fantasies to the centre ground.

[Enormous laugh]

There's a way!

The third way!

The third way. There is a way, of wording the left field, the far right, in order to make the floating voter think 'he's all right . . .'

'in spite of being a Europhile . . . he's the one for me . . . '. There is a third way. Don't feel afraid to try your best to read the ebb and flow of lovemaking. In that regard it's very much like a game of Test cricket.

It is.

The vibe is gonna change over the course of five days' lovemaking.

Just because an early wicket falls . . .

[Laughter]

Doesn't mean you're not gonna spend the afternoon slogging in the heat of the sun as numbers two and three really dig in.

Yeah, and do take time for tea.

And if you're running out of ideas . . . why not bring on a spinner?

[Laughs]

Just to disrupt them . . . do what they least want you to do . . . That was always Michael Vaughan's approach to Test captaincy, do what the opposing team least want you to do . . .

I mean if you've got that in your back pocket it doesn't matter if you don't win the toss.

And don't tamper with the ball . . . I've just realised that Michael Vaughan's advice only applies to Test captaincy, and not to lovemaking.

No.

At this point I halted the recording, posed the question 'Why are we telling people how to make love?' whereupon Elis and I laughed for a full two minutes. Two men, lost in a riff matrix of their own design.

Birds Eye

J:

John's Shame Well

It feels good to do the impossible. In the old days, it was impossible to know if you'd been given the right change in a shop until the invention of the calculator watch, it was impossible to order a Chinese takeaway from the toilet until the invention of the mobile phone, it was impossible to predict just how many people held reprehensible views until the invention of Twitter. John Robins has done something that was previously considered impossible. He has caused a nation to reflect on the concept of shame via the medium of commercial digital indie radio.

As someone who knows John, I am aware of how often he feels he has done something bad when he hasn't, and how many sleepless nights he has had turning over conversations that might have happened 10, 15, or even 20 years ago. John isn't alone in this, but we hadn't realised how prevalent a feature of the human condition it was until we started talking about it between Kasabian tracks on the radio. We turned this into a feature on the show called John's Shame Well, where anonymous listeners would admit to the incidents from their past they were embarrassed about, and John and I would relieve them of their shame and allow them to continue with their day-to-day lives, free from embarrassment. In order to placate our editor, who found this chapter far too heavy-going, we have included a few of our favourite shame well entries at the end but for a more detailed examination of how shame can affect people, I will hand you over to the master . . .

Thank you, Elis, and hello readers. You join me here at the dark, damp base of a well. But this is not just any well: this is John's Shame Well. It's somewhere between the terrifying, fingernail-scratched well belonging to Buffalo Bill in *The Silence of the Lambs*, and the slightly more comforting well of Haruki Murakami's fantastic novel *The Wind-Up Bird Chronicle*. There is a shelf, of sorts, for me to sit on, and damp walls run some 30 feet up to a circle of sky, where clouds saunter past by day and the moon is sometimes visible on clear nights. And what do I muse on at the base of this well? Historically low ISA yields? The risk/reward ratio of bitcoin? The tyranny of the uninsured driver? No, dear friend, here I muse on shame.

O Shame! O Shame! O flushing of the cheeks! O restless nights! O memory flashing through the cloud of a hungover mind! O school-day woe! O words spoken without thought! O inappropriate present and unlocked door!

I'm no expert in what shame *is*, but I'm certainly well versed in what it feels like. I'm sure there are scientists, psychologists and experts in behaviour and evolution that could tell you what function shame serves, but what fascinates me is how debilitating it is, and how often the heaviest feelings of shame attach themselves to the lightest instances of transgression or error.

One broad definition I think I can make without a degree in psychology[135] is that guilt is public, whereas shame is private. If I steal £20quid from my mum's purse I feel guilt. If she finds out

---

135 My degree (received from Oxford University) is in English . . .

I feel shame.[136] Interestingly, one of my earliest shame memories is, aged about 10, finding £10quid in my wallet. I told my mum and she asked if I'd taken it from her purse and even though I ABSOLUTELY HADN'T, I still felt, and feel, shame to this day. I mean, it was by far the most likely explanation. As a child who would count his pocket money again and again, frequently asking for it to be changed into different types of coin so he could experience all the types of coin, the idea that something as life-changing as a £10quid-note just appearing was unthinkable, and yet it had done.

However, I think what this episode goes to show is that shame isn't attached to events; it's attached to other people's reaction, or more potently, the reaction you *imagine* someone else having. It wasn't my mum's reaction to my explanation that caused me shame (she gave a kind of light 'hmmmm', as I remember). It was her subsequent interior monologue that I had no access to and, therefore, had no end or limit to its potential negative analysis of me. And it's in that imagined analysis that shame spreads like a virus, because only I can fill that narrative with my own insecurities and anxieties.

My relationship with burning shame led me to spearhead a campaign to try to banish it from the UK. After a record-breaking week of restless nights dwelling on things I'd said or done at school in the late 90s, I told some of these shameful memories on air. Sharing these anecdotes lessened their impact on me, and those restless, blushing, sweating nights came to an end. I invited listeners to anonymously submit their most shameful stories, which I broadcast here from the base of the well, so that as the words rise up into the sky, the shame disperses into the atmosphere to haunt them no more.

---

136 And also guilt.

A large part of shame is, I think, a feeling of being misrepresented by your actions, words or someone else's interpretation of those actions or words.[137] 'What must that person have thought of me?!,' 'What does that person think of me now?!,' 'They must have thought I was so insensitive,' 'They must think I'm some kind of racist!' And so on and on into the wee small hours of the night, with no end to the spiral. In so many cases, every last remnant of shame would dissipate immediately with the arrival of the other party to say, 'Hey, don't worry, I knew what you meant!' or 'Oh God, that was totally my fault for not knocking!' or 'You had no idea the eye patch in Secret Santa would go to the only person in the office with one eye!' But, for those of us who are naturally down on ourselves, sensitive to what other people think or lacking confidence, in place of those comforting words come our own fears and social anxieties. The brilliant author and poet John Burnside remarks on this contrast between imagination and fact in a passage from his memoir *I Put a Spell on You:*

> . . . later, when you go back to assuage or confirm your shame, there is nothing to see but a few scratch marks or bloodstains that anybody could explain away in a matter of moments. That's when you begin to understand that you can't go back, you can only repeat – and this is what we do, occasionally for an entire lifetime.[138]

If only we could go back to that classroom, to that office party, to that moment when our words stuck in our mouths in front of the person we were enchanted by. If only they could know it

---

137 [EJ] Occasionally, John Robins nails something. And he has absolutely nailed shame with this sentence.

138 John Burnside, *I Put a Spell on You*, Jonathan Cape (2014).

My first official headshot, c.1985.

Ever the rule breaker, I smashed birthday party convention by wearing my Dennis The Menace boxer shorts outside my trousers, 1992.

In West Wales it's a Christmas tradition to ward off evil spirits by handcuffing the eldest child to railings surrounding the tree.

Wales home shirt, 1994–6, Umbro.

This is not the photo of Elis' 18th birthday gold catsuit I specified be included. In the one I wanted he is stood outside a video shop with a visible erection.

Proof of the versatility of the Mohican haircut, providing an imposing look both informally (Reading Festival, 2001) and in white tie (Oxford University matriculation, 2001).

Smoking a pipe like a complete tool, Oxford 2002.

Traditional west Walian university initiation, 1999.

Pour away that youth, Mike and Chris. The Star, Oxford, 2004.

St Anne's College Bar, 2002. I attempt 'The Centurion' with friends: 100 shots of beer in 100 minutes. Depending on how accurate the measure, it works out anywhere between 4 and 8 pints in a little over an hour and a half. Ever the renegade, I'm doing it with Orange WKD. I am smoking a fag. Bliss.

Oxford, 2004. In a cab travelling down Walton Street on my way to the final night out of my university career. Opposite me sits James, on his phone, and I have never forgotten the look in his unanswerable eyes.

The North Bank, The Vetch
Field, Swansea City Vs
Shrewsbury, 30 April 2005.

Welshman's Thigh ft. VHS,
c.2006.

Two men, two microphones, one love.

Early advice from Robins . . . ouch.

May

28 Monday

148–217
Spring Holiday (UK)

Gig: Taunton, Brewhouse theatre
6/10. John Robins told
me to gig more, to write more, that
I was funnier off stage than on,
and that I ~~needed to~~ needed to find
'my comedy voice'. Ouch.

£30 — invoice.

29 Tuesday

49–216

Valentine's Day, 2017.

Goodbye rum.

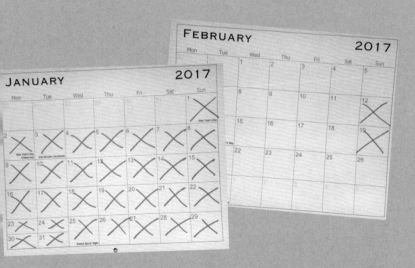

Dry January 2017 ranks as one of my all-time greatest achievements. February, however, was a total write-off.

A selection of some of my favourite empty pubs. Clockwise from top left: Kings Arms, Roupell St, London; The Ravensbourne Arms, Lewisham; The Highbury Vaults, Bristol; The Dundee Arms, Bethnal Green; The Dachre Arms, Lewisham.

was our enchantment that made us say something that offended them. If only we could burst into that moment and shout, 'That wasn't what I meant at all!' If only.

That said, I think there are things we can do, very trans-formative things to lessen the impact of shame. Firstly, telling someone. Telling a friend about something that has irked you for years puts it into perspective. So often their nonplussed response will wash over you like a healing anti-shame tonic. Also, they may display empathy with the situation that you were in, and, folks, empathy kills 99.9% of all known shame! Because, through empathy, the person you were that was so misrepresented, who had their intentions misread by some-one else, finds a companion who understands them. Also, we can have empathy with ourselves, especially if you're feeling ashamed about something that happened years ago, or as a child. Visualise that child, have a vibe-exchange with them, take into account all the things that were going on in their head at the time, how they might have been naive of etiquette or learning what behaviour is acceptable or not, and forgive them. Let's face it, if you didn't make mistakes as a child you'd never learn not to make them as an adult. I once made a joke that implied the word 'coin' in front of a family friend. My mum was not impressed, and quite right too! I haven't used that word in an inappropriate setting since![139]

In terms of other genres of shame, there is also basic embar-rassment. If your trousers fall down when you're alone at home, you wouldn't think twice. On a bus, however, the stakes are much higher. But think on those trousers for a while. Would any

---

139 Save for one voiceover audition for Carphone Warehouse, when I was, to be fair, very hungover and dealing with an unusual level of personal turmoil. I would like to apologise now to all those shocked executives, clients and brand representatives. It was definitely an overreaction to dropping my pen.

person on that bus think anything more than 'Haha, that was a funny incident'? Or, more likely, 'Oh no! That poor person!'? Maybe you even brightened up their day or made them smile in a tough time. No one is going to witness that and think: 'I hope that person feels ashamed of the existence of their legs/undergarments for the rest of time.'

I think one of the best pieces of advice I have for someone afraid of public speaking, can also help to alleviate shame. If someone says to me, 'I have to give a talk at work – got any tips?,' mine is thus: a lot of your fear is worrying about what happens if it goes wrong, you stumble over words, you forget a stat or figure. But imagine you're in the audience – you're not willing anyone to make a mistake in a talk, nor would you judge them for doing so. Accept the possibility that mistakes might happen, and have a plan. Something as simple as saying, 'Sorry, I've forgotten the number, let me just check the sheet, wouldn't want to give you the wrong blimmin' info!' and people won't even notice anything has happened. As a comedian, the vast majority of tough gigs or moments of tension are turned around by addressing the issue in a light or playful way: it's the elephant in the room that crushes us, but turns into a mouse when we address it.[140]

There are also instances where shame is just deserts for actions or words someone genuinely regrets. Here it can be quite useful to say to yourself, 'Yeah, I should feel like this. I went in too hard on that tackle and I knew what I was doing.' You may find you come to terms with the feeling, like it's an appropriate sentence for the crime.[141]

---

140 [EJ] Whenever somebody asks me about public speaking, I always say: 'After my first bad gig I realised that nobody I loved had died, and that my friends thought no less of me, and then it was fine.' I think John's paragraph here is slightly more helpful.

141 Unless you have committed an actual crime, in which case hand yourself in to the police and let the Crown Prosecution Service decide what charge is appropriate.

By reminding us of times we have transgressed or done wrong, shame keeps us in check; it is the officious warden of a sensitive mind. But let us take action against unwarranted shame! Let us guard against those times the warden loses their shit about the coffee stain when they should be focusing on serious crimes like murder, tax evasion and people who drive right down to the end of a lane that's being closed then nip in at the last minute at the start of roadworks.

Below are six of my favourite shame well entries. I would like to thank absolutely everyone who has submitted a shame well to the show. Reading them is one of my favourite parts of the week. The humour, sensitivity and honesty that every single person shows are an inspiration to us all. And here, as ever, the correspondants have been kept anonymous. I hope, that by reading them, they bring a smile to your face – and just as you forgive and empathise with the people who sent them in, so you forgive and empathise with yourself for your own shame wells.

SAT NAV

Fifteen years ago, while in the first few weeks of my first proper job, for some reason still unknown to me I told my colleagues that my dad had a sat nav. I'm ashamed to admit that this was a lie. I instantly started panicking that my web of deceit would become untangled and I would be exposed as a fraud. I worried so much that I gave myself a panic attack and was driven to A&E by a kind colleague named Lyn. Someone from the office phoned my parents and my dad was dispatched to A&E to collect me. On arrival he apologised for being late due to 'getting a bit lost'. Lyn commented, 'Your sat nav on the blink then?' My dad looked confused and replied, 'Sat nav? What sat nav?' Commence instant unbearable shame!! Lyn gave me a funny look, quickly changing the subject and was kind-hearted enough to never mention anything about it. I, on the other hand, tried my absolute best to never speak to Lyn again, instantly started looking for a new job and 15 years later still think about it late at night, on a regular basis, during episodes of cold sweat and regret!

SOUNDS JUICY

This incident occurred almost 14 years ago while I was at university. I was quite shy at the time and tended to keep to a small group of people whom I knew well. On one particular occasion, however, I arrived ahead of time at our lecture and couldn't see anyone I knew.

*I took a seat near to a couple of my fellow students, a guy and a girl, whom I recognised but with whom I'd never really spoken. Both were sharing some strawberries and chatting about the new Muse album (*Absolution*). They were friendly, said hello to me and began to include me in their conversation. I had recently bought the new Muse album and so had opinions to share with them! 'Great,' I thought, 'this whole getting-to-know-people thing isn't as hard as it seems!'*

Everything was going well and the conversation subsided into a comfortable, convivial silence between us, which was broken only by the sound of them enjoying their strawberries. It was at this stage, for reasons still unknown to me, that I chose to break the silence by saying the following two words in reference to the fruit they were eating:

'Sounds juicy.'

SOUNDS. JUICY. I don't think I'd ever used those words to describe someone else's food before and it didn't occur to me how strange (and creepy) this would sound when said aloud.

They both looked at me, confused. 'Sorry, what did you say?' the girl asked.

'The strawberries,' I said, face reddening, 'they . . . sound juicy.' I accompanied these words by pointing at the punnet of strawberries.

THEY. SOUND. JUICY. Why? Why? Why? Why? Why? WHY DID I SAY THAT?!

I can still recall the looks on their faces as they looked towards each other and then back at me. The guy sort of smirked and shook his head, while the girl remained silent, apparently unsure of how to respond to this strange (unintended) critique of the auditory volume at which they consumed food.

The lecture promptly commenced, leaving me no opportunity to defuse the awkwardness. With hindsight, this may have actually been a mercy as my awkwardness-defusing tactics to that point appeared to solely consist of pointing and repeating different combinations of the words SOUNDS and JUICY.

At this, I was left to wallow in a pit of my own grief for the following two hours. As the class ended, I slunk out quickly and wordlessly. I never spoke to either of them again.

Looking back, I think that my intention was to make conversation, and complimenting their food choice seemed like a good idea at the time. I've thought about this a lot over the intervening years and feel I would have been on safer ground by commenting on how the strawberries looked rather than how they sounded when being eaten.

A further consequence of this shameful incident is that, to this day, I cannot enjoy strawberries without experiencing a Proustian rush of historical shame.

PENGUIN ICE CREAM

When I was 25, and shortly after I started a new job at a fuel company, I was attending an expo in Geneva. Although nervous and apprehensive as to how I would cope meeting people face to face whom I had been in E-Mail dialogue with since I joined the company, I felt that the first two days of the expo were going rather well. I seemed to perform really well when meeting high-flying executives.

On the final evening of the expo, I was invited to a dinner that was being hosted by one of the world's largest oil companies.

The setting for this event was in a very exclusive Swiss restaurant that was below street level. The venue was small and very intimate. I found myself sitting opposite one of the head directors of the company. The evening was going very well. Again, I felt I was holding my own among the bigwigs. After an amazing Swiss cheese fondue and other amazing dishes, it was time for dessert. Although the first seven courses were pre-ordered by the event organisers, we were able to choose our dessert. I was rather full and the prospect of cake, dark chocolate or anything other than ice cream wasn't that appealing. After scouring the dessert menu, I found what I was looking for. Although the name of the dish was in French and German, the description was in English. Plain vanilla ice cream. Perfect.

After watching the 50 or so other guests receive their desserts, I wondered where mine was.

It was at that moment when I noticed the lights starting to dim.

The saloon-style doors swung open and the waitress appeared with her unnecessarily large entourage brandishing a large serving plate with what I can only describe as a two-foot-tall plastic penguin on it.

They then proceeded to light the wick poking out the bottom of the penguin, which ignited multiple sparklers – just to make sure those who hadn't noticed were now paying full attention.

Everyone, including the staff, were scanning the room, trying to identify which lucky seven-year-old's birthday it was. After a brief moment of confusion, the headwaiter pointed to me.

As the two-foot-tall sparkling penguin was placed in front of me, I thought things couldn't get any worse. All the staff began to clap. The waitress then removed the head to reveal a single scoop of ice cream.

To this day, the sparkling Pingu-like ice-cream surprise haunts me. No matter how well I progress in the industry, I will still be that guy who ordered a child's toy for dessert.

SEXY CURRY

It was the heady days of 2008, and at the tender age of 17, I had fallen madly in love with a boy/man, (he was 24, I think it was broadly fine, though?) that I'd met on holiday in Tenby that summer. Since I'd gone home, ▉▉▉ and I had been corresponding frequently via SMS and we had grown very fond of each other. I was so desperate to see him again, but I knew my mum would never in a million years let me go on a six-hour, £60 train back to Tenby to meet up with a random west Walian bloke I'd snogged on holiday.

So, I took matters into my own hands. ▉▉▉'s birthday was coming up and I told him I was coming to see him. I told Mum I was going with my mate Laura to her dad's in Birmingham, and off I went. But not before swinging by the local Ann Summers in Basingstoke to pick up some, what you might call . . . top-shelf nighttime attire.

All set, I hopped on the train and a short six hours and three changes later, I was nearly there. As the train passed through Narbeth, I headed to the on-train toilet cubicle, Ann Summers bag in tow. Several uncomfortable minutes later, I was resplendent in

129

my saucy get-up, complete with a fetching trenchcoat that (just about) covered the naughty bits . . .

The train rolled into dreary Tenby, and there was a wonderful, manly, muscular ▮▮▮ waiting to whisk me off in a flurry of passion. I hopped off the train and sauntered over to him. As I'd hoped, he did indeed sweep me up into quite the wooze-inducing kiss. So far, so good. He told me he was so happy I'd come, and that I looked 'lush'. Nailed it, I thought.

But then, gorgeous, sweet, clueless ▮▮▮ said: 'We've just gotta go by my dad's house to pick up my birthday cards – he's dying to meet you!' He took me by the hand and off we went. Just like that.

I was so stunned that I just followed, dumbfounded: 'Ohh great, yeah, I can't wait to meet him too!' For some reason unbeknown to me now, I decided against mentioning my (what I thought was fairly obvious) state of undress. I figured we'd just stop in, say a quick hello and pop off back to the boudoir to get down to business, easy. But NO. Of course, his dad insisted on making us a cuppa and giving us the full house tour. I have to say, walking up a flight of stairs in front of your prospective boyfriend's dad while wearing nought but a thong and a trench coat is a traumatic experience.

You'd think that would be enough hell for a silly, reckless teen to endure in one night. But oh no, it did not end there.

We said our goodbyes to ▮▮▮'s dad and I thought, finally! The big reveal is close! I just have to keep quiet a big longer . . .

But no sooner had we crossed the threshold of his house than there was his mum (▮▮▮ still lived at home . . .): 'Hello, love, oh it's so nice to meet you finally! Do you fancy a curry? ▮▮▮ do you fancy a birthday curry, love? Shall we all pop down to Bengal and grab a takeaway? Aw yeah, that'd be nice. Let's do that, off we go!'

▮▮▮, still completely oblivious, smiled and followed his mum back out the door to the car, pulling me along by the hand despite my wide-eyed terror and (admittedly internal and completely

silent) protestations.

After an excruciatingly awkward trip to the takeaway (main-taining any modesty en route in and out of the car was particularly challenging), we proceeded to eat our curries off lap trays during Britain's Got Talent *and while I rebuffed increasingly alarmed offers from* ██████*'s mum to 'Please, let me hang your coat up, love.' Understandably, I was sweating profusely throughout the ordeal – partly because I ate a curry wearing a coat in a very warm house, and partly from unbearable, heart-twisting, face-melting shame.*

When the time FINALLY came for us to retreat, I was a broken woman. Not one to miss a meal even in the direst of circumstances, hefty portions of bhuna, rice, naan and poppadoms had rendered me bloated and immobile. As soon as the bedroom door clicked shut, I threw off the godforsaken coat and belly-flopped face down onto the bed, mortified, in all my sparkly, black-lacey regalia. ██████*'s little face lit up at first sight of the undergarments, but very quickly his expression darkened as the realisation of what had just occurred over the past three hours dawned on him.*

To his credit, ██████ *was horrified and apologised profusely for his obliviousness. Quite rightly, he did point out that had I alerted him to the situation as soon as he suggested going to his dad's, he would have cancelled in a heartbeat and whisked me off to the boudoir immediately. To this day, I have no idea why I kept my mouth shut.*

We eventually found the funny side of the situation, and after a giggle and a substantial rest and digest, we were able to partake in the, erm, activities I had gone there to pursue . . .

██████ *turned out to be a lovely bloke and we stayed together for nearly a year, until the long-distance thing inevitably got a bit tedious.*

My relationship with his parents, though, remained some-what distant, with a distinct air of mistrust. Had they seen what they thought they saw? Could she possibly have thought that appropriate behaviour for meeting her boyfriend's parents? Do teenagers really behave like that nowadays?!

It's been 10 years, and I am still haunted by the memory of sweat dripping down my corseted back as I tried to yank the lapels of my trench coat across my bosom without dislodging the lap-curry or flashing my fishnetted nethers at ███'s *mum.*

BIKE LOCK

It was around three years ago that I was recruited for a dream job and started with a huge sense of excitement. Day 1 had gone well and I was looking forward to Day 2 when I would meet the rest of my team and the senior managers at their weekly meeting. The only downside to the job was the hellish commute from home through some of the most congested parts of west London. As a keen cyclist (like Elis), I thought I would try a different routine on Day 2. I studied the map and saw that I could park up and cycle the rest of the way to the office, thus missing the worst of the traffic via a canal path. I left early with my work clothes in a rucksack and a substantial bike lock secured around my waist for ease of carrying, just like a cycle courier. All went well at first – the canal was easy to find and was cycle friendly. However, the path was meandering and, before I knew it, I was very late for work. I eventually arrived and parked my bike . . . which is where the problems began. I rummaged for my keys to release the bike lock from around my waist and realised in horror that I had LEFT THE KEY IN THE CAR . . . 15 miles away. My blood ran cold. What should I do? I was so late, there was no hope of going back to fetch the key – half the day would be gone by the time I made it back to the office. So I decided to plough on. I left the bike unlocked and went to the changing room, where I tried to get undressed without my new colleagues noticing the issue, but of course this wasn't possible. Someone started laughing and pointing and all the other ladies took a look at the shameful sight. It was painfully embarrassing. I showered avec bike lock (with the added problem of oil and grease running everywhere) and emerged from the changing rooms fully dressed with a conspicuous bulge around my middle underneath my dress, which made me look like I had a large muffin top/was wearing a chastity belt.

The events of the rest of the day were a blur of shame involving one of the office technicians trying (unsuccessfully) to pick the lock, a trip to a bike shop, who suggested trying an angle grinder (they said they were reluctant to use it anywhere near an actual person), and finally the team meeting over lunch, which was truly uncomfortable for many reasons, not least that the bike lock was so tight around my waist that I couldn't sit properly and couldn't eat much. There were some odd glances (probably thinking I was intensely nervous about meeting everyone for the first time). Miraculously, my new managers didn't seem to notice the lock and I made it through the rest of the day, eventually cycling back to my car and unlocking with an immense sense of relief.

The next day, the story spread like wildfire through the office and I was greeted with inevitable remarks from colleagues. Thinking that everyone had heard, I thought I would bring up the topic at afterwork drinks with my managers a few weeks later. As I started recounting my Day 2 tale, their faces looked blank and tumbleweed blew across the table. It was clear that they had not heard the story before and appeared genuinely stunned by my unprofessionalism. They have never looked at me in the same way again.

'HEY ALL'

On the 11th of November last year I went to work a couple of hours late because of a prior doctor's appointment. I was into my third week of working at a new office and I was beginning to cement a few relationships among my colleagues and become part of 'the team' a lot more. As I got into my office, I noticed that the room was very quiet; the radio was off, no one was engaging in small talk about the previous evening and everyone was sitting down at their desks. 'Hmm,' I thought, trying to think of what to say to break the silence as I assumed everyone was in a lethargic mood.

I decided that I would raise my hand to say hello and hopefully get visual recognition at my entrance to the office. However, instead of waving I kept my hand still and raised. I still hadn't received a greeting from anyone; instead a few people seemed to look at me with shock. 'Well, that's odd,' I thought. 'Maybe I should say hello too then.' I went with my usual greeting when I enter the office and said, 'Hey all'. It didn't sound like 'Hey all' at all.

It was at this moment when a room full of 30 people looked at me in utter dismay and disbelief as I was standing there with my right hand raised at the 10 o'clock angle after seemingly saying 'hail'. As I looked at my colleagues with a confused expression I heard our line manager's phone beep, after which she said we could carry on as normal. I felt my stomach burn, churn and turn as I realised I had just done a Nazi salute in the middle of a minute's silence.

I have since transferred to another branch and have not told any of my new colleagues about it, although I am E-Mailing from my work PC so the IT guys are probably having a good laugh right now.

potato!

K:

Keep It Session™

For some years now Elis and I have encouraged listeners to 'Keep It Session™'. For the avoidance of doubt, the term refers to the practice of drinking ale, lager or cider, equal to, or below, 4.5% ABV.[142] It is without doubt the most successful, and unlikely, commercial digital indie radio health campaign of our times. People often say to me, 'Why do you always Keep It Session™, John?' . . . 'John, do you really need to examine every pump clip individually?' . . . 'Christ, man, the barman thinks you're weird!' . . . 'John, I'm bored of this, just get a pint, any pint!' . . . 'OK, I'm going home now!' So I've decided to offer a brief history and examination of the practice of Keeping It Session™ in the hope of bringing on board the last few doubters.[143]

---

142 Alcohol by Volume (ABV), a measure of how many ml of ethanol there are in 100ml of liquid.
143 Though, I doubt, bringing back on board listener Andrew, who E-Mailed to say he had stopped listening to our podcast around episode 34 because it had become 'too beery'. We still miss him.

Origins

The beginning of my personal session quest came about quite by accident. As a teenager, trips to the pub were fraught with anxiety, not just because there were other people there, but because I didn't like lager. In fact, I hated it, and still do. When I say lager, I'm talking your classic cans: Fosters, Grolsch, Kronenbourg, Stella, et al. Over the years I've found the odd lager I don't mind: Pilsner Urquell, Carlsberg from a bottle at my friend Sam's, 1998–2002, and those stubbies you have at family barbecues called things like Biere d'Or, Biere de Luxe and, the undisputed king, Biere Des Moulins. But as a rule, put a four pack of Beck's in my dressing room and I'll torch the joint.

Then, one night in 1998, at The Knot of Rope pub in Thornbury, a mohicaned Queen fan in a velvet jacket tried something called Worthington's Bass Smooth and one of the great romances of modern times was born: Robins and ale. It also led to an affair with Guinness that would supplement my Bass obsession, and all was well, until, however, I ventured into pubs further afield. Finding myself in increasingly un-Bassed environments, and a victim of the ongoing competition to be the first landlord to serve Guinness at Absolute Zero,[144] I needed to branch out, but the range of ales was downright baffling. Long before the days where I could afford to adopt the motto, 'Life's too short to drink bad wine', a pint of ale I didn't like could deprive me of half my spending money and thus ruin an evening. Tasting beers before buying wasn't really an option before the craft beer revolution,

---

144 Fun fact: the origins of the unpalatable Guinness Extra Cold and Lord-knows-why Guinness Super Chilled come from Irish pubs where so many pints were prepped to settle before selling, that the first three-quarters would warm up. Some clever clogs had the fantastic idea to use a colder keg to fill up the top quarter, thus creating a pint that was at normal temperature. How that abomination came to be made available on its own is beyond me. It is utterly undrinkable.

or certainly wasn't something I was confident enough to ask about, so I had to find something that connected all the beers I liked, or at least gave me as good a chance of making the right choice between the ones on offer. The terms 'malty', 'hoppy', 'bitter', 'full-bodied', 'golden', 'amber', 'best' all kind of seemed the same to me. I liked ale that tasted of very little. At university, the Tetley's Smoothflow available in the bar, Fuller's Chiswick at The Harcourt Arms and Greene King IPA (pre-2002) at The Eagle and Child were enough to keep me happy but, on returning to Bristol, I needed a system.

And then, one fine evening, like that scene in *Lorenzo's Oil* where Nick Nolte realises the paperclips he's been stringing together hold the cure to his son's disease,[145] it hit me.

I LIKE WEAK BEER.

Not all weak beer, you understand, but if you hand me a 4% ABV ale, the chances of me liking it are, I would say, 65 per cent, and the chances of me being happy to make do with it around 85 per cent. Add to this the more recent finding that I don't like 'malty' ale (London Pride, Doom Bar), anything made by Greene King[146] and the majority of ales whose names make reference to the clergy, World War II, woodland animals and sexism, and you can up those numbers to 80 per cent and 95 per cent respectively.

So, from that moment on, if a favourite ale wasn't on tap, I would scan the percentages, filter the names for references to the above, and usually find myself with a pint I enjoyed. The below is a list of some favourites:

- Arbor Motueka 3.8%
- Beavertown Neck Oil 4.3%

---

145 Not literally. I cannot stress this enough – alas, paperclips do not cure adrenoleukodystrophy (ALD).

146 Apart from, ironically, the 'Amplified' Radio X beer, which was genuinely fantastic.

- Darkstar Hophead 3.6%
- Darkstar Session IPA 4.2%
- Harvey's Sussex Best Bitter 4.0%
- Moor Revival 3.8%
- Moor So'Hop 4.1%
- Oakham Citra 4.2%
- Oakham JHB 3.8%
- Otter Bitter 3.6%
- Otter Bright 4.3%
- Purity Bunny Hop 3.5%
- Redchurch Paradise Pale Ale 3.7%
- Sambrook's Pumphouse Pale Ale 4.2%
- St Austell Tribute 4.2%
- Truman's Swift 3.9%
- Truman's Zephyr 4.4%

One note on the above: broadly they are 'hoppy' ales. Though I would now be classed as a 'hophead' on grumpy CAMRA forums, it wasn't always the case. I used to like beer that tasted of nothing, or next to nothing, and was as scornful of the citrus revolution as the next person. However, I must admit my palate has changed. I'd much rather have the lipsmack of a mild grapefruit aftertaste than the dusty leathery taste of darker ales, or, God forbid, some godawful chocolate porter or rich Christmas ale. That said, if you offer me a 'sour' ale, I will knock you clean out. Stop trying to impress everyone and go and live in a bin.

However, something was happening – there was an unexpected side effect to increasing my chances of liking a beer: I was able to drink more, and for longer. And if there's one thing that's true of I, John Robins:

I WANT TO DRINK MORE, AND FOR LONGER

Whack that on the digital gravestone while you're at it. There's a quote I heard long ago, that I now can't find, but it was something like:

'The best thing about drinking is not *being* drunk, it's *getting* drunk.'[147]

That's the heart of it for me: long nights in quiet nooks as open fire flames sing from the brass on bars unimaginable. As a teenager, too many evenings were ruined by getting hammered off two drinks and being sick and missing all the fun or embarrassing myself.[148] These days, I'd much rather embarrass myself on my own terms, and with zero sick.

Not only does opting for a weaker (or frequently, *the weakest*)

---

147 [EJ] Unlike John, I used the early years of the Radio X show to pursue and promote my 'maximum shunting' agenda. For the uninitiated, 'maximum shunting' was a term used by my school friends to describe irresponsible binge drinking. Contrary to popular belief, it's not a Carmarthen or even a Welsh term; it was only used by my year at school. Its origins spring from us laughing at the way people from nearby Llanelli would say 'going on the shant', when they meant 'going for a drink'. 'Maximum shanting' became 'maximum shunting' and the next thing you knew you were saying it every time someone got a round of Jägerbombs. They were great days, and I look back on those hangovers with fondness – a ham sandwich, four pints of Ribena and the *Hollyoaks* omnibus. My maximum shunting days now seem like they belong to a different lifetime. For some reason, in the last year or so, even three pints of commercial lager mean the next day is written off with symptoms that make the Spanish Flu Pandemic of 1918 look like brain freeze from eating too much ice cream. Unlike John, I used to think that drinking was all about the destination and not the journey, and I wanted to get to the stage where I was falling out of a tree (Adelaide, 2010), or falling asleep, face down in my meal in front of the promoter of the Australian stand-up tour I was doing (Melbourne, 2010) as quickly as possible. Nowadays, I cannot think of anything worse. If I take off my top with sheer joy (Scotland 1, Wales 2, Hampden Park, March 2013 and the Super Furry Animals' reunion show, Brixton Academy, May 2015), I will feel shame the next morning that burns into my soul. I am a 37-year-old father of one, for crying out loud. To be honest I'm a bit frightened of heavy drinking now and, if it weren't for John's guidance on Keeping It Session™, I would probably quit altogether. However, unlike his advice on ISAs, investing in bitcoin and general punctuality, I am proud to say that I have taken John's teachings on board and I endorse them wholeheartedly.

148 Once, having been sick through booze in front of a girl I liked (at what turned out to be an illegal drugs party), I passed out on the A38 and was driven home by a man in a Toyota Avensis. It is a shameful episode covered in *A Robins Amongst the Pigeons*, which is available from all (our) good (only) bookshops (merch website).

beer mean you can drink more, it means you can talk more, sing more, see more, stay out later, wake up fresher and sometimes save a few quid too.[149] But why?

The Science

A pint of 4% ale contains 2.27 UK units,[150] a pint of 5.2% lager contains 2.95 units. That may not seem like much of a difference, but it is. In fact, the 5.2% lager is THIRTY PER CENT STRONGER. That's right, for every pint your 5.2% hooligan consumes, you get 1.33 pints of our 4% friend. And that's before you've walked into a Brewdog and found that a beer as weak as 5.2% is the stuff of a madman's dream. A pint of Brewdog's 5.8% Punk IPA (one of their weaker selections) comes in at 3.3 units. That's a whopping FORTY-FIVE PER CENT STRONGER than our 4% friend. Now, if you're having one or two beers, this might not be a huge issue, but what if you're talking to The Lovely Robin about remorse over five pints? Now, the government would warn you against this,[151] but, let's face it, it happens, and when it does, it is the BEST THING IN YOUR LIFE. So you'd ideally like it to not be ruined by drooping, slumping or crying off early, thus missing out on key remorse chat. All this can all be avoided by Keeping It Session™.

---

149 In theory, weaker ale should be cheaper in a pub, though many modern bars couldn't give an eff about passing that saving onto Johnny Weak Pints. There is, however, less than half the duty on beers 1.2–2.8%, which results in the fantastically cheap Sam Smith's Alpine Lager (2.8%) (£2.20quid a pint).

150 Many online unit calculators are useless for working this out in detail. Often designed to be user friendly, they'll generalise that a pint of lager contains three units and a glass of wine contains two, not allowing you to specify strength or quantity. The best unit calculator I've found online is: http://www.cleavebooks.co.uk/scol/ccalcoh3.htm.

151 That is to say, drinking this much alcohol. The Tories have yet to pursue an anti-remorse agenda.

The crucial factor is how quickly your body processes alcohol. As a very broad figure, the average person, having eaten an average amount, processes about one unit of alcohol per hour. This can vary according to gender, age, weight, health, medication, etc., but I'll take it as a decent average. The stronger the beer you consume, the more alcohol backs up in your system as you drink, ipso facto, you get drunk.

The chart below is based on a graph drawn on the back of a beer mat by Joe Stange, celebrated booze writer and author of beer blog thirstypilgrim.com, which I originally came across as part of an article on this very topic for *Draft Mag*.[152] What it shows is the excess alcohol building up in your system drinking 4% ale, 5.2% lager and 5.8% IPA, with a one unit per hour reduction for the amount you burn off. It assumes that, like The Lovely Robin and me, you average about a pint every 45 minutes.

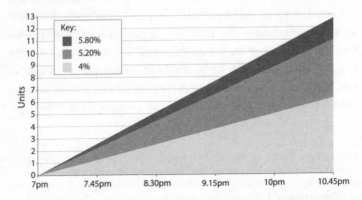

As you can see, after a five-pint session with The Lovely Robin, simply by choosing what you may think is an innocuous lager, you're almost twice as drunk! Choose the Punk IPA and you're MORE THAN twice as drunk.

---

152 http://draftmag.com/science-session-abv-processing/

Among the young there is a belief that you want the best 'bang for your buck'. They may ask, 'Why pay £4quid for a pint at 3.8% when you can have a pint at 5% for £4.50quid?' But, oh shadow from the past, after a certain age, the bang is chat and the buck is time. Also, I don't want to regret either bang/chat or buck/time. I want to wander home thinking, 'God, that was a good laugh! Isn't Robin lovely?! Aren't I lovely?!' and not 'Oh man, I'm a mess.' The system works.

Suffice to say none of the above is completely accurate for any individual person, and certainly may not be used as evidence in court, but it serves as a useful illustration for most folks.

Hangovers

I've never really suffered that badly from them physically. I've had the odd sore head, never really felt nauseous, and it's nothing that couldn't be solved by a cup of tea and six toilets. However, I must admit that most mornings after drinking I wake up with a crippling sense of shame and dread, an inability to focus, concentrate or feel any hope, happiness or self-worth, a kind of furnace fear of anxiety and self-loathing. But no nausea . . . So . . . every cloud . . . I thought a lot of this was that, due to my career, I've always been able to sleep through the worst of them. However, since turning 30, I've woken relatively early (7.30am–8.30am), and still not felt the sore head or nausea. I think the above graph gives a clue as to why.

Were each of the three subjects to pass out at 11pm and wake at 7am after drinking their separate drinks, the 4% legend would have been alcohol-free for about an hour and a half before waking, the 5.2% lager drinker would still have three units in their system, the Punk quaffer a whopping 4.75 units. Just to put that into perspective, both would be over the legal drink drive limit, and the Punk IPA person probably double the legal drink drive limit! That's quite a stark fact. How many times have you had five pints, been in bed by 11pm, and driven to work the next morning? After watching well over 400 episodes of UK-based traffic-police documentaries, I cannot emphasise enough the horror and grief caused by drink drivers, and the long-lasting impact their own actions have on their own lives. In the (rightful) eyes of the law, our Punk pal above is no more innocent than someone who drinks two pints of Doom Bar for breakfast and then hops in the Audi.

Afterward

Having banned spirits in my house from April 2017,[153] the power of my 'moral' hangovers or, in Norwegian, *Fylleangst* has lessened. Yes, I still have the odd cloudy day that I have to write off, and spend ignoring the self-doubt and seeking emergency crying nooks[154] in central London, but these are rare. I have had to admit that spirits, rum especially, had a large part to play in the end of every relationship I've been in, numerous shame wells and all my major career failures/plateaus 2007–14. But I have now reached a happy medium where, by sticking to session ale, and having the odd day off booze marked in red Sharpie on my official Queen calendar, I'm genuinely able to enjoy my drinking and my life. So, go forth dear friends, examine those pump clips, spread your alcohol over longer nights, extended chats and deeper nooks. Forgo wasteful units, erase shame from your mornings and Keep It Session™.

---

153 Due to factors.
154 Unused studios at Radio X HQ are an absolute godsend for any tearful digital DJ caught short welling up in public. For example, after a watching the film *Arrival* at a central London cinema in January 2017.

L:

Living, Grief Is

Little did I know, on the 27th of October 2017, when sat on the toilet finishing my tenth bag of pickled-onion Space Raiders, that I had started a movement.[155] When stumbling downstairs to a pile of eight empty cans of Beavertown Neck Oil (4.3%) and my laptop paused on the fourth episode of *Mindhunter* I'd watched that evening, I wrote three words in my notebook:

'Grief Is Living'

These words soon became the rallying cry for anyone who has ever opened a packet of Cadbury's Mini Rolls and thought, after immediately eating two: 'You're gonna eat the whole bloody pack, aren't you? Oh Lordy . . . here we go again.'

*   *   *   *   *

When Elis and I began broadcasting together, it never occurred to me to be anything other than as honest with him on air as I was in person. If he asked me how I was and I was sad, I would

---

155 Both literal and metaphorical.

say so. If he asked me, 'How was your week, John?' and I'd had a tough time, I might exclaim, 'AWFUL!', before playing Green Day. It soon became clear that this wasn't very common in the world of commercial radio and, as a result, over the years our Radio X show has contained many references to, stories about, correspondence concerning, all kinds of things one might place under the broad heading of 'mental health'. I must admit I'm even slightly uneasy using terms like 'mental health' or 'depression'. Maybe because I worry that other people, whether rightly or wrongly, might cringe, tense up or think, 'Oh, this isn't about me' or 'I don't want to hear someone being all "open" about stuff.' So thank the Lord for our old friend Elis James, who, with a common touch like no other, coined the term 'The Darkness of Robins'.

Little did that man on the street know that not only was he predicting the title of the 2017 Perrier Award-winning show[156] and, by extension, predicting that one day I would be crowned the funniest comedian on earth,[157] but he had found the only word I feel totally comfortable using to 'describe my vibe'.[158]

I was reluctant to write about darkness. I'm far more comfortable describing how it manifests itself, and then having a laugh about it. I would never want to suggest that my experience was in any way unique, or that my take on it was in any way authoritative. I think perhaps what I feel most acutely is a fear that anyone suffering from any form of mental health problem may read what I write and think, 'That's not my experience; maybe I'm even more unusual/alone/weird than I thought.' What I have learned is that the more subjectively one talks about such things, e.g. 'I ate ten bags of Space Raiders before writing

---

156 Sorry Fosters, If.com, Lastminute.com, that's what I'm calling it.

157 Plus Australian support.

158 Note to self: potential gameshow title? Get Elis to pitch to one of his TV friends?

"Grief Is Living" in a notebook,' the more people can see themselves in those stories. Yet, when you try to speak generally, e.g. 'Depression is like running up a hill through treacle,' you immediately exclude most people, because our experience of mental health is as varied and individual as our experience of physical health. Just because I get pains in my left hamstring after long drives[159] doesn't mean your eczema isn't real.

I wouldn't say I'm depressed, or suffer from depression. I don't think I do. However, I do feel dark at times – and my general outlook and baseline mood is often one of darkness.

I felt a connection to the word when I first heard Bonnie 'Prince' Billy's masterpiece *I See a Darkness*. It's a flawless album, and the title track speaks to me very personally, as I'm sure it does to everyone who has heard it. Have a listen and then a read of the lyrics. It's not as bleak as it first sounds – it's a song of honesty, friendship and hope, but it's still sad, mournful and dark. I love that balance: there is light in the darkness, but also darkness in the light.

There's an interview with Will Oldham[160] on the music website Pitchfork. It's a characteristically stupid interview, where, hilariously, the interviewer begins by asking why Will Oldham doesn't like interviews and, having heard his reasons (nuance impossible, detail glossed over, interesting topics rushed or edited, complex topics not pursued), then spends the rest of the interview proving Will's point. There's a great bit where he asks if Will Oldham has had much experience of karma. He answers, 'Tons and tons', to which the interviewer simply responds, 'Johnny Cash played "I See a Darkness" on his last album . . . What was that like?' I mean COME ON! Maybe dig a little deeper on the interesting thing he just said! It's like that bit in *Knowing Me,*

---

159 The sole downside to being one of the world's most accomplished clutch balancers.
160 AKA Bonnie 'Prince' Billy.

Knowing You where Alan Partridge asks the racing driver if he gets bored of the same old questions before asking, 'When did you first want to be a racing driver?'

Anyway, if you don't want to be annoyed, don't go on Pitchfork, but there's one really cool thing Will Oldham says in the interview. He's asked, 'Do you think that you're more depressed than most people?' Which, speaking as someone who has given a few interviews over the last year, is a really horrid question (and I've had some stinkers[161]). There's no way out of that question without: A. Your answer becoming the story, e.g. 'Bonnie "Prince" Billy has depression!' or 'Bonnie "Prince" Billy's melancholic persona all a lie!' or B. Sounding self-important. Answering either 'yes' or 'no' would make him sound like he thinks he's somehow special and separates him from his audience. If you fudge it, it sounds like you don't want to engage with depression or mental health. And, in fact, it's impossible to answer because HOW DO YOU KNOW HOW EVERYONE ELSE FEELS?! Such a dumb, unanswerable question. However, somehow the brilliant Will Oldham finds the perfect answer.

'Not today.'

I absolutely love that answer. I love it so goddamn much! Because in one exchange, something of the experience of mental health is captured without anyone claiming ownership of what that experience is like. Everyone has mental health, both positive and negative experiences of it, and everyone's experience is not only different, but different day to day. In that answer, we have a world where everyone is depressed and not depressed; we're all experiencing emotions in different ways at different times.

I would say, broadly, that since the age of about 12 my

---

161 NO IT'S NOT ABOUT HER AND NO SHE'S NOT SEEN THE SHOW AND YES WE DO SPEAK.

baseline mood has been one of melancholy. It was also about the age I first started getting quite hung up on girls. I'm sure for most people those two things go hand in hand; this huge new emotional world opens up, it's like getting a new sense. As a fan of Philip Pullman, I would say 'the dust has begun to settle'. And those infatuations are rarely fulfilled (unless you're an absolute secondary school playa), so with those emotions arrives a sense of loss and loneliness into your teenage landscape. For me, there were other factors too: an absent father once led to a troubling experience after watching the film *Cocoon* at about the age of eight. So deeply did it chime with my feelings of loss that I think I cried for the next two days. And once, aged seven, after discovering I had stepped on a worm in the garden, I ran to my mum, absolutely inconsolable. Male role models and worm-empathy have been an Achilles' heel ever since.

But one thing that has stood me in pretty good stead is I've never felt like sadness is a bad thing, a negative. Now, let me be very clear, depression is a destructive and real cause of suffering in people's lives, and if you feel it is stopping you from enjoying life, functioning or living up to your potential, then some numbers and links you can use to seek help are available at the end of this chapter. But I'm not talking about depression, I'm talking about (my own) darkness.

When I think about the world, and I'm very lucky to have the free time to combine this with some really excellent periods of sitting, I often see it through a kind of sad lens. I'm sure a lot of you do, too; the world is rife with injustice, abuse, intolerance and cruelty to people and animals that I'm want to dwell on. Grief *is* living. The final nail in the coffin is I do nothing about this. I do not protest, I do not write letters and, as of the Brexit Referendum, I don't even tweet about it. I look back on that flurry of online activity before Brexit as one of the saddest, most misguided movements of our age. About 100,000 people retweeted and agreed while some 17.4 million just went out and voted for something so preposterous it makes me want to bury my head in the sand. And I do.

That said, I also do very little to alleviate this cloud. I'm happy to look at it, content to let it bring me some of the music, literature and films I hold dearest to me. I'm not envious of people who wake up in the morning and jump out of bed to go for a run and fill their life with endorphins and positivity. I enjoy the world around me in small ways: the jackdaws that wake me up scrabbling on my roof in the morning; the intricacies of service stations and motorway maintenance; a full pint glass in an empty pub; silence. And I'm hugely fortunate in that this outlook can play a part in my work, that as soon as I find myself about to break down, or check myself having done so, I can laugh at myself, and be paid to tell people about it onstage. Which is also why I'm very wary of being absolute about what sadness, depression or darkness is like for other people. I cannot imagine how much courage it must take for someone to hold it together for a class of pupils, an office, a fire department, a patient when their life is falling apart. I salute absolutely every person who has ever put themselves second for the good of their work or their family, but I also believe, very strongly, that we are often only one or two decisions away from vastly improving our mental health, and even if those decisions are hard, they can be made in seconds.

How many lives would change in an instant by using one of the following sentences:

'I'm quitting'

'I'm leaving'

'I love you'

'I'm going'

'I'm coming back'

A counsellor once said to me, 'People come to me, sometimes very desperate people, and they say: "I'll do anything to feel better." But after a few sessions of talking and weighing up their options it emerges that what they actually mean is: "I'll do anything to feel better, just don't make me change."'

It's so true, we find ourselves overcome by unhappiness in lives we never wanted but are too afraid to change. Something my mum calls 'the fur-lined rut'. I know the pain of being in a relationship you know is wrong, in a job that isn't for you, being drawn into a situation where you think: 'How did this happen? This isn't my life!' Often changing these things causes other people pain, or hassle or inconvenience, but what is the cost of not making change?

There is a book of poetry I adore called *Stag's Leap* by Sharon Olds. It tells her experience of being left by her husband after thirty years of marriage. What is so striking about it, aside from the descriptions of her grief, is her kindness: deep down she knows that to love him is to accept the changes he has made for his own happiness. For me that is true love, and is encapsulated by the line, from the title poem

> . . . *When anyone escapes, my heart*
> *leaps up. Even when it is I who am escaped from,*
> *I am half on the side of the leaver.*[162]

That, for me, is empathy at its finest. So, if you're feeling like you're stuck in a rut, make a list of half a dozen things you wish you could change in your life. Try to ignore the cries of 'But what if?', 'I can't' and 'What will Doris think?!' You may be surprised by how simple those changes could be to make – and Doris will have to like it or lump it.

---

162 Sharon Olds, 'Stag's Leap', *Stag's Leap*, Jonathan Cape (2012).

Sometimes it's not life changes, or lack of, that make me feel dark. In fact, most of the time when I tot up all the things I have in my life, I realise I'm absolutely Living My Best Life™, but still that sense of sadness returns, floating in for an evening. I'm lucky in that I find it as much of a motivator as an obstacle, if not more so. When I was at my absolute worst following the end of a relationship, I found myself crying while sat on the toilet. The tears fell onto my penis, and then fell from my penis onto shit. I don't think my life has ever been that starkly bleak. Just to repeat: MY PENIS WAS CRYING ONTO SHIT. And as soon as I'd clocked that, as soon as that image was seared onto my brain for eternity, I started to laugh. I sat on a toilet laughing as tears fell from my penis onto shit. Not bad for a day's work.[163]

The things that infuriate me about myself, my onerous interior monologue that I am trapped with, the moments when I'm on the edge of losing it at myself as I stand in front of the bathroom mirror, comparing prices and reviews of things I need online until I am beside myself with loathing at my own indecision, all these things frequently end up with me sighing ruefully, or giggling, or texting The Lovely Robin or telling Elis/the nation on a Saturday.

---

163 [EJ] I have known John for 13 years, and one of the things that struck me about him when we first met was how he wasn't ashamed of his melancholic outlook and embraced sadness as a part of life. This was totally new to me, as until then the people I knew tended to pretend at all times that everything was great. A few family members of mine have had serious problems with depression, and I don't talk about it on the radio as I'm frightened of misrepresenting them, and I also don't feel it's my story to tell. However, if I had to sum up John, it would be a conversation we had around ten years ago when he was a bit down about his stand-up career. At that stage in stand-up, you value yourself and try to establish your place in the perceived pecking order of things based on the gigs you do and the promoters you work for. A promoter John wanted to 'get in with' wasn't answering the phone, and he was also worried about his first Edinburgh show. He called me and was clearly down, and jealous that I was off out to do something exciting. I asked him what he was doing, and he replied, 'I'm watching mince defrost in real time.' When I asked why, it really made him laugh. He felt better after our chat, and I realised that I have never met anyone who had such a combination of humour and self-awareness.

And for these pressure valves I am eternally grateful. I'm aware I don't have a family to support, kids to organise, a department to run, but I do have responsibilities to people, events, organisations and HMRC, and when the darkness threatens to encroach on these responsibilities there are things I do to help.

Earlier I spoke about how making big changes can be simpler than you think. But also, the more I think about it, the more I find I can really improve my mental health with very small acts, little things that make big differences. So I thought I would write them down here, make a list of some of the small things I do to get through.

1. Make a to-do list

This is often my first port of call, and many of the things listed below will be on such a list. Feeling like you've achieved things, even very small things, in spite of how you feel, can be incredibly empowering. Often on my worst days I'll say to myself, out loud, before bed, 'Hey, you did well today, man! You felt like shit but you got stuff done!' There's a wonderful instruction from 'Just for Today', a list of motivational advice from *The Twelve-Step Programme of Alcoholics Anonymous*. I discovered it many years ago through Gamblers Anonymous, when seeking help for a gambling problem I had in my late teens and early twenties. The whole list[164] is a great place to look for help at dark times, but this one is relevant to the above:

> Just for today I will have a plan, I may not stick to it but I will have it, I will save myself from two pests, hurry and indecision.

---

164 Google 'Just for Today Alcoholics Anonymous' (the link was way too long to go here).

And when I say small things, I mean SMALL things. Rule number one for to-do lists is never to write something like 'Tidy the house' or 'Sort accounts'. It's too much and you'll feel annoyed for not solving it all at once. Break it right down: some of the things might take ten seconds, but the more I get crossed out the better I feel. Right now I have a to-do list in front of me for today. It says:

~~Unload dishwasher~~
~~Take out recycling~~
~~Gas meter reading~~
~~Listen to last night's gig recording~~
~~Write up last night's gig recording~~
~~Call Chris~~
~~Remove spoon from lawn~~
Work out why there's a spoon on the lawn

As you can see, I'm not there yet, but I have my suspicions that the local pigeon community is currently experiencing some kind of major drug epidemic. Time to put a Robins among them!

My point here is this: you are enough. You did something. Too often we feel like we aren't in control, aren't capable of things. And it doesn't matter whether it was writing a symphony or emptying the dishwasher – you did it. And hold on to that for dear life, because when it's all you can do not to bang your head against the wall or stay in bed all day, or drink into oblivion, emptying the dishwasher *is a symphony*. And it's with these small, seemingly insignificant hand holds, that we can begin to pull ourselves out of the swamp.

2. Look after the basics

This is my mum's first question whenever I'm in a state. Though my teenage self would often roll his eyes at the dreaded 'basics', she was right. These basics are:

Food
Sleep
Drink
Excersize

If I were a woman, I would add menstrual cycle to the list. These four or five things have drastic effects on our mental health, probably more than anything else. Let's look at them briefly in turn:

Food

Fun fact: there is not a food, product, pill, shampoo or face mask on earth that can 'detox' you. It's one of the great marketing scandals of our age. If you buy something that claims to 'detox' you and it is not your own liver, kidneys, lungs or skin, then you've been scammed. These organs are the only things that can cleanse your body and they're doing it right now. How well they do it can be helped by all of the 'basics' above. If you're the sort of person who skips meals, then try to keep a check on when you last ate, as all sorts of things associated with hunger (blood sugar, insulin, headaches, low vitamins) can affect your mood massively. I'm insanely irritable when I'm hungry, and the only way I could understand the extreme mood swings experienced by women in my life as they waited for/got/recovered from their periods, was to imagine myself hungry all the time, and from that moment onwards I was better able to empathise with what it must be like to feel out of control of your mood. I also find planning, shopping for and making a meal relaxes me. I'm not going to tell you what to eat, but I used to get really low and tired after eating processed fast food, and I don't after eating more healthy food. It's not rocket science.

Sleep

Elis is rightly obsessed with sleep after reading the article in this footnote.[165] It's not just the length of sleep but the quality that affects your mood. During my 'rum years' (2008–11 and 2013–17), not only was I hungover every single day, I also never had a decent night's rest. Unbeknown to me, while my body should have been recharging it was fighting an unending battle to process alcohol. I was the equivalent of a boss making their employee work every evening, day off, weekend and bank holiday. Not cool. And no wonder I often woke up feeling absolutely bereft and hopeless.

Also, try not to 'electrify the bedroom'. And I don't mean hold back on your feminine allure/twig and berrymanship.[166] But unnatural light can make it hard to sleep. Close your screens earlier or get an app to soften the tone of the screen. I use one called f.Lux for my MacBook and it's ace.

Drink

For me alcohol has the biggest negative impact on my world view/ability to concentrate/capacity for joy/capacity to relate to people/motivation/career/relationships ... the list goes on. I know I don't drink enough water and I will pay for that when I hit 50 and my face falls off. But I've been too busy trying to cut back on booze. It has been a real struggle and one that is ongoing. I'd

---

165 https://www.theguardian.com/lifeandstyle/2017/sep/24/why-lack-of-sleep-health-worst-enemy-matthew-walker-why-we-sleep.

166 See **Appendix i: Glossary of Terms**.

say I'm now at a point where I've found a balance I'm comfortable with: I'm drinking weaker booze, in smaller quantities, less often. But any one or combination of those will make some difference to your mood. And if you need to stop, there are some organisations listed at the end of this chapter that can help. You can do it. I haven't gambled since the 6th of December 2002. If you'd told me on the 5th of December 2002 that I would go sixteen years without gambling, I'd have thrown up at the horror of that idea/burst into tears/started gambling. But that's perhaps, for another book.

Excersize

I'm not an excersise guy. You might be able to tell that from the fact I've spelled it wrong three times so far in this chapter. Elis is your one-stop shop for that. But I have had periods of my life where I've done it, and I know it does good, I know I feel better. But, alas, I also know I can't be arsed. That said, as a small addendum to Elis's wonderful chapter, 'Body, Shock Your', for those of us who can't be arsed: do something, do anything. Two brisk walks of ten minutes a day do make a difference. They also get you out of the goddamn house/office. Get yourself slightly out of breath a couple of times a day. Walk to the shops. Take the stairs. If you're in a city, often the distances between public transport stops (especially tube stops in London) are eminently walkable. And when you take into account changing lines, waiting, delays, getting in and out of stations, it's often a matter of minutes' difference. Pound. That. P.

Menstrual cycle

'Hmmmm, isn't this the very definition of mansplaining, John?'

I sincerely hope not. I'm not going to even attempt to explain or advise, but I also don't want to exclude something that I have witnessed have a monumental impact on the mental health of women in my life. It affects half of the population for sometimes half of their lives, and I want it to be recognised how completely wretched and tiring and frustrating and damaging it can be when your own body is making your life hell. All I can say is, if you're suffering then seek help, and if your GP is an ass about it, then go to another GP and then another and then another and DEMAND they refer you to a specialist hormone/fertility centre. And, if your partner or colleagues or friends don't understand, then don't feel you can't keep telling them, in as punishing detail as you like, what you're going through. Just because someone doesn't get it, doesn't mean you don't get it!

3. Get out/find your space

I really think the room and house where you live, plus the mile radius around it, have a huge impact on your mood. I've lived in city centre areas where I couldn't control how depressed the endless bookies, amusement[167] arcades and kebab shops made me feel. But I could control the nice pubs I found (eventually), the little parks, the churchyard you wouldn't know was there unless you were in it, the really nice Turkish restaurant that didn't look really nice from the outside, the walk to the nicer part of town. Similarly, I could control the calming stacks of books in the living room, the fairy lights on the bookcase, the signed Bonnie 'Prince' Billy posters arranged just how I liked them, my favourite mug. In these small things, these little places, you can find a moment of calm, a bit of nourishment, and maybe a little island in the sea of life.

---

167 There's a criminal piece of false advertising if ever I saw one. Never have I seen someone crippled by addiction to fixed-odds betting terminals display anything approaching amusement.

They also get you out and about. I know I'm never going to average 10,000 steps daily, but 3,000 steps taken somewhere you like, on a day when you'd otherwise have stayed indoors for 24 hours, can make a real difference.

4. Find your thing

I'm a firm believer that our niche interests and passions brighten the corners of our lives. In a way that's why this book exists at all. All Elis and I really do is talk about things that obsess us, annoy us and amuse us. If you pitched The Elis James and John Robins Show now, I very much doubt even the most open-minded radio exec would back a show with a mainly Queen/O'Sullivan/farthing/Gorky's Zygotic Mynci/Wim Hof/Sherlock Holmes/*Traffic Cops*/shame-based agenda. Never, ever be embarrassed about the little things that you enjoy doing. Just because you may not feel you're changing the world doesn't mean that your farthing collection, Queen Fan Club magazines or four-hour-long *Traffic Cops* binges aren't making a big difference to your mood. If your partner thinks crocheting is lame, tell them Robins says it's 'cool as eff'.[168] If you feel like a failure because your sister is in the top tax bracket and all you seem to get a kick out of is taking apart bikes, then to hell with her income! After all, who's the one doing the important work of taking more bikes off our roads?![169]

5. Write stuff down

I'm a huge fan of beginning things. In that tiny act of creation so many powerful forces are set into play. Whatever you feel like, write

---

168 And once developed quite an intense crocheting habit for about two months in 1994. I even took my bobbin to Scouts.

169 I'm really, really pleased with that joke.

it down, and I mean physically write with a pen and paper. It could be a letter you will never send, it could be a diary, a poem, the start of a story, a list, a play, absolutely anything. You don't have to show anyone. I have a whole sack of stuff in the loft labelled 'John's Bag of Death'. It's a big Ikea bag full of scraps, notebooks, poems, letters and all manner of stuff that, were it to be made public, would cause me to spontaneously combust. But that's not the point. It doesn't have to be good. And you can tear it up or burn it in a ceremonial pyre when it's finished. And it doesn't even need to be finished! Indeed, the words 'Grief Is Living' aren't finished, they're not a play or a novel, but that didn't stop them beginning a UK-wide revolution[170] that would change the lives of the entire population and might, one day, see me honoured by the Queen, or, should my petition for reform of the monarchy be successful, Queen themselves.

In all seriousness, it did make a few people laugh, and a few people feel a bit less embarrassed about their low moments. And I genuinely didn't know that would happen when I stumbled back pissed from the toilet, covered in pickled-onion maize-snack dust. So the point stands.

There's a book called *The Artist's Way*, which I was recommended years ago. It's excellent. And if the slightly New Agey language puts you off, then do ignore it and persevere. Because at its heart is a message of using creativity to improve your relationship with yourself and the world. Though I've never stuck at it to complete the whole programme it outlines, the excersises it sets are really transformative and the core practice of writing three pages of stream of consciousness every morning has been where all of my last four Edinburgh shows have come into existence. I haven't done it for a year, and might only do it for a week or two, but it's there when I need it.

---

170 Commercial digital indie radio-receptive areas only.

6. Talk and get help

My first port of call for help is usually my friends and family: Elis, The Lovely Robin, my friend Damion, a text group of like-minded legends, my mum and stepdad. I know from experience the last thing you want to do when you're in the pit is to reach out of it, but doing so sets all manner of positive things in motion. If you think about it, the only way anyone's mental health ever improves is by talking, by beginning to communicate your problem in some way. Even if medication ends up suiting you, that road will have begun with a conversation. Begin that conversation now, think about who might be best to approach and say the thing that's been banging round your head since forever.

If you don't have a Lovely Robin or Elis of your own, then maybe be one for someone else. As powerful as finding help when you need it is giving help to someone else when they do. And it doesn't have to be someone you know. Many places are desperate for volunteers to reach out to those who are lonely or need support, and there might be a place near you! Even a brief chat with a stranger in a shop can change your mood. Just ask Elis's fiancée; it gives her brain orgasms.[171, 172]

Finally, some experts to hand you over to. I was very reluctant to write this chapter, but I'm glad I did. I hope you don't feel I've tried to tell you what your life is like, or set myself up as any kind of wisdom merchant. Nothing I've written here is in any way new. And everything I've said here has been expressed far better by other people. One thing I like is that none of the above costs a penny. It's all free! Some of the things take time. Some effort.

---

171 This is no veiled criticism of Elis's twig and berrymanship. I know for a fact he is a competent lover.
172 [EJ] It's called Autonomous Sensory Meridian Response (ASMR) and she made a programme about it that may or may not be available on iPlayer.

But we have more time than we think, and more effort than we thought ourselves capable of.

All of the numbers and organisations below are free. However, seeking regular help from a therapist near you may cost money, but it could be the best money you've ever spent. I've seen a handful of counsellors in my time; none of them were perfect, but all of them were incredibly useful and helped me effect real change. The British Association for Counselling and Psychotherapy has a great deal of information on BACP.co.uk and you can search for therapists there or at counselling-directory.org.uk. Make sure the person is accredited, and, depending on qualifications and area, the cost of a counsellor should be somewhere between £40–£70quid per hour, perhaps more for a psychotherapist. Read their profiles, see what areas they specialise in, get a read of their vibe. And if it doesn't feel right after a few sessions, find someone else.

CONTACTS

Alcoholics Anonymous
Phone: 0845 769 7555 (24-hour helpline)
Website: www.alcoholics-anonymous.org.uk

Anxiety UK
Charity providing support if you've been diagnosed with an anxiety condition.
Phone: 03444 775 774 (Mon–Fri, 9.30am–5.30pm)
Website: www.anxietyuk.org.uk

Beat
Eating-disorder helpline.
Phone: 0808 801 0677 (adults) or 0808 801 0711 (under-18s)
Website: www.b-eat.co.uk

Bipolar UK

A charity helping people living with manic depression or bipolar disorder.
Website: www.bipolaruk.org.uk

CALM

CALM is the Campaign Against Living Miserably, for men aged 15–35.
Website: www.thecalmzone.net

Depression Alliance

Charity for sufferers of depression. Has a network of self-help groups.
Website: www.depressionalliance.org

Gamblers Anonymous

Website: www.gamblersanonymous.org.uk

Men's Health Forum

24/7 stress support for men by text, chat and E-Mail.
Website: www.menshealthforum.org.uk

Mental Health Foundation

Provides information and support for anyone with mental health
problems or learning disabilities.
Website: www.mentalhealth.org.uk

Mind

Promotes the views and needs of people with mental health problems.
Phone: 0300 123 3393 (Mon–Fri, 9am–6pm)
Website: www.mind.org.uk

Narcotics Anonymous

Phone: 0300 999 1212 (daily until midnight)
Website: www.ukna.org

No Panic

Voluntary charity offering support for sufferers of panic attacks and OCD.
Offers a course to help overcome your phobia/OCD. Includes a helpline.

Phone: 0844 967 4848 (daily, 10am–10pm)

Website: www.nopanic.org.uk

OCD Action

Support for people with obsessive compulsive disorder (OCD). Includes information on treatment and online resources.

Phone: 0845 390 6232 (Mon–Fri, 9.30am–5pm)

Website: www.ocdaction.org.uk

OCD UK

A charity run by people with OCD, for people with OCD. Includes facts, news and treatments.

Phone: 0845 120 3778 (Mon–Fri, 9am–5pm)

Website: www.ocduk.org

PAPYRUS

Young suicide prevention society.

Phone: HOPElineUK 0800 068 4141 (Mon–Fri, 10am–5pm & 7pm–10pm. Weekends 2pm–5pm)

Website: www.papyrus-uk.org

Refuge

Advice on dealing with domestic violence.

Phone: 0808 2000 247 (24-hour helpline)

Website: www.refuge.org.uk

Relate

Marriage and relationship counselling.

Phone: 0300 100 1234 (for information on their services)

Website: www.relate.org.uk

Rethink Mental Illness

Support and advice for people living with mental illness.

Phone: 0300 5000 927 (Mon–Fri, 9.30am–4pm)

Website: www.rethink.org

Samaritans

Confidential support for people experiencing feelings of distress or despair.

Phone: 116 123 (free 24-hour helpline)

Website: www.samaritans.org.uk

SANE

Emotional support, information and guidance for people affected by mental illness, their families and carers.

SANEline: 0300 304 7000 (daily, 4.30pm–10.30pm)

Textcare: comfort and care via text message, sent when the person needs it most: http://www.sane.org.uk/textcare

Peer-support forum: www.sane.org.uk/supportforum

Website: www.sane.org.uk/support

YoungMinds

Information on child and adolescent mental health. Services for parents and professionals.

Phone: Parents' helpline 0808 802 5544 (Mon–Fri, 9.30am–4pm)

Website: www.youngminds.org.uk

M:

Mind Scenarios, A Guide

During the Edinburgh Fringe Festival of 2012 the mind of Robins was in a state of high agitation. I had met a girl in the weeks before the festival and had been overcome with a very potent fondness (obsession) for her (the idea of her). We would soon go on to have an intense relationship lasting five months,[173] but I was yet to know that I'd fully secured her affections. Also, I had started using an artificial stimulant, street name 'Red Bull'[174] before my shows. I would arrive, order a pint of Diet Coke, a pint of Red Bull and down both before going onstage at 7pm. Little did I know that this was the equivalent amount of caffeine used by zookeepers to keep a small elephant, or large pig, awake for 72 hours straight. This, coupled with the stress of a career that had recently flatlined,[175] meant that, regardless of what time I went to bed, I would awake between 6am and 7am daily, my

---

173 [EJ] Classic Robins!
174 AKA 'Motion Lotion', 'Twerp Petrol' and 'Coffee 2.0'.
175 Some three years previously.

heart racing, as the previous night's alcohol wore off, revealing the lovesickness/caffeine/overwhelming sense of failure it had masked.

Not only was this a real spanner in the works to my career as an LNL,[176] it also had the unwanted side effect of making me super-tired at around the 3pm mark. There was no choice. I would have to perfect the art of something I had previously scorned/not been capable of.

Napping.

Pre-2012, if you'd told me you were the sort of person who took a nap, I would have turned my back on you, sparked up a fag and hailed the nearest taxi home, told the taxi to wait outside my house while I changed into an even cooler leather jacket, before taking me back out, but to a place where you, with your cocoa and weirdly soft blanket, were nowhere to be seen (perhaps The Legend Society, Caution to the Wind 'R' Us, or some form of winners' enclosure). How wrong I was.

Napping is now one of the great[177] pleasures in my life.

I used to find the late mornings and lie-ins one of the great upsides of finding self-employment as a part of the night-time economy. However, since the purchase of a beer fridge, I'm now much more likely to stay at home of an evening, alone, railing into the abyss, but at supermarket (or brewery shop) prices. And this means I'm usually in bed by 1am. It's now not the 9am-midday snooze I value, but those hours between 3pm and 5pm, where my mind is my oyster.

I've spent most of my life perfecting the art of thinking.

The arrogance of this sentence! Plato, Descartes, Sartre . . . Robins!   *EJ*

---

176 Late-Night Legend.
177 [EJ] 'only'.

I have a great deal of time and few people to speak to, so like a call from a volunteer to a pensioner, my own mind is a lifeline, a charity I have set up to save myself from loneliness. Thoughts, however, can be a double-edged sword. Lie down for a nap at 4pm worrying about the effect of historically low interest rates on your cash ISA, and you'll be up till dawn. Add to this a rumination on how to secure a 6 per cent return on your savings, and you may never sleep again, bemoaning the vast sums of money you've lost in a stocks and shares ISA following a bad stock recommendation from your friend's brother in 2014.

So, it was clear I would have to devise a system to regulate the topics my mind had access to in order to fully relax pre-nap. Fantasy was in, and the real world of once-promising (now bankrupt) alternative energy companies were out. And so, I developed a selection of what I call 'mind scenarios',[178] places, realms and situations my mind could turn to when I needed to relax. These places are not the sole domain of the late-afternoon nap; they are vital for helping me sleep at night on the rare occasions I don't drink and find sober sleep so stressful I've twice called NHS Direct thinking I was having a heart attack.

I will now describe some of my favourite mind scenarios. Feel free to try them out and come up with your own. If you do come up with a potential belter, do E-Mail it in to the show. Perhaps the thought might, itself, be about the possibility of setting up your first E-Mail account and entering the futureland of electronic communications? If so, make it a reality. After all, the idea of a letter you could send instantly without a stamp or post box was once the mind scenario of another visionary. Today it is a reality for some 40 per cent of small businesses, and 65 per cent of large ones.

---

178 Rejected names include 'Brain Films', 'Thought Maps' and 'Imagi-Nations'.

The Indian Star

This began as a mind scenario in which, finding myself suffering from locked-in syndrome (LIS), I kept my conscious mind occupied by writing my own Sherlock Holmes stories – a kind of fan fiction for the persistently vegetative. I would lie down (in the actual world) and imagine myself waking up (in the mind world) to another day in my hospital bed, staring at the clock and ready to begin again the Sherlock Holmes story I had been writing in my mind for the last few months.

Pretty soon the premise became self-defeating as concerns about if and when I would recover from my locked-in state began to dominate. I became distracted and disheartened by desperate attempts to try and move a thumb or toe, move my eye on rare occasions I had visitors or communicate with the nursing staff. Annoying noises such as a ticking radiator, a TV on too loud or an itching sensation, none of which I could change in my locked-in state, turned the whole exercise into a truly dreadful experience. I also became somewhat obsessed with locked-in syndrome and, as a result, read half a dozen memoirs written by those who had recovered, and some by those who had not. It was a deeply disturbing period of my life, but I've come through it, one step at a time.

In order to de-stress the scenario I ditched the hospital storyline altogether and simply focused on my own Sherlock Holmes story. It begins with Watson looking out onto Baker Street on the first warm day following a bitter winter. As the snow thaws, he reflects on the many tragedies in the newspapers due to the effects of the cold. His eye is then caught by the sight of a horrifically deformed man with, to his professional eyes, 'the most severe curvature of the spine I have observed'. Despite his military and medical training, Watson is disturbed when the man makes for the front door of 221B Baker St. He turns his back on the door as he hears the uneven step on the stairs. The man asks for Dr John Watson and Watson replies, 'I'm afraid he is not in at present.' The reply comes, in a familiar voice, 'Well, my dear Watson, I hope you offer a warmer welcome to our actual clients.' Watson turns to find Holmes standing before him, disguise in hand. 'Holmes!' he cries, before apologising and then quizzing him on his get-up. It turns out Holmes needed to be unseen, and the great detective states, 'Sometimes the best way to pass unnoticed is to be so visible that people look away.'[179]

Holmes then has to smoke loads of fags and a pipe before giving Watson the lowdown on his latest case. These are my favourite moments in Sherlock Holmes, when they are settling down in armchairs, or in the nook of a country inn, and Holmes is about to describe the case in hand. To drink a pint at his table! Or three! Or six! But not ten, I'd make a fool of myself.

A famous diamond, known as the Indian Star, is to be exhibited in order to distract from dissenting voices about Britain's involvement in the subcontinent. Holmes is concerned that Moriarty plans to steal it.

'But Holmes, that stone has over one hundred guards. Never has a stone been so well protected!' I exclaimed.

'My dear Watson, you find yourself guilty of being too trusting. Whereas you see a hundred guards, I see a hundred links in a chain, any one of which could be weak. I would rather know it was guarded by one trustworthy man, than one thousand regulars.'[180]

Then Holmes lays out his plan to steal the gem BEFORE Moriarty can, and replace it with a fake.

179 CLASSIC HOLMES!
180 CLASSIC HOLMES!

Eventually the prime minister comes to ask for Holmes's help. Holmes catches Moriarty after he has stolen what (he thinks) is the diamond, but the stone is nowhere to be found as Moriarty has disposed of it. At the denouement Holmes observes:

'It has been sold, most likely on the continent, to a private collector. There really is no hope of recovering the stone Moriarty stole.'

The prime minister is dismayed. Holmes, ever the dramatist, goes on:

'The real stone, however, should prove much easier to find.'

The prime minister's face reddens with impatience:

'What on earth are you talking about, man? Her Majesty is ruined and you stand there making jokes of a most caddish nature!'

Holmes is the picture of calm.

'Prime minister, control yourself. Please do me one small thing; reach into your breast pocket.'
'By Jove!' the prime minister exclaimed, and from his pocket he withdrew a stone of such brilliance that its light seemed to shine on every wall of our humble lodgings.

You guessed it. THE DIAMOND IS IN HIS POCKET. CLASSIC HOLMES! I never really get beyond the opening scene, as the very thought of Holmes smoking a fag in an armchair is usually more than enough to get me to sleep. Another story, 'Porlock's Revenge', sees Holmes receive an unmarked envelope full of tobacco, with no name or message attached. Through intense thought alone, he solves an elaborate mystery and brings down an entire criminal empire, all without leaving his rooms. But this is in its very early stages.

The Vanished People

I am well aware that 'post-apocalyptic' is a contradiction in terms; by definition there can be nothing after the end of everything. However, I deem it correct by usage, and have a degree in English from a little-known institution revered for its teaching on the subject.[181]

What could possibly be more relaxing than the end of all responsibilities, save the responsibility of survival itself? What more calming prospect than the end of all interaction with all other human beings? The idea of being truly alone on the planet chills me out no end. Sure, I would miss weekly badinage with Elis, and I would mourn his extinction as much as the next man, more so! But I'm sure I would soon fashion a solar-powered iPhone charger so that I could revisit old podcasts; no replacement for the real thing, but close enough.

Cheers, mate

One favoured scenario is that I wake up and all the people on earth have disappeared. Cars are still in the street, electricity still on, clocks still ticking, and yet it's like the entire human race has vanished, perhaps filming six and a half billion cameos for an episode of TV sitcom *Josh*. Anyway, I have to make a trip to the supermarket to stock up on supplies to see me through an indeterminate period of time. I'm allowed to use a trolley but *not*

---

181 Oxford University, BA (Hons) English Literature Course II. MA (Oxon).

a big trolley, the one that is the perfect size for a single recluse doing a big shop. In my mind I enter the supermarket and it is deserted. I browse the aisles before stocking up on tinned tomatoes, dried pasta, jalapenos and cuppa soups while pondering issues of legality. Does this count as theft? Do I leave change on the self-checkout? I have no access to tills so can't get change for notes. I don't want to *overpay*. But I also don't want this society of one to descend into lawlessness, a tragedy that would see me having to declare martial law over myself! But then who polices the police?[182]

At this point I usually become distracted by considerations of whether the CCTV is still recording, and feel burning shame for what would happen if everyone returns and sees that I've been shopping/pilfering on my own. So I agree to compromise and leave money on one side that I will collect the following day if no one has taken it, which they won't. A win–win scenario.

I will then imagine how to get the shopping home, not wanting to take a trolley beyond the boundaries of the Tesco car park. Hopefully, I'll be fast asleep before the pain of all the ale in pubs going bad within a week begins to stress me out.

Time Pause

Another scenario kind of related to the one where the rest of the world's population have disappeared is the time pause. In it I am able to pause time for as long as I want, as many times as I want. Everything stops, people freeze, cars stop in their tracks but the natural world continues as it was (water flows, food spoils, beer can be extracted from the pumps in a pub and I, unfortunately, age). I rarely visit this scenario, though, as after the first

---

182 Both me, in this scenario.

few trips to the pub it inevitably takes an unpleasantly top-shelf turn, not dissimilar to situations outlined in Nicholson Baker's *The Fermata*, a book I have not read, but am told is very, very rude.

Nuclear Attack

It may not sound like the most relaxing thought exercise to have, but what could be more relaxing than knowing you are prepared for a nuclear explosion? Try giving yourself three different amounts of warning. An hour, fifteen minutes and three minutes, for example. Practise different scenarios each time. If you're quick, an hour will give you time to shop for bare essentials nearby, fifteen minutes might just be long enough to take shelter in a pub beer cellar (my dream location) and three minutes will see you form a tight schedule for how to hunker down in your own house. For reference, here's a decent three-minute plan:

- Run a bath full of cold water
- Close all windows
- Get as much material between yourself and the outside world
- Grab a torch, first-aid kit and moist wipes
- Press play on Queen's anti-nuclear anthem, 'Hammer to Fall'

Snow Cave

I once watched a Ray Mears video where he made an igloo from scratch, then demonstrated how to create an emergency 'snow cave', if there was no time for an igloo. Like all Mears's vids, it captured my imagination. I often like to imagine I am caught in a huge snow drift on a slight incline (not up a mountain, I'm not mad) and I have to dig a snow cave about 10ft long, 4ft high and

4ft wide – like a kind of wintery coffin, but with room to turn round. I then stock my bag with ten things to help me survive for a week. You get the clothes you are wearing and a snow shovel for free, and each item of food counts as one thing, as does a sleeping bag. An example list would be:

- Self-igniting gas stove with in-built pan/lid (for melting snow into water)
- Massive Toblerone (like in duty-free shops)
- Head torch
- Sleeping bag
- Breathable bivvy bag
- Sleeping mat
- Massive bag of salt-and-vinegar peanuts (really, really massive)
- Berocca
- Candles (remarkably good for warmth in enclosed spaces)
- Pipe and tobacco

The Million-Pound Question

My most common and most valued mind scenario: what would I do with a million pounds? If I'd spent as much time trying to earn a million pounds as I have fantasising about how I would spend it, then this fantasy would be a reality many times over. The answer to this question is clear to anyone with half a brain:

1. Pay off as much of the mortgage as is possible without triggering early-repayment charges
2. Invest £700,000 in a mix of savings/Premium Bonds/peer-to-peer lending sites and use the interest to live/buy ex- out of house/provide family with income

3. Pay off friends' debts
4. Buy The Lovely Robin a flat nearby and charge reasonable rent[183]
5. Buy a second hand 1.6d BMW 1 Series achieving c.70 mpg combined
6. Buy a bed with under-mattress storage
7. Buy Queen's *News of the World* limited-edition box set

You might like to try your own distributions of money. Maybe you don't want the maximum in Premium Bonds? Maybe you want to drip feed an ISA to maximise tax efficiency? Maybe you're a Gilt guy? Or a Bond girl?[184] However you choose to maximise your investment, give it a go. It's also a treat to imagine you've won the million pounds on the Premium Bonds. Imagine the knock on the door on the first of the month. A gentleman introduces himself (always called Paul when I imagine him), and you immediately twig what he's come to tell you.[185] You offer him coffee, and all the time you're making it you know exactly what he's going to say, but you tease out the time as this is the very best bit. After the moment comes you imagine the kind of leaflets and reading materials they provide for big winners, like special investment advice, or an appointment that can be made for you with a financial advisor. You opt to remain anonymous to prove a point Elis made that if you ever won a million pounds he wouldn't notice any change in your behaviour/clothes. You then tell Elis on the first anniversary of your windfall that you have been a millionaire for a year, and he laughs and he laughs and he laughs. To celebrate you shout him a PizzaExpress.

---

183 'Like I said, I'm sure we can come to some arrangement.'

184 Government, not James.

185 NS&I always send a representative to tell the main prize winners in person.

I am actually suspicious that John has already won a million pounds, because quite recently I supported him on tour in Coventry, for which John kindly paid my expenses. When I told John that I had got the £16quid train (which was over an hour longer) as opposed to the £77quid Virgin train, he was less pleased with me than I had anticipated.

EJ

This scenario can work with any amount of money, from, I would say, £2000quid to £2,000,000quid. Though after that it just gets silly. (I always imagine I'd run a fund that made monthly payments to charities. I would research and select them, before going on the road to deliver cheques to tearful volunteers, essentially becoming a 'secret millionaire' for the rest of time.)

The Night Shift

Here is a recent one, I think inspired by a passage from *London Belongs to Me* by Norman Collins, about a guy who lived a very basic life in a rented flat. It might also be based on a scene in Mike Leigh's film *Naked*, where David Thewlis talks to a security guard about the devil.

Basically, I'm some form of night watchman or security guard. I have a small room, perhaps like one of those people who monitor barriers at the entrance to big offices. Though small, the room has some home comforts: a fridge, a microwave, a two-ringed hob and a sink. My job is not dangerous – I'm some kind of middleman who alerts a bigger boy if he sees anything suspicious on CCTV, so I don't actually have to leave the room. Anyway, I work midnight–8am and there are maybe four CCTV screens in front of me that I need to keep an eye on, but very little happens. In this mind scenario, I populate the shelf and gaps on the worktop with all the things I might need. Maybe a dozen books, meals I could make on the hob, a cheeky bottle of whisky in the filing cabinet. However, this scenario does have one limitation in that, in order to turn up sober/not fall asleep, it does preclude me from going to the pub ever again, so I tend not to pursue it too far. I usually am quite happy to imagine myself watching a late-finishing World Snooker Championship on a portable TV while eating pasta, the silence of the industrial estate around me, or having a little nip of Glenlivet in my cup of tea as the sun comes up.

* * * * *

So there you have a selection of mind scenarios to get you going. A psychologist might suggest that taken as a group they are evidence of a mind that suffers from an acute fear of responsibility. Or, perhaps, someone whose self-imposed isolation would cause them less concern if the reason for their isolation were taken out of their hands, by snow or the rest of the human population suddenly disappearing. Well, that's as may be, but does anyone really trust what 'so-called' psychologists say about 'so-called' minds anyway?! And, as Bonnie 'Prince' Billy so rightly sang:

'When you have no one, no one can hurt you.' [186,187]

---

186 'You Will Miss Me When I Burn', *There Is No One What Will Take Care of You.*

187 [EJ] I would say 'keep it light', but it seems a little late at this juncture. Reading this chapter confirmed everything I had secretly known about John, but it reminded me of something my mother used to say about a cool kid misbehaving when I was at school: 'Don't feel you have to be like him, Elis.' If you are interested, I try to empty my mind of all thoughts before going to bed – my brief foray into mind scenarios (I was always replacing Aaron Ramsey in the semi-final of Euro 2016 against Portugal, and laying on the pass for Gareth Bale to score the winner) meant that I was too excited to sleep and would usually have to have a bottle of lager to calm down. Annoying, when you've already brushed your teeth.

N:

Normal, How to Be

And lo! A crowd formed. By the port gathered merchants and lenders, farriers and farmers, tailors, beggars, concubines, artisans, clerks, washerwomen and men at court. And behold, raised on a rock at shore sat a man in a Queen hoodie, vaping, and the crowd did sit before him as he gazed out to sea.

An old woman approached him, holding a tartan shopping bag on wheels and smoking a fag.

'Speak to us of public transport.'

The man turned, placing his e-cig on the rock.

'My child, when enter ye the bus or tram, train or plane, be not as the wolf before the babe, snarl ye not to announce the presence of your stag do, but, I say unto thee, be as the babe before the wolf. Does the babe bray loudly about how much they've already had to drink so the whole carriage can hear? No. Nor does the babe swear loudly even though there are children travelling home late from a trip to the panto. Just as the parents of those children yearn for those youths to halt their mouths, so do I yearn for radio-friendly language to be used on the carriages of our country.

'Indeed, when Elis James did pronounce the Thai holiday

destination Phuket as "Fuck It" live on national radio, did he not think he was being culturally sensitive? And lo! When Producer Dave did subsequently unleash all hell on him, did he not ensure it was during a Stereophonics track? When the mics were down?'[188]

A minstrel stood, with his lute in hand and did address the man.

'What of music on the carriages of the plains? What say ye to the listeners and performers of song?'

The man stood on the rock and vaped longingly. He held the minstrel in his gaze and the minstrel cowered.

'Fear ye not, songstrel of the western lands. Do I not stand before you now, my torso emblazoned with depictions of the four cornerstones of rock? Music is to mine ear like berries to the morning lark. Does not the morning lark sing for you? So, I too speak now with the food of Queen in the belly of my heart. However, the lark does not sing on the train, nor outside of hours laid down by the local council. Likewise, I do decree that no man nor woman should play music on any train, bus or plane. Unless that music be dimmed by the outer silence of the earbud. Aye, and not only music, but YouTube videos, adverts or funny videos you have taken on a night out. For I myself was tested on the bus to Bristol, whence I was sat in front of two girls who scrubbed through a half-hour video of the previous night's karaoke, taking in the region of fifty screengrabs with the screengrab sound effect still on, and it was as much as I could do not to put out mine own eyes.

'Furthermore, should you take a call wearing headphones, remember ye that ye needst speak no louder than normal. Does not the responsibility of amplifying your voice lie with our old

---

188 For once.

friend the microphone? And if ye speak of personal matters, your own success, anecdotes of drunkenness or using business lingo, remember that the annoyance is increased tenfold should others be forced to listen to your braying. Do as I do, brethren, tell the caller: "I'm on a train, I will call you back to discuss unresting death at a later point."'

A glutton stood and as he spoke crumbs fell from his lips, still chewing, as he was, a Pret tomato and brie baguette. 'What of eating, sire? Must we starve on long travels?'

'My son, no man nor woman nor child nor beast can roam the plains without sustenance. Do not our termini provide an increasingly pleasing range of food halls? What would Marylebone be without its M&S? What traveller would seek Manchester Piccadilly if it had not an Upper Crust and dual Costa Coffees? What coach driver would hold out for Tebay services without its genuinely fantastic farmshop and delicatessen? I say unto you, eat, drink and enjoy your meal deals. But in the name of the Lord shut your mouths when you eat.[189] Am I not amazed by how many of even my closest friends and disciples have never been taught to eat? Mouth breathers! Be as your quieter cousins the nose breathers! Combine not eating and breathing for 'tis genuinely abhorrent before the Lord.'

A cooper approached, his hands stained with polish. 'Speak to us, if you see fit, of pubs.' There was a murmur in the crowd. The man bowed his head into his hands, a silence fell, and as he raised his eyes to the congregation, tears welled in his eyes. He looked skyward, towards clouds tinged pink with the first glimmer of sunset.

---

189 [EJ] I agree. Although I must also point out that steps have been taken in America to ban hot food on the subway, and it's not unheard of in London to sit next to someone on the tube who's working their way through a takeaway paella.

'O my people. O faith. O hope. O time to do and not to do.

'Brethren, you ask of me to speak of pubs, but how to speak of that which is the heart's stillness? How to voice the silent mind of that which transcends silence, and is silent still?

'To be born into a land of pubs, blessed is thy luck, for you are the chosen pub-goers, the pint holders, the drinksmiths and ale lords of your own destiny.

'As you enter a pub, so a pub enters you. And as you enter, remember these words: "Every pub has its own vibe. Do not bring your own vibe to a pub lest the Holy Bond of vibe and pub be rent asunder." Rail not against the loud music, sports broadcast and plastic glasses of cold John Smith's in the Walkabout chain, for though the vibe is terrible, that is its vibe.[190] Likewise, in the quiet sunlit pub, where gentlefolk seek solace and reflection, as light sings through ale in glasses held by silent hands, do not be as the management consultant bringing four clients to squawk about nothing in pink shirts with white collars at 5pm. For they have created an abomination. I say unto you, just as a mother seeks shade for her child in summer and wraps swaddling cloth about her child in winter, enter not a quiet pub when your heart is raging, nor a loud pub when your heart is still.'

A moneylender stood and spoke. 'What of buying rounds?'

'Like a cart without wheels, or a hawk without wings, a pub cannot be driven/fly without its rounds (wheels/wings). Surely you know the fable of the man and his round? No? Then let me repeat it, for its message is good.

'A wise man approached a bar that was mildly busy. In front of him a foolish man was placing an order.

---

190 [EJ] Again, I agree, but am absolutely astonished at the uncharacteristically permissive attitude he preaches here.

"I'll have two pints of Stella, please."

The barman poured his pints and named the total. "That'll be 7 pounds 90," he said.

The man paused, adding, "Oh, and a glass of red wine."

"Which red wine would you like?" asked the barman.

Dazed at the question, the man turned to his table. "What red do you want, Carol?"

Carol, seemingly surprised at the question, asked, "What red have they got?"

The man passed the question on to the barman. "What red have you got?"

"We have Rioja, Cab Sav and a Merlot," the barman replied, patiently.

The foolish man relayed this list to his table, but in his foolishness he forgot the selection.

"They've got Rioja, Cab ... What was it?"

The barman's patience was being tested, and the wise man grimaced like he was about to burst into flames.

"Cab Sav and a Merlot," the barman repeated, making eye contact with the wise man to communicate that he, too, wanted the fires to engulf him.

"Cab Sav and a Merlot!" the foolish man shouted across the now-formidable queue.

"Cab Sav!" Carol shouted back.

The barman tensed. "Medium or large?" he asked, knowing the trials that lay ahead.

"Medium or large?" the man shouted.

"Oh, go on, I'll have a large!" Carol barked back.

The barman poured the wine adeptly, and rang up the new total. "That'll be 12 pounds 70."

The man replied, "Can I also get two gin and ton ... "

But he spake no more for the Lord was watching, and so angered

> was the Lord by the foolish man's inability to follow basic bar
> etiquette that he turned him into a pillar of sand. The wise man
> stepped to the bar and said:
>
> "I'll have a pint of Hophead, please."
>
> "Is that all?" The barman asked.
>
> "Yes it is," the wise man replied. And God was pleased.'[191]

The crowd gasped at the tale, and the man stepped down from the rock. He walked amongst them, and raising a clay pot, weak session ale sprang from his hands.

'Children, be not the foolish man. Memorise your round, and trust in the barman's training. Why not use an iPhone note if it's a big one? The staff can quite easily memorise four drinks, and let them decide in which order to most efficiently pour them. Be not the fly in the pint of the person behind you; be as the head on the pint of the person inside you.'

By now the sky was blazing a deep pink, and the sun half set over the horizon. A woman on horseback rode into the centre of the crowd. She dismounted and spoke to the man in a powerful voice.

'Give us now your teachings on driving, and general motorway etiquette.'

The man smiled, before turning his back on the crowd and walking into the shallows of the water. He bent down and thrust his hands into the sea, which parted around them in a tumult of sand and salt water. From the ocean he drew a giant sign. It was the direction sign[192]

---

191 [EJ] I was with John in The Harp in Chandos Place when this happened and saw God smite this man with my own eyes.

192 To give it it's proper title, a Worboys directional sign, after the 1963 committee chaired by Sir Walter Worboys, which reviewed traffic signage in the UK and which resulted in the document that defines Britain's traffic signage to this day: *Traffic Signs Regulations and General Directions* (TSRGD).

from M4 Junction 13 Eastbound detailing the interchange where the M4 connects with the A34.

He placed the sign in the sand, and lo, splashing salt water onto the sign there emerged ten rules, written in the standard motorway sign font.[193] He turned to the crowd and addressed them.

'Attend me now, and attend these ten commandments. These commandments are passed down from the Almighty Traffic Officers and Transport Police. Heed their rules in all you do . . . on the roads.'

1. Obey the Speed Limit

2. Keep your distance (one metre per mph, two if wet)

3. Indicate

4. Get in lane. Stay in lane

'This is especially true when warned of a lane closure or approaching a queue on a slip road. See the heathen who races down the outside and then indicates and dives in at the last minute. Shame on him!'

The crowd trembled as it seemed a storm was raging in his voice.

'For he is the reason there is a queue in the first place.'

5. The inside lane is the driving lane, the middle lane is the overtaking the driving lane, the outside lane is the overtaking the overtaking the driving lane

'My children, if you are not in the inside lane, and you are not in the process of overtaking, then what are you? For you are not of the Lord . . . of traffic. Your speed is irrelevant. They are not 'slow''

---

193 Known as 'Transport Medium' and 'Transport Heavy', these are the only two fonts allowed on UK road signs (save for motorway route numbers, which are allowed in the font 'Motorway'). They were designed by Jock Kinneir and Margaret Calvert after the Ministry for Transport appointed an advisory committee on traffic signs for motorways in 1957. The font was rolled out under the Sir Walter Worboys committee mentioned above.

or 'fast' lanes. Though exceptions can be made when moving over temporarily when traffic is joining from a slip road or junction.'

6. Never take a risk, never miss an opportunity

'Brethren, be assertive, but be not rash nor aggressive. Be not as the fool who fails to build up speed when joining a motorway. Be not as the wild man who moves across and not diagonally forward into a space. Be not too hesitant, nor too hasty. Be, in all things, part of the smooth and effective flow of traffic, for it is good.'

7. Never use your proximity, your lights or your horn to bully another driver

'Is there a greater fool than the fool who puts themselves and others in danger to prove a point? If the Nissan Micra goes slowly on the country lane, might that not be because it is unfamiliar with the road? Why then does the Audi A4 get within a foot behind and flash their lights?! To startle the Micra into sudden familiarity with the road? The driver may be elderly, or already tense and anxious. BACK OFF, YE COIN! Calm down, and go and sit in yonder bin.'

8. Never drink and drive

9. Never drive tired or after smoking/taking/experimenting with/riding the dragon of, doobies/any illegal drug/prescription drug (when taking of said prescription drug can cause drowsiness or slow reactions)

10. Don't park on the pavement/by a dropped kerb

'Did it not occur to you that somebody might be in a wheelchair or blind? And thus it is for those A-frame/swinging shop signs businesses put on the pavement now I come to think of it.'

He paused, and vaped awhile.

'Ye drivers bemoan the curse of the traffic jam, blaming roadworks, the Highways Agency, private companies or ye local council. But what part do you play in the formation of long queues? Let us imagine a common cause of a traffic jam: the M4 (eastbound) has gone down to two lanes due to roadworks in the outside lane. If all the rules above are followed, there would be no jam. At a restricted 50 mph and everyone 50 metres apart, with 800 yards warning of the closure, indicating to move lanes and not then jumping from lane to lane to gain an advantage,[194] and no one racing down the outside lane to force their way in at the last minute, then we would all slide into two lanes with a minimum of fuss, just at a slower speed. Did I not once see with mine own eyes two lorries conspire to block the lane that was closing by going slow, parallel to each other, in the middle and outside lane? It was a joyous miracle far beyond the capacity of my powers. For there was no queue when the closure came. Blessed are those lorries. That said, lorries overtaking each other when there's only one mile per hour difference in their speed, effectively closing off two lanes, is an abomination. With no bullying on the lanes, no drink taken, no doobies smoked, no drivers excessively tired, would not the accident that caused the traffic jam in the first place never have occurred? See not the speck of dust in the Highways Agency's eye, but miss the rock in thine own!'

He turned to leave, then stopped. Many in the crowd were weeping.

'I am leaving you now. I am passing on to the further place, the silent realm. Do not weep, child, for in your heart lies the strength to *be normal*, as it lives in the heart of every person in this land. I say unto you, *BE NORMAL*. Through love and patience and charity will we tone it down, rein it in, slow it to an economical 50 mph on a smart motorway, keep it in our headphones.'

---

194 A completely fictional advantage!

Now he turned for one last time, his back to the crowd. He knelt on the sand and spake as if unto the sea itself.

'Ready, Freddie!'

And Lo! A cloud approached. A great tumult ensued and the people lay on the ground before a terrifying storm. The seas exploded into waves ten-oxen high. Then a shaft of light broke through, and an enormous arm reached down from on high. It was clad in leather, a leather sleeve as yellow as the sun itself, the fist clenched around the man, and he was raised unto the heavens, as a voice with what sounded like a four-octave range cried out, 'EYYYYYYYYYYYYYYYYYYYYYY OH!'

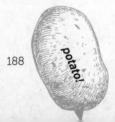

O:

Oxford Pub Crawl, The Ultimate

Between the years of 2001 and 2004 I was a student at St Anne's College, Oxford.[195]

(Brookes). *EJ*

Terms were torturously short at eight weeks long, thrice yearly, which gave the experience of being there an intensified, almost alternative reality. As soon as you arrived, the clock began to tick towards the moment you would once again return to your childhood bedroom, no bar downstairs, no friends next door, no music from a farther room.[196]

---

195 Unsuccessful in my first attempt, I took an unplanned year out where I worked at a Virgin Megastore and developed a chronic gambling problem.

196 Cf. T. S. Eliot 'The Love Song of J. Alfred Prufrock', 49–53, *Selected Poems*, Faber & Faber (1986). When I was about 14 I borrowed a copy of T. S. Eliot's *Selected Poems* from the school library. In an uncharacteristic display of lawlessness I never took it back; I still have it now and it accompanied me to all my tutorials on Eliot. It was the reason I studied English and I thoroughly recommend it to anyone.

Over the last decade, I have had countless conversations with fellow alumni The Lovely Robin about why this period of time had such a profound effect on us. For many people, university was a fun three years, perhaps a time when they first had sex, their first serious relationship, or got up at 6am every morning to go rowing like a complete fool. Then, life brings with it bigger things, like children, jobs, mortgages. For me, and I daresay The Lovely Robin, our time at university *was* our life – to quote Elis, we were 'too good at being young'.

> I wish I'd never said this, because he doesn't half bloody go on about it.

Indeed, when thinking about this chapter, a Bonnie 'Prince' Billy lyric sprang to mind. It's from a song called 'I Am Drinking Again':

And life is a tribute to you,
And so is dying,
And drinking in this way,
To die is what I'm trying.

Intense, huh?! Well, imagine how intense it is when you play it to a girl you fancy in your college room?![197] To put it plainly, it was like being at Hogwarts, and everything since, a life among muggles.

> I don't get this reference because I am 37, and was 17 when the first Harry Potter novel was published.

That's not to say people who didn't go to Oxford are muggles, you understand. Any university could have had this effect on me, but there's no escaping that it *was Oxford*.

---

197 V. v. intense.

The college system certainly played a part in creating a kind of Pullmanesque realm. You were cut off from the rest of the world, you had to enter through a porter's lodge, had your own pigeon hole for post, your own canteen, bar and library, and every college came equipped with a 'quad', an area of grass that varied from the magnificent (Trinity, Christ Church) to the modest and tree-lined (St Anne's). In fact, in the summer months our quad was dominated by the smell of semen, not an indicator of loose morals on the lawn, but the distinctive aroma of a tree known colloquially as 'The Cum Tree'.[198]

For me, two words that explain the intense experience of college life are 'freedom' and 'uncertainty'. Imagine a place with 400 18–21-year-olds, their meals provided, their bedrooms private, the bar open every night, where Guinness is £1.60quid a pint and a bottle of wine an irresponsibly priced £3quid. This wasn't a bar in town, this was a bar directly below my bedroom. Guys, I cannot emphasise this enough:

I LIVED ABOVE A FUCKING PUB

An album I listened to a great deal during my time at uni was *Summer Never Ends* by The Anomoanon. The title of a song from that album sums it up perfectly: 'Night Is Most Uncertain'. In later life, certainty seems to take over somehow: doing things you don't want to do, overtime, rent, getting food from the Tesco Express because your train home was delayed, cooking late and going to bed early, *Blue Planet II* on iPlayer, what Philip Larkin, in his devastating poem 'The Life with a Hole in it', called:

The unbeatable slow machine
That brings what you'll get.

---

198 *Pyrus calleryana*, or the Callery pear.

And though, looking back, the weeks and months of that time now seem to have fallen away at a breathtaking pace, for those three terms a year we shone.

That is, in reality of course, absolute bollocks. I have never been so depressed as I was at times at Oxford. 'But how could you be depressed at HOGWARTS, John?!' I hear you cry! Erm, I mean, have you read *The Half-Blood Prince*?![199] I mean, come on! Am I right, guys?![200] But, in hindsight, it feels like being depressed *in the right way*. By which I mean it meant something, it had a purpose, it was a reaction to life being lived.

A common habit was to get depressed about a girl not fancying me, pressurise Mike The Barman to sell me a bottle of red wine after hours and take it to my room where I would listen to 'Nomadic Revery (All Around)' by Bonnie 'Prince' Billy far too loud, have a brief cry, perhaps a bit of sick and then pass out. I was *hard work*.

Was?

Though I never involved myself in any comedy or theatre at uni, it was where I got my first taste of comedic performance. After being elected 'Bar Rep' on the JCR Committee (an election I won by downing three bottles of orange WKD at an afternoon hustings) . . .

You really brought an air of *Ibiza Uncovered* to the dreaming spires, didn't you?

---

199 [EJ] I had to google it, and No.

200 Though, luckily, cursed amulets and the possibility of He Who Shall Not Be Named rising to power were not threats during my time at Oxford, there were many reasons to get down at that age, things that resulted in a lot of bad poetry, the odd hunched cry over a barstool at last orders and, once, an overnight stay in A&E.

I would put on events and inevitably find a role for myself as compère, in spite of the fact that no compère was ever needed. I mean who commentates on karaoke?![201] And, as much as those first forays into pseudo stand-up undoubtedly set me on course to become the best stand-up comedian in the world,[202] so did the life of late nights, lie-ins, drink and uncertainty. I guess what I'm trying to say here, guys, is it meant a lot, and every single other thing to happen in my life has been a pathetic, vain, failed attempt to recapture one ounce of what it felt like to be nineteen, listening to 'We Are Not Alone' by Frank Zappa in my top-floor room in Bev 5, applying copious amounts of CK Be, before heading out into youth's vast, unending night.

So, what better way to recapture absolutely none of that feeling of freedom, and absolutely all of that feeling of loss, than by returning for a pub crawl over a decade after you left! That's right, guys, what follows is the Ultimate Oxford Pub Crawl, calling at The Regrets Arms, The Lamb and Sadness and Grief Tavern. But first, a few general tips on pub crawls:

Pub crawl tips

1. Ten before eleven
The below crawl was originally planned to take in eight pubs, but ten is the dream. You may well not have access to ten or you may want to specialise in a smaller number of pubs that fit a certain criteria, 'Pubs I've Cried In', for example. But for the ultimate, hit ten.

---

201 This legend!
202 See picture section for details.

2. One and done

Never, ever have more than one drink in each pub. Momentum is your friend, 'The Slumps'[203] your avowed enemy.

3. Stroll to success

Include a couple of decent-sized walks of 10 mins plus along your route. Fresh air and the pinch of cold is nature's Red Bull.

4. Pick yourself up

A good alternative to nature's Red Bull is actual Red Bull, and in the form of a Jägerbomb it's an absolute godsend. Ideally pop into a generic bar in between pubs – no one wants to be the guy ordering a Jägerbomb in a dreamlike pub that is all desire, all loss.

Only in your hands could Jägerbombs and melancholy combine.

5. Line your stomach, but not too much

The timing of food is perhaps the most important element in a successful pub crawl. Curry after pub seven? GAME OVER! Starting on an empty stomach? SEE YOU LATER, SLUMPY! Straight to pub one after Pizza Express? GOOD LUCK FINDING ROOM FOR NINE MORE PINTS! No, complete a decent (but not enormous) meal 60 to 90 minutes before you embark. A Pizza Express pizza (classic base) plus dough balls or bruschetta to start is ideal fare. Take some form of snack with you in case you're caught hungry: a bag of seeds, a Mars bar, a banana. And make sure one of the later pubs offers something less than a meal, but more than crisps. Nibbles or tapas-style side plates are ideal.

---

203 'The Slumps' describes the state you are in when your friends look round to find you with your head in your hands, or face drooping, having misjudged the pace, strength or start time of your drinking. Also known as 'the Droops'.

Good advice from John here. For some insane reason, when I was at school a common bit of advice was to line your stomach with milk. No, no, no, no, NO. Milk will curdle and the colour of your vomit will give you a panic attack. I would advise something with potatoes, though, as drinking on an empty stomach will give you a nuclear hangover.

EJ

6. Don't start early

I'm not a fan of early drinking, but even if you can happily drink a midday pint and not immediately want to sleep, don't let excitement get the better of you. Yes, you're excited! You're about to commune with every ghost of your past! Who wouldn't be excited?! But under no circumstances should this translate into a quick pint at the station before you leave.[204] It will be your undoing.

Technically, in Wales, an all-dayer (a 'Mike Rayer' or 'Gary Player', delete as applicable) needs to start at midday, preferably 11am. Anything after 2pm is simply regarded as a 'heavy session'. These events offer a slightly different vibe to John's pub crawls, however. More fun, you could argue. Less 'communing with the past', more 'communing with the sick in your bin'. I totally accept that binge drinking causes a myriad of terrible social problems but I can't change where I'm from.

EJ

7. Have a schedule

This is basic stuff, people. As enjoyable as the day itself is, the process of planning and carrying out that plan is just as, if not more, exciting. Imagining pubs! Comparing longlists! Honing

---

204 On Oxford Day II, Robin had a bottle of Moretti in Pizza Express and a pint of Carling before getting to the first pub. It is something for which I will never forgive him.

[EJ] Unfortunately, I am on The Lovely Robin's side here. The 'tsssst' of a can being opened on the train is where an all-dayer in a different town should begin.

shortlists! Wildcards! Classics! So, prepare the pubs, prepare the route, prepare the timings. As the saying goes, 'fail to prepare, prepare to fail (to commune with the ghosts of your past)'.

> Sounds good, but this is where John and I diverge. Part of the fun is not having a plan, and then the inevitable argument when you end up in an All Bar One. In fact, I would say the 'spontaneous all-dayer' (sadly something that hasn't happened to me since I left university) is one of the most fun things a human can do. But by all means, if you have been lumbered with a personality like John's, laminate your plan three months before the fun is scheduled to happen.

8. Keep up the chat

If you're in a small group, or perhaps with one friend, have pre-planned discussion points throughout the crawl. Perhaps mark the pubs out of five in different criteria, for example Vibe, Beer Selection, Beer Quality, Nostalgia, Staff, and discuss your choices. Or maybe prepare a quiz about the local area, your past or the pubs themselves. Or why not do all three?!

9. Stay over

If you don't live in the city of your crawl, there are few things as depressing as getting the last train home after the final pub. Knowing you have a bed nearby stops the increasing doom of the real world rearing its ugly head around pub seven.

10. KEEP IT SESSION™

In the name of all that is good in the world, don't drink anything above 4.5%.[205] Over the course of ten pints, the difference

---

205 For a full analysis, see **K: Keep It Session™**.

between 4% and 5% ABV will break you. It's 25 per cent more alcohol, or the equivalent of nearly three extra pints at 4%, and believe you me, a pub crawl on strong imported lager is not a laughing matter. Just ask my friend Phil what he remembers about pubs six to ten on Oxford Day III. That's right, sweet Fanny Adams! Towards the end you may need to substitute a short, or short and mixer, for a pint. There's no shame in that, it's like dessert! But do beware wine. A 250ml glass of wine at 14% contains 3.5 units, whereas a pint of 3.8% ale contains 2.16 units, a single shot of spirits, 1 unit.

OK, them's the rules. And here I sit, alone, preparing to delineate the Ultimate Oxford Pub Crawl. Looking out of my living room window the sun is brightening the falling autumn leaves. I could well be looking out of my university window onto the quad. And, in a way, I am. I always am.

Arrival

Meet your friend Robin at Oxford train station at 1.30pm. If you are coming from the same place, by all means sit with him and discuss the day ahead, though you may like to sit opposite in silence, pretending you haven't seen the other person, so that when you alight you can pretend you've bumped into each other with an entire day to kill.

When you get to the station, converse only in excited giggles and single words for a good five minutes. E.g.

ROBIN: 'Hehehehehe . . . pubs . . . '
JOHN: 'Hehehehe . . . pints! . . .'

Then speak in the voice of a West Country pub bore something along the lines of:

Oh dear! Oh dear, Robin! It seems we have found ourselves in an environment full of establishments that specialise in the licensed sale of ale! Oh dear! Oh dear! Whatever shall we do?! Oh dear!

Keep this up for way too long, before you head for your PizzaExpress around the 2.30pm mark.

Following your PizzaExpress (no alcohol consumed of course), you make your way to your lodgings. Ideally you'll be staying in a university college booked via universityrooms.com or through the individual college. Not only are these rooms cheap, but they allow you the crucial luxury of pretending you are still a student.

John, you are 36 years old. This is saaaaaad.

After you've checked in at around 3.30pm, stand for a while in the quad speaking about the coursework you have on and when you might be free.

JOHN: I finished my Saussure essay this morning, and my tute[206] was cancelled this afternoon, so I'm free till our lecture next Wednesday.[207]

ROBIN: Yeah, that's weird, I was meant to have a tute on Langland this afternoon, but Gillespie[208] cancelled and said just put the essay in his pidge.[209] I finished it last night so I'm good until Wednesday too.[210]

---

206 Cool Oxford slang for 'tutorial'.

207 For clarity, this scenario is taking place on a Thursday.

208 Dr Vincent Gillespie, J. R. R. Tolkien Professor of English Literature and Language, and Fellow, Lady Margaret Hall (formerly of St Anne's) AKA Total Legend.

209 Cool Oxford slang for 'pigeon hole'.

210 The sense, real or imagined, of having a number of days with nothing to do, no responsibilities, no cares, is absolutely crucial to the Ultimate Oxford Pub Crawl.

Now take the opportunity to spill over into hyperbole:

> JOHN: I might have a little lie down, then sit at my desk for 20 min-
> utes and gaze longingly down the long vista of the past! You?
> ROBIN: I'm going to read a while by lamplight and then open the
> curtains onto that other realm where memory and desire mix
> perpetually before an ever-present dusk!

> John, you are 36 years old. You need to get over this. You are a
> cool digital DJ with some of his life ahead of him.

EJ

Return to your rooms and do the above. Set your alarm for
4.20pm. Sit at the desk. Browse the copy of Philip Larkin's
Collected Poems you brought with you.[211] Lie on the bed and
stare at the ceiling, letting the sounds of college life mingle with
the afternoon sunlight: cutlery jangling on a trolley pushed over
paving stones towards a conference; children departing a distant primary school; the leaves of an oak tree rustling in a light
breeze; the spin of a bicycle wheel as it meanders down the road
beyond the college walls. Engage in a mind scenario.[212] Nap.

ALERT ALERT ALERT! Your pub crawl has begun!

Did you sleep? Was that a dream? Those thoughts were so
vivid! Yes you did! You had the ideal nap[213] and it's time to pub!

Well, almost . . .

Departure

Meet at 4.30pm at the porter's lodge and walk across the
University Parks. Remember the times you would trudge

---

211 Make sure it's the 1990 Faber edition with the yellow cover – FOR CRYING OUT
LOUD.
212 See **M: Mind Scenarios**.
213 11–19 minutes.

towards lectures across frosty grass at 10.45am in Michaelmas[214] Term all those years ago. Remember the Pub Porn[215] you wrote about being put in charge of the cricket pavilion for some complex stipend, which allowed you and The Lovely Robin to live and drink in Oxford for five years, that ran to over 13,000 words.[216] Remember the party she had on the grass all those summers ago, stumbling into bedrooms, drinking red wine from plastic cups, full ashtrays on your desk, afternoons in The Rose and Crown, hungover trips for Ribena and bacon baguettes from 'On The Hoof', that essay finished as the sun came up and the birds began to sing, those lost weeks after finals. Remember. Remember.

5pm The Star

Up St Clement's Street and past The Half Moon (not yet!) you take a right, or is it left? Why is it always one road further along, or one road back? Do the roads shift and slide when your back is turned? And then, after another 'Are you sure it's up here?' it reveals itself. There is no greater sight on earth than the glow of a pub revealing itself in the half-light of dusk. Nothing close to it on earth. You are breathless with desire, and you sit on the table where that photo was taken in 2002,[217] the one of Chris and Mike sitting in the summer sun, the light throwing shadows across the table, the same table. Stacks of CDs line the shelves behind the bar; you once noticed a copy of Frank Zappa's *Jazz from Hell* sitting there. Not just any Frank Zappa album, but *JAZZ FROM HELL*!

---

214 Cool Oxford slang for 'winter'.
215 See **Appendix i: Glossary of Terms**.
216 Twice the length of any essay you wrote when you were actually a student, you mad, mad bastard!
217 See picture section.

5.50pm The Half Moon

Doubling back on yourself, you hit The Half Moon. What a juke-box! Not only *The Best of Frank Zappa* but *Bongo Fury. BONGO FURY!* It's like the pub knows who I am! The beer range isn't great, but the Guinness is well kept. You remark, 'Why didn't we come here more often?!,' and The Lovely Robin replies, 'It feels like I've been robbed of something.'

6.45pm The Grapes

A decent long walk back into town, across Magdalen Bridge, cutting through Catte Street, past the Radcliffe Camera, Brasenose Lane, Turl Street, Ship Street, down the passage which we did not take, towards the door we never opened.[218]

Oh loss. Oh grief. The pub has changed.

History is the dark magician inside us tearing at our liver.[219]

It was once an actors' pub; no doubt the playbills on the wall were not originals, nor did any actors still grace its booths, but it was the pub I first loved in Oxford – a dark slice of the bright high street. I once lost my heart to the sight of a barmaid in The Grapes. She had long, bouncing, frizzy hair, and such was my shock I remarked to the landlord about how beautiful she was. He grinned with a strangely smug expression, as if humouring a child. It turned out she was his girlfriend and I was a child. I cannot remember her face, her features slipped from my pocket somewhere in the labyrinthine corridors of memory, but I will remember her hair, and how I felt, the light hitting my eyes with a start as I stumbled out, earlier than I thought it was, drunker

218 Cf. T. S. Eliot, 'Burnt Norton', *Four Quartets*, Faber & Faber (1969).

219 Deborah Levy, *Hot Milk*, Hamish Hamilton (2016).

than I thought I was. Though I only saw her once, I will remember that barmaid as long as I live.

It's a craft beer pub now and it's too fucking bright and the beer is too fucking cold and it's five fucking fifty for two-thirds of a fucking pint.[220]

7.15pm *The Eagle and Child*

Up St Giles now, that familiar walk past Hassan's kebab van, the smell of chicken donner hits you like walking into a lamp post. Past the Oxfam bookshop that once had an entire display of Frank Zappa books, all of which now sit on a shelf on Double Billy.[221]

On the shelf below those books there is a pump clip. It is a Greene King pump clip from when Greene King IPA was one of the best beers around. Long before it turned into a corporate behemoth peddling rip-offs of better beers branded so garishly in Union Jack-embossed middle England nostalgia and tasting so breathtakingly similar to a pint of dust that you'd think they were secretly trying to use up all the malt in England, Greene King was a fantastic ale. I found out that the company was being rebranded when I walked into The Eagle and Child in 2002. They'd just bought the Morrell's brewery and with it sold The Horse and Jockey pub opposite St Anne's College to be made into flats. An act of barbarism attested to by The Lovely Robin himself in his wonderful song 'The Brewery Tap':

Now it's a different pub,
they took out the old bar
and the tiled floor,
oh I want it to be back then.

---

220 At time of going to press. Seriously, a pint of Neck Oil is £6.20quid.
221 See **Appendix i: Glossary of Terms**.

The Horse and Jockey too,
it's now a block of flats
and so I wrote a song
as if that could help bring it back,

as if you could listen closely,
closely enough
that you could order a drink,
oh I want it to be back then.[222]

Well, 'back then' I walked into The Eagle and Child and they were changing the old Greene King pump clips for newer ones that looked like a shield or a Spitfire or a UKIP councillor or something. Well, I asked if I could have the old clip, and now, years later, it sits on my bookcase, among other ephemera: photos, ornaments, scraps of paper, postcards from the past.

The Eagle and Child is still a good pub, though. It's where Tolkien, C. S. Lewis and the rest of 'The Inklings' would sit and read each other drafts of their work, *The Hobbit* among them. And where, in my first term at university, I went one evening to read an Old English poem called *The Seafarer*, sat alone in a corner booth, my mohican haircut still intact, drinking a pint, smoking a pipe and looking like an absolute weapons-grade bellend.[223]

7.45pm The Lamb and Flag

You cross the road to The Lamb and Flag, Larkin's pub, directly opposite. Robin declares, 'The past is myself!' as you approach the door. St John's College memorabilia fills the walls, and you wish to God you'd spent more time in this glorious pub. The beer

---

222 Robin Allender, *Above the Dreamer's Head* – www.robinallender.bandcamp.com.
223 [EJ] Oddly self-aware joke from John, there.

is very well kept and lecturers mingle with students who probably go to special recitals and readings because they're the absolute best of the best, the 1% of the 1%. God, how you envy them, and simultaneously the idea of a life in academia brings a sudden and intense sadness. Perhaps the one thing bleaker than returning to a university you left 14 years ago is never leaving at all. Robin says, 'How can I be nostalgic about buying a baguette?!' and you write it down in your little book.

8.15–9.15 Pencilled slump/food break

Any serious pub crawler will make allowances for the unexpected. This buffer period could well be the making of the whole venture. Someone flagging? Take a longer stroll. Is hunger an issue? Take time out for a SMALL SNACK. Or, find yourself in fine fettle, cancel the break and head to AN EXTRA PUB!

Into Jericho

Between Great Clarendon Street and Juxton Street around a dozen small lanes lined with small terraced houses intersect in an area known as 'Jericho'. I don't think there is an area of the world that holds such magic, for me, as Jericho. Jericho contains five 'true' Jericho pubs: The Jude the Obscure and The Jericho Tavern sit on Walton Street, what I deem as the boundary to Jericho. No map will tell you that, but I am navigating with a map of the mind, an Ordnance Survey of the soul. Behind Walton Street a mere three pubs reside: The Rickety Press (formerly The Radcliffe Arms), The Harcourt Arms and Ye Olde Bookbinders. This haven was the district we most frequently wandered into, being a short walk down Observatory Street from college. Although, in reality, only a handful of pubs are located here, at the time they seemed infinite, shifting position, constantly unfolding, revealing and disappearing before your eyes. Is there a more perfect prospect, a more powerful proposition, than a dozen quiet streets in which pubs constantly reveal themselves?

8.40pm The Jericho Tavern

Woah, this is not on your schedule! You are really playing with fire here. But confidence is high and there is simply too much history in this venue. While not a pub that holds particular mystique, it's probably the pub we spent most time in, bizarrely. At the time it was a Scream pub, and afternoon drinking would take place during football matches on the big screen, before gigs, or just because it had enough space for larger groups. We had a drinking song based on their drinks selection at the time:

A Red,[224] a Veba,[225] Bacardi Breezer
A Carling Premier! A Carling Premier![226]

It is where, later in life, Robin played with his band, Gravenhurst, and where I, in a past life, hosted the Bar Oscars. The Bar Oscars were a glorified popularity contest in which every student could have one vote in various categories, from the charming 'Sweetest Couple' to the downright unacceptable 'Fittest Girl' and 'Hottest Bloke'. It was 2002, and if we weren't very PC, we were at least even-handed in our sexism. I hired myself to DJ at the event.

'Why, John? Did it really need a DJ?'

---

224 An alchopop whose existence I cannot, now, verify online, but which I'm convinced I haven't dreamed. My friend Phil, who did Classics, once claimed to have drunk 41 bottles in a sitting. A claim which I am sure he dreamed.

225 Vladivar Veba, a vodka-based alcopop released by Maxxium UK, the marketing arm of Jim Beam Brands, in spring 2001.

226 Still available in cans from some outlets of 'Bargain Booze'.

What?! Sorry, didn't hear you. I also compered. Gave myself an award for funniest man, and passed out on a bench on the way home, leaving a wallet containing 250 CDs in a green box on the street the night before recycling day. When I went back the next morning to retrace my steps they were gone. It remains one of the worst 48-hour periods of my life to date (and I've had a few STINKERS!). I placed notices, offered a £100quid reward[227] and two days later received a call (ironically while en route to The Star) to say they had been found. How I hugged that old St John's College porter in his workshop, how he found that uncomfortable and how, ever a man of my word, I wrote him a cheque for £100quid.

You eat a snack, drain your pint, feel slumpy and have a brainwave.

9.41pm The Jude the Obscure

Given that you've added an extra pub, it suddenly dawns on you that you can now return to the original plan, albeit slightly later than scheduled, with ONE PUB IN HAND. Incredible scenes. Also, given that the extra pub is one you don't like that much, though Robin does for some inexplicable reason, something about having 'once met a girl there in the grief-stricken recess of my past', you could substitute a pint (it also has a poor beer selection) for mankind's Red Bull: Red Bull. This is the perfect stop for a Jägerbomb, as it's the sort of thing they're used to selling in this slightly indistinct pub that always seems to have a half-drunk pint of Guinness on an empty table next to a white oval dish containing three chips.[228]

---

227 £149.29quid in 2016, taking into account inflation.
228 Honestly, Robin, what are you thinking?!

9.51pm The Harcourt Arms

How has this happened? You're now ahead of schedule! I mean, who sips a Jägerbomb?![229] So you're now a pub in hand AND ahead of time. This is the kind of thing that only happens in Jericho. Time means something different here, Walton Street is like a wardrobe into another realm, and we are well and truly through the looking glass.[230]

The Harcourt Arms, as it was between the years 2001 and 2004, remains my favourite pub of all time. It was silent and sunlit by day, warm and still relatively quiet by night, the perfectly suitable selection of jazz (Django Reinhardt, Sidney Bechet, Art Tatum) at the perfect volume. John the Landlord was an ever-present figure, making toasties behind the bar for £1.50quid[231] and proudly displaying an A4-printed sign detailing 'Some of the games that can be played here' (Scrabble, Risk, etc.). It had a log fire and did four-pint pitchers of Fuller's Chiswick bitter for £11quid or something insane. It has sadly changed hands, but has crucially not been ruined. There are no longer toasties sold at cost price,[232] but nor has it been gutted. And as you sit down to your rum and Diet Coke (you've made the switch), you notice the barman from St Anne's College sitting across from you. It's Mike! It's Mike The Barman! Some ghosts, dear reader, are not ghosts at all. This could only happen in Jericho.

You speak to Mike The Barman far too enthusiastically and take selfies[233] and he still works at St Anne's College Bar and says that 'there aren't as many mavericks as there used to be' and that 'we've never taken as much money as we did in your day'

---

229 This legend!
230 Of the wardrobe.
231 And I'm not jokin'!
232 Cancel the minibus, Dave!
233 See picture section

and inside something like pride glows for an instant. It's not like it was anymore! You're not missing out! The experiences you had are not being relived perpetually by others, they were for you and you alone, and you lived them. One small victory in the unwinnable war against time.

You check your watch . . . damn, still 2017 . . . but it's 10.15pm. Your final pub, Ye Olde Bookbinders, might be closing soon. You check online. Hang on, it closes at midnight! We've got so long. You look up at Robin, he looks at you, you couldn't . . . could you?

10.20pm The Rickety Press (formerly The Radcliffe Arms)

You cannot believe this is happening, you're going to do TEN PUBS! In all the discussions, the E-Mails back and forth, the routes planned, screengrabbed and redrafted, never in your wildest dreams did you believe it was possible. IT WASN'T EVEN ON THE CARDS! Only, dear friend, in Jericho. You decide to have gin and tonics in the venue where, if dinner in hall was rubbish (e.g. pizza night[234]), you would go for cheap, honest pub fare: The Radcliffe Arms. Alas, because, as yet, science has not found a way of stopping time, the name, management and decor have changed. Yes, dear reader, gastrofication has again waved its bare-wood wand.[235] The worn furniture has been replaced with brand new (yet somehow even more worn) furniture at great cost, a cost they are happy to pass on to their customers in the form of grievously overpriced drinks, though thoroughly worth it for the joke you make:

JOHN: Six fifty for a gin and tonic?!

BARMAN: It's Hendrix.

JOHN: I'd want his guitar for that!

---

234 Bases too thick/bready.

235 Ten and three-quarter inches, dragon (no) heartstring. Great Potter banter!

Great, great banter.

10.47pm Ye Olde Bookbinders

Here you are, at the boundary of Jericho. St Barnabas Church looms out of nowhere, so distinct, like a watchtower at the end of time. Beyond it lies Port Meadow, the River Thames, The Perch, The Trout, all time, all beauty, every lost afternoon, every smell of perfume, every electric glance, the warmth of the sun on your back, the smell of vodka on her lips, the taste of cigarette smoke and cherry on her tongue, bold winter nights, chance happenings, coincidence. As the pub reveals itself, so too does the unrepeatable past, the bittersweet tumult of intensity and innocence that Philip Larkin called:

> The strength and pain
> Of being young[236]

You chill out and head in. Ye Olde Bookbinders is undoubtedly a historic pub, claiming to be 'Oxford's Best Kept Secret Since 1869'. But so many secrets haunt these streets. And anyone who's watched *Inspector Morse* will find Ye Olde Bookbinders unrecognisable from its drab, canteen-like appearance in many an episode. It looks now like it has been untouched since 1869, but, like so many pubs, the historic décor is probably not much more than 20 years old. It's such a perfect reflection of our own sense of nostalgia. Pubs try to look like you want them to have been, but never were. They are memory incarnate, recreations of a time that never was, attempts to haul back what was lost, lost only because it was never there in the first place. And therein lies

---

236 Philip Larkin, 'Sad Steps', *High Windows*, Faber & Faber (1990).

their appeal. The Lovely Robin sent me a text recently, a quote from a book called *The Outrun*:

One reason alcohol is addictive is that it doesn't quite work.[237]

It's heartbreaking and true. We attempt to get to an unobtainable state with an imperfect tool, again and again and again. We get close, so close, a scent, a glimpse, a sense memory, and then it goes, a phantom in the mind's eye swept away. I think the same could be said of pubs. On a trip to New York[238] I described this observation to 'diabetic comedian'[239] Ed Gamble, and he replied with something that floored me:

You never quite get to where you remember being the last time.

Ed, I salute you. It's where you remember being, not where you were.

Adrenaline alone got you through that final drink. Mulled wine?! Lordy. You step out. It is later than you thought it was, you are drunker than you thought you were, soberer than you hoped you'd be. It is finished.

Ending

You return back to halls.[240] The conversation is fragmented. You remember that photo of your friend JC you took in the back of a cab on your final day at university.[241] Driving through Jericho he

---

237 Amy Liptrot, *The Outrun*, Canongate.
238 See Reuters for details.
239 BBC News website.
240 [EJ] Halls, Halls! Absolutely hilarious. The man is 36.
241 See picture section.

is on his phone, and, though usually a positive, upbeat guy, the look in his eyes is one of total resignation. 'It's all over' they seem to say, 'what do we do now?' Even 14 years later, I have no idea how to answer him.[242]

What you do right now, however, is return to your accommodation, sit on the toilet, AND FART YOURSELF TO DEATH. You've had seven pints of ale, a Jägerbomb, a rum and Diet Coke, two gin and tonics and a mulled wine, for Christ's sake. You brush your teeth. Fill an impossibly small glass with water, drink it, repeat twice more (like that'll do any bloody good) and place a final full glass next to your bed. You lie down, begin the opening salvos of a mind scenario and immediately pass out. You wake at 2.34am desperate for a piss (nice one, Poindexter).

In the morning you rise, head for breakfast and recount the night. It was good, so good. We did ten pubs! TEN! You sip your coffee and realise you've got ≤120 seconds until you SHIT YOURSELF TO DEATH. So it's a hasty jog back to the room.

Then to the train station, you are headed back to London and The Lovely Robin makes for Bristol via the purgatory of Didcot Parkway, 'trapped in Didcot' you both say. Going your separate ways, you temper the gloom of returning to reality with plans for the next trip, but sobriety's nameless dread is beginning to course through your veins, you leave.

Meanwhile telephones crouch, getting ready to ring
In locked-up offices, and all the uncaring
Intricate rented world begins to rouse.
The sky is white as clay, with no sun.
Work has to be done.[243]

---

242 /his eyes.
243 Philip Larkin, 'Aubade', *Collected Poems*, Faber & Faber.

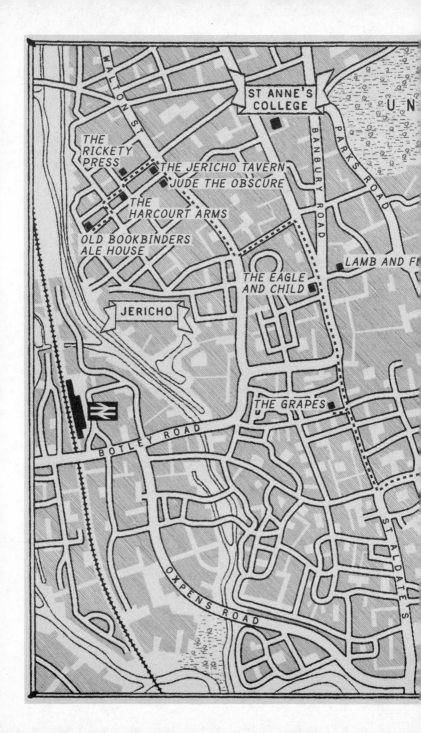

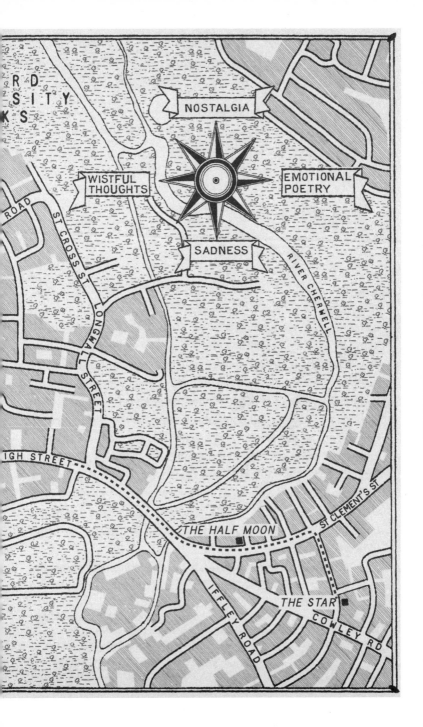

P:

Producer Dave

The setting: Ye Olde Mitre public house, Holborn, central London. A damp, blustery Monday night in January 2014. The pub, a favourite of John's, dates from the mid-16th century and is frequented by an older, professional clientele, who want to relax after work with a quiet pint and a pork pie. John and I have been sent here by Chris Baughen, then head of Xfm, to meet the producer he has assigned to working with two unproduceable comedians – two comic minds that will not be restrained by the conventions of commercial, digital, indie radio. They are free thinkers: radicals in the best tradition of Lloyd George and Antony Worrall Thompson. 'I'm sending you my best man,' Baughen assured us. 'He's very experienced, runs a tight ship but can think on his feet. This guy lives and breathes radio. He understands our audience but I know he'll just *get* you. You're going to be very impressed.'

As John and I walked into the pub, the other drinkers were wearing suits, and nursing pints of Hobgoblin[244] over that day's copy of the

---

244 [JR] Doubtless Elis's memory has been clouded by time. Ye Olde Mitre is actually a Fuller's pub, so Hobgoblin wouldn't have been available. More likely these patrons would have been drinking London Pride, Seafarer's or Oliver's Island (all session).

Financial Times. One man, however, stood out. Shirtless, save for a Burberry scarf tied around his neck that obscured a plethora of Sergio Agüero tattoos, one of a giant bee to represent his beloved Manchester and the Lacoste crocodile stretched across his shapely pectoral muscles, he deposited something like a small package in his sock while arguing with the barman about the combined price of a pint of Carling and a toasted sandwich.

Scanning the room for likely producers, John walked up to a fragile-looking elderly gentleman who was sitting in the snug, peering over his reading glasses at a two-day-old copy of the *City AM*. 'Excuse me,' John enquired hopefully. 'Are you Producer Dave?'

'Pardon?' replied the gentleman, before looking down at his paper, rolling his eyes at his own inattention and nodding, pausing only to readjust his glasses. 'I don't know where I'd be without these damn things! Yes, you're right, the situation is very grave.' He motioned at the paper's headline.

'Er no . . . ' John spluttered. 'Er . . . are you Producer Dave . . .?' All the hope in John's voice that this 80-year-old man could run the desk at a commercial digital indie radio station had now extinguished.

'These investors are dumping equity in favour of safe havens,' the old man said. 'I've not seen a situation like this since . . .'

'FOOOOOOOKIN HEEEEEEEEEELL!' the topless man exclaimed, rearranging himself in his trousers as he approached us. 'Have you seen the prices in here?! £4quid for a pint of foookin Carling?! It's a good job I've got half a gram . . .'

'Nice to meet you, Dave.' I offered my hand. This must be the man. It hadn't escaped my attention that Producer Dave had a Stockport accent capable of cutting glass. He sounded like Liam Gallagher trying to escape from a bag of gravel. The Stopfordian accent wasn't a problem for me, personally, but I knew how the Oxford Brookes-educated Robins would react. I tried to gauge the response of the friend I knew so well but unfortunately John's poker face had completely failed him. The anguish in his eyes spoke volumes, as Robins floundered between fancying a brief chat with an old man about bond analysis (a conversation he would have thoroughly enjoyed), and making small talk with a producer he was scared stiff of but couldn't ignore. We knew that Producer Dave was a gatekeeper at Xfm. This guy was Baughney's best man. He was to be our George Martin. Our Malcolm McLaren.[245] Grasping a nettle for the first time in his life since he stopped wearing Converse trainers because they gave him a bad back,[246] John offered his hand. 'Nice chest,' he said, before adding as an afterthought, 'I like football too.'

The evening passed in a blur. Producer Dave got the barman who'd asked him to put a shirt on in a convivial headlock and led Ye Olde Mitre's regulars in a chorus of 'Blue Moon' and 'Slide Away', even insisting we all hummed the solo. Producer Dave strummed air guitar in ecstatic reverie as the six people in the pub reached Noel's high notes. 'I'm Bonehead, that's my job, just keeping things ticking over,' he assured us, his arms draped around our shoulders. 'You two are Noel and Liam.'

'Thanks,' I replied. In south Wales, like Manchester, this is a huge compliment and I was happy at how things were going. I sent John a quick text from under the table:

NOEL = GUITARIST
LIAM = SINGER V FAMOUS + V ARROGANT

---

245 [JR] Our Roy Thomas Baker.

246 [JR] Actually they gave me a bad big-toe joint, which was misdiagnosed as gout just long enough for me to pen an award-ignored stand-up routine concerning the ailment. And a good job too, as even I would have struggled to find the funny in cartilage damage caused by a lack of arch support in Converse All Stars.

John nodded a thank you. He was keeping a mental note of things to google when he got home. (Guigsy[247]/Meow Meow[248]/ AGÜEEEEERRROO[249].)

Having attended close to a thousand football matches and spoken to cab drivers, I was totally comfortable in Producer Dave's company. We chatted Man City, toastie prices, stag do etiquette, whether Georgi Kinkladze was better than whizz, the parallel universe where Oasis released their B-sides as a third album instead of *Be Here Now*, the difficulties in navigating the Ben Sherman website and improbably, the challenges of selling commercial quantities of teak in the north-west when the construction industry is in recession.[250] The Carling flowed as easily as the conversation, and within minutes I was put at ease by Producer Dave's manner. Despite me feeling comfortable with the shirtless King of the Kippax,[251] John was clearly uneasy. I can tell when my old companion Robins is nervous, as he goes red and starts babbling about interest rates. The radio show was a life changing opportunity for us both and Producer Dave was to be a huge part of it, but John was way out of his comfort zone and, cruelly, it was to be three and half years before he'd have the Edinburgh Comedy Award[252] as the screensaver on his phone to calm him. I was worried about my old

---

247 Guigsy: nickname of Paul Francis McGuigan, founder member of Oasis and the group's bassist between 1991 and 1999.

248 Just say no.

249 A reference to the famous Martin Tyler piece of commentary, as Sergio Agüero secured Manchester City's first league title since 1967 with a last-minute winner against QPR in May 2012. Up to and including January 2014, this was the best moment of Producer Dave's life (they have since won the league again).

250 For the benefit of people reading this book because of John's comedy award or my appearance on *James and Jupp*, Producer Dave's dad is a timber magnate in Stockport. Like Scrooge McDuck, but he swims around in a silo of sawdust.

251 The Kippax was the best-known and most vocally active terrace at Man City's original Maine Road ground, which they left in 2003. It was Man City's equivalent of the Kop at Anfield or Old Trafford's Stretford End.

252 [JR] See picture section.

friend. I had to act. I have seen enough penalty shoot-outs and read enough middle-brow fiction to know that it was all down to me.

'Dave, do you like Queen, Chris de Burgh, interest rates, Ronnie O'Sullivan, T. S. Eliot, farthings, total silence, post-apocalyptic survival fantasies, bushcraft, exploring the concept of historic shame, Meat Loaf, eating crisps on the toilet, Frank Zappa, vaping, the ebb and flow of Test cricket and Poirot?' I asked, laying John's frightened cards on the table.

'No?' replied Producer Dave, understandably.

'But do you think those things have a place on commercial digital indie radio?' I asked firmly, conscious that my entire future could implode in front of me.

Producer Dave raised an eyebrow. And with that raised eyebrow, I knew we'd be OK.

* * * * *

This unlikely meeting of minds heralded a beautiful three-year working relationship. Very quickly it became apparent that Producer Dave knew what he was doing, we absolutely didn't, and it was probably best if we spent most of the time behaving like he was our cool dad. With kind words and patient gestures, Producer Dave taught us how to be commercial digital indie DJs, occasionally using phrases like:

'You've got to try!'

'You've been getting that wrong for six months, Elis. You don't introduce adverts like they're a song!'

'Why don't you try writing your login details down?'

'Stop showing off that you've written down your login details, John.'

'It's probably best if you get here more than three minutes before the show starts, El.'

'But what's in it for the listeners?'

'If you do that we'll all get sacked!'

'I don't think there's a feature in ISAs, John.'

Of the two of us, John is the one who struggles most with author-ity figures. This instinctive broadcaster dealt with having his wings clipped by going red a lot and insinuating that Producer Dave was very right-wing when we should have been advertising the new Samsung Galaxy. But Producer Dave took this in the broadly good-humoured spirit with which it was intended. Producer Dave is the first person I have ever met who doesn't need to sleep or eat, doesn't suffer from hangovers, never loses his temper, doesn't show he is stressed in any way or is anything less than unfailingly polite.

I must interrupt this wonderful account of Producer Dave to pick Elis up on these last three observations. Yes, Dave was truly a Masterman, mastering the arts of commercial digital indie radio, mastering the Farah shirt and chinos combo, mastering the early mornings required to produce a breakfast show, mastering Chris Moyles's complex 6am Bubba Gump Shrimp breakfast order, mastering just the right level of laddish hijinx as captured on *Booze Britain: Binge Nation 2*. However, there were two occasions where temper, stress and politeness went out of the window, occa-sions that I will, for the first time, put into print.

JR

1. ▆▆▆▆▆▆ Southampton-Based-Singer–Songwriter-Gate

One bright summer morning we were broadcasting from a tem-porary studio. The restricted functionality of the studio, plus annoying sound overspill from the band recording a session in the room below, had put me in a bad mood. Any number of things can put me in a bad mood before or during a broadcast, including, but not limited to:

- Elis's lateness
- Elis's excuses for lateness (trains, lost wallet, daughter ill)
- Elis on his phone when he should be reading the papers to prepare the only feature he's in charge of
- Elis on his phone when he should be reading the papers to prepare the only feature he's in charge of after being late
- Elis eating mango 15 seconds before a link
- Elis eating mango
- Anyone else eating too loud
- Anyone else eating
- Anyone else
- Realising I've not bought enough food from Pret
- Realising I've bought too much food from Pret
- When my favourite vegan options in Pret are not all available in the same store so I have to go to three different stores and even up to the Veggie Pret in Soho, which, AMAZINGLY, sometimes doesn't itself have all the vegan options available
- Being told I can't play Queen[253]
- Being told I can't play early Queen/Queen deep-cuts[254]
- Excessive security to enter the building
- Too hot
- Too cold
- Centralised air conditioning that you can't control from the studio
- Overly paranoid password-renewal protocols
- Too much to drink the night before
- Not enough to drink the night before
- Factors
- Playing Southampton-based singer–songwriters

---

253 2014–15.
254 2015 to date.

The day in question was a perfect storm. Not only was I battling the studio functionality (it didn't have the chairs I can put up really high to make me feel superior) and sound overspill, but a number of the above criteria for a mood had been met. I can't remember if Elis had been late but statistically it would have been likely and he would definitely have eaten some mango. It was sunny outside and too cold inside, I had 'under-Pretted', my password had expired for the second time in a month, and a fourth request (this one in writing) to play Queen's 'My Fairy King' from their debut album *Queen* had been turned down. And then . . . then we had to play a Southampton-based singer–songwriter.

I remember the scene. As the S-BSS's dulcet tones faded out I was staring out of the window at the coin shop on Charing Cross Road. I mused about how nice it would be to browse the coins, I wished I were out there browsing florins, shillings, groats, I'd even give the foreign coins a go, they looked so shiny, so shiny and collectable. Then I remembered how hot it was, and not being a PE teacher or in Blink-182 I wasn't wearing shorts. Drat it, damn this heat! And all at once all my frustrations came out in a description of said S-BSS's outro as 'leading us into the abyss'. Elis remembers seeing Dave's face harden into chiselled Stopfordian rage. I, unaware, continued the short link, teasing forward to our regular features. When the mics went down, all hell broke loose. I was subject to a piercing lecture about 'responsibilities', 'professionalism' and 'who pays our wages'. It was a tense exchange. As a man who is paralysed by guilt whenever he's told off and remembers all eight occasions in his life when he's been shouted at:

1. Removing legs from a dead daddy-long-legs (1986)
2. Urinating on a compost heap from a garden wall with the

son of a Beavers' leader[255] (1988)

3. Describing shepherd's pie as 'shepherd's poo' (1989)
4. Asking if I could play cow bell in Year 3 music lesson (1991)[256]
5. Making a suggestive comment in French homework about a teacher's private life (1996). Direct quote: 'That's not behaviour I expect from you; frankly it's the behaviour of a thug.'[257]
6. Breaking my friend Robert's ruler in DT after using it as an improvised drum stick/writing an offensive slur about Ryan Giggs on his DT folder (1996)
7. Making a suggestive comment about a History teacher's private life in a class discussion about Italian culture (1997)
8. Making the audience rowdy before bringing on an act at Bath Komedia (2012)

I dealt with it in the only way I could, by going red for half an hour. I have since apologised in writing to the Southampton-based singer–songwriter and he has accepted my apology. He even invited me to his Southampton estate to witness a recording session, which I politely declined.

2. Phuket/Chang Gate

The full story of Phuket/Chang Gate is one that perfectly illustrates the dual nature of our unproduceability, on the one hand an inability to follow basic instructions, on the other an inability to rein in our creativity. It was the perfect mixture of incompetence (Elis) and devil-may-care audacity (Robins).

---

255 'Son of a Beavers' leader' does sound somewhat like a radio-friendly swear, but he genuinely was the son of my Beavers' leader.

256 Who chastises someone for enthusiasm?! Mrs Barr, that's who. And she used to slap us with a ruler (illegal).

257 I'd like to meet the 'thug' who could make innuendo in a foreign language (GCSE A Grade).

It was a day like any other, and, as is often the case, Radio X were running an exciting competition. A lucky listener could win a holiday to Phuket in Thailand in association with Chang beer. Now, as an experienced producer attempting to produce the unproduceable, Dave had rightly identified the pronunciation of 'Phuket' as a potential flashpoint. Dave had selected Elis as the more responsible tiller-hand for this link, so he began a comprehensive guide on how to handle the topic, and, more importantly, how to pronounce 'Phuket' ('Poo Ket'). Elis nodded along and provided a couple of his trademark 'Yeah, yeah, Dave, I get it!'s. However, what Dave had failed to notice was that Elis's eyes were dipping down to below the desk, where he had his phone concealed, displaying multiple open tabs concerning John Charles's away record, a link to buy tickets for a tour of 'Big Pit' and a *Guardian* Long Read concerning the Paris Accord. I, eagle-eyed as ever, could spot from a mile off that Elis was taking in none of the swear-avoidance tips, and, annoyed by my request to take the link being denied thricely/secretly desperate for Elis to get shouted at for once, I remained silent.

As the track ended, Elis piped up and nonchalantly said:

'Exciting news, folks. Radio X in association with Chang beer are giving you the chance to win a holiday to fuck it.'

Now, when I say nonchalantly, I mean nonchalantly. I think it's the most nonchalant I've ever heard anyone speak. It was as if he were commenting on an unexpected spell of warm weather, or telling an aunt he was OK for a cup of tea as he had just had one.

Dave was gobsmacked. For a moment he was lost for words – it reminded me of when Father Ted kicked Bishop Brennan up the arse. In his head he was clearly confused as to whether he had just hallucinated Elis James saying 'Fuck it' on live radio or whether Elis had just committed the most brazen act of insubordination in the history of live radio. Neither explanation made any sense whatsoever.

'ELIS!'

'What?!'

'What did we spend the last two minutes discussing?!'

'Oh God, is that not right?'

'OF COURSE IT'S NOT RIGHT. THAT'S WHAT WE DIS-CUSSED! I JUST TOLD YOU TEN SECONDS AGO!'

Still live on air, I was pleased as punch. Elis was being shouted at and Dave's decision to entrust Elis with sensitive-place-name pronunciation had blown up in his face. The first trait of our unproduceability, incompetence, had been well and truly ticked off the list, and the second was just around the corner. Giddy with both my dreams coming true, I stepped momentarily beyond even the accepted lines of devil-may-care rule-breaking, and exclaimed:

'That's what you get for trusting Elis, Dave! All I was going to say was, "Here at Radio X we love a night out on the Chang!"'

Dave. Went. Ballistic.

I've never seen such an instantaneous 'step-up' in anger. The mics went down and the walls shook. Despite having learned that 'Chang' was a slang word for cocaine only weeks before, a fact I'd learned FROM ELIS AND DAVE, MAY I ADD, all his ire was now directed solely at Robins.

'You knew what you were doing!'

'Elis made an honest mistake.'

'That was intentional.'

'I could lose my job!'

'They're a big sponsor!'

Vin was immediately dispatched to delete the link from the podcast, hard drive and back-up hard drive. And Dave's fury knew no bounds, lasting, as it did, for four consecutive Stereophonics' tracks. A record for consecutive plays that remains to this day.

Anything else to add, El?

Well, I'd say his capacity for listening to Oasis is only rivalled by his capacity for telling me the same thing a thousand times because I keep getting it wrong. He is patient, passionate, professional . . .

Producer . . .   *JR*

Producer Dave. After a fantastic three years, Dave decided to depart for pastures new, a decision that was sad, but understandable. He would have been irreplaceable, had it not been for one quiet man from Croydon . . . [258]

Birds Eye

---

[258] See **V: Vintern/Vin, Producer**.

Q:

Queen

My parents split up when I was young, by the age of six my dad had moved abroad, and so, as a child, I developed very powerful bonds with a number of male heroes: family friends who would take me fishing or go-karting or let me help them build/knock down/sit on walls, or more famous figures like Roald Dahl, Ayrton Senna and Bruce Grobbelaar. The problem was that the famous ones, at least, kept bloody dying/being implicated in match-fixing. As soon as they had captured my heart, they went away.

On the 25th of November 1991 I saw on the news that a man I kind of recognised, who made music that was kind of familiar, with a band I kind of knew, had died of bronchopneumonia brought on by AIDS. I was nine years old.

I have two memories of Queen prior to this. Once I saw a TV advert for the 1989 album *The Miracle* and remember declaring to myself in my head that it was 'too loud'. The second was reading the liner notes to *A Kind of Magic* on cassette to avoid talking to a friend of my mum's (also one of my earliest shame wells).

I don't know why, but something awoke in me the day I heard

that Freddie Mercury had died. Perhaps the cassettes my mum had played in the kitchen had subconsciously done the ground-work. Perhaps I was just ready to start liking music at this time in my life. Or, perhaps, Freddie Mercury was the ultimate unob-tainable male hero.

I wonder if part of my attraction to Queen was that they were an absence. Over the following decades, the more I loved the music, the further it moved away, and the further it moved away, the more I loved it.

I know I have false memories of early Queen incidents. I remember talking to someone at secondary school about 'Bohemian Rhapsody' and bringing in the CD single where it was a double A-side with 'These Are the Days of our Lives'. But that single was released in December 1991, and I didn't start sec-ondary school until two and a half years later. What must have happened is that three years after the event, I brought a CD sin-gle of 'Bohemian Rhapsody' into school and talked at someone about it. Very on-brand.

One thing I am sure of, though, is that my childhood book-shelves soon swelled with Queen cassettes. My first was def-initely *Greatest Hits II*, then, in no particular order, *Queen II*, *Sheer Heart Attack*, *Jazz* and *A Night at the Opera*. The imagery of Queen began to enter into my daily life. This came to a head, when, some time in 1992, a ten-year-old Johnny Robins wrote a handwritten letter, enclosed a cheque for £15quid and asked, were he to be found a suitable candidate, could he 'have the hon-our of joining the Official International Queen Fan Club'. And for the next ten years, I devoured the quarterly glossy magazines and merch catalogues and gazed longingly at details of fan club conventions which, alas, as a pre-teen, I was never to attend.

Why did you stop subscribing, out of interest?   *EJ*

Well, partly it became much easier to subscribe to the mailing list; E-Mail's gain was the fanzine's loss, I'm afraid. But I kind of had a nostalgic view of those 'wilderness' years, and by the early 2000s they were doing proper big projects like *We Will Rock You* (the musical) and touring with Paul Rogers and Adam Lambert. So that was all over the press anyway. The magazines from the 1990s had been a mixture of local events, things like a PC-ROM game they did the soundtrack to, and because no other outlet covered this you felt like you were a true fan for finding out. Then the whole thing moved online anyway. It was quarterly, after all, and there's not much to be said for finding out about a tour three months after the tickets have sold out.

By the age of 12 I was well and truly head over heels, which is clear from even a cursory glance at my Year 7 DT folder, a two-sided A3 masterpiece of fandom.[259] I remember vividly the two afternoons spent meticulously cutting, arranging and sticking images from Queen calendars (this was pre-Photoshop) to make the haunting collage.

> Hang on, John! Defacing official Queen calendars?! It doesn't sound very Robins!

I bought duplicates.

> Now that is *very* Robins.

I arranged the rear photos around a brief biography taken from the back cover of *Queen: A Beginners Guide*,[260] so that anyone admiring the folder could at least get a potted history of the band as a starting point, before finishing the front with the *pièce*

---

259 See picture section.
260 Again, duplicate.

de résistance: I took a photo of Freddie c. 1989,[261] where he is pictured reclining on a chaise longue[262] and has his arm outstretched along the back,[263] and, cutting carefully around him, I superimposed this image on top of a photo taken from the rear-sleeve artwork of *Made in Heaven*. This image features the remaining members looking out over Lake Geneva[264] in Montreux, and the two together provide a moving tableau where the intention was to show Freddie embracing his former band mates, as if to say, 'I'm with you guys, you did good.'

It took me nearly eight hours to create this masterpiece, and, within ten minutes of arriving at school I realised this was not going to impress any of the girls I fancied. They were not interested in Queen collages one bit. It turns out what they were interested in was a kid called Dean stealing shoes for them from Footlocker where he worked,[265] selling them marijuana his older brother had grown[266] and fingering them at parties.[267] But I maintained my Queen fascination regardless, and it burns as brightly, if slightly moderated by interest in other musicians, today.

So, 'Why Queen?' Good question. Part of me is tempted to say, 'I dunno, I guess it could have been any band really,' but then the ten-year-old inside me screams, 'NO IT COULDN'T! IT'S QUEEN! QUEEN ARE THE BEST!' And he'd be right.

Firstly, I will never tire of the name 'Queen'. It's just so cool! I love saying it, I love seeing it written in different fonts. Say it

261 The stubble and waistcoat place it firmly in *The Miracle* promo period, so probably Jan/Feb 1989.
262 Of course he is!
263 Of course he has! (A man in Freddie Mercury's position can't afford to be seen falling off a chaise longue!)
264 Fun fact: the very same water that 'smoke' was 'on', as attested to by Deep Purple after a casino caught on fire during, fun fact, a Frank Zappa gig.
265 Which is illegal.
266 Which is also illegal.
267 Which is legally a grey area.

out loud now. 'Queen.' Feels good, eh? It feels shiny, like a polished piece of steel. It sparkles.

Secondly, and I know this overshadows other elements of the band, but Freddie's voice is, I think, one of the seven wonders of the musical world. It's not the range as such, it's the power in that range. It's not his high notes that are hard to replicate, it's the force and character of the mid range. Having seen Adam Lambert perform with Brian and Roger twice now, I can confirm he's a phenomenally talented singer. But there's an awful lot of very *X Factor*-y cooing and running up and down scales, which, though accomplished, shows him to be a singer and not a frontman. His voice is not individual. Also, the softness of Freddie's voice, though not showcased as much on the *Greatest Hits* albums, is really breathtaking on some deeper cuts, 'Love of My Life', 'My Melancholy Blues' and 'You Take My Breath Away' being three good examples.

Thirdly, it's the melody, stupid! Elis has said he likes music that sounds 'wrong', like punk and Can and The Fall. That's all well and good, sometimes I like music that sounds wrong too (the difference being that the music I like that sounds wrong usually turns out to be right).[268] But it's clear that the music my mum played when I was very young made me an absolute sucker for melody: Dire Straits, Fleetwood Mac, Chris de Burgh, Paul Simon. It's a classic late-80s divorcée playlist, and I love it! To me, Queen are just the most consistently melodic band;[269] the harmonies, the overdubs, the guitar hooks, all of it just sounds as if it came from somewhere inside me. I remember, in the glory days of being able to hear Queen songs for the first time, it was like they were already in me when I heard them.

---

268 Cf. Captain Beefheart.
269 [EJ] Er . . . The Beatles?

EJ

You have said this in the past, and I'm always surprised you don't like soul music a bit more. Come on, man, what could be more melodic than Aretha Franklin or Martha and the Vandellas! Put some Northern Soul stompers on!

Fourthly, May. Oh Brian. I wish I had the musical knowledge to fully understand what he does, but his guitar solos are not 'solos'. It's not the band pausing for the guitarist to noodle away for 32 bars in the same key. It's a short 8- or 16-bar section where a counter melody appears on the guitar, somehow completely of the song and yet different. His ear for this is second to none. A really good example of this is 'Killer Queen'. I know it's so familiar, and because of that it's easy to turn off when listening, but put it on, actually listen to what's going on in that song, especially the guitar. The guitar, when it appears, becomes part of the melody, even though it's using it as a springboard to solo. Brian May, though he has rock in his heart, has got a phenomenal ear for pop hooks, and never, ever, outstays his welcome. I think the fact they used to let him do 13-minute guitar solos halfway through live gigs meant no one was ever frustrated. Brian got to go crazy, and the rest of the band got to have a beer.

Fifthly, our old friend John Deacon. If I got hold of the master tapes from all Queen's back catalogue,[270] the first parts I would listen to would be the bass tracks. He wasn't fussy as a bassist, but accented the rhythm just enough, just at the right time. Again, like Brian's solos, the bass lines often become an integral part of the melody, you just have to listen much closer. Check out 'Save Me', it's all Deacon! Driving the melody like a legend! The little flourishes in the verse are just heavenly. And then the little four-bar solo from May at 02:36! I mean, it's so modest,

---

270 And I'm not far off.

so utterly fitting. I love how the band allow each instrument to drive different songs, and different parts of the same song, but they're always contributing to the whole Queen sound.

Sixthly, the drum fills in 'I'm in Love with My Car' and 'Brighton Rock'.

Finally, it's the story. I never knew Queen as a band whose story didn't end in a heartbreaking tragedy. It's part of who they are. And it's a part of so much of the later music, which, the older I get, the more moving I find, *Innuendo* especially. If *The Miracle* was an album recorded on borrowed time, then *Innuendo* was an album *about* borrowed time. I will concede that a little filler did creep in,[271] but these were four men working against the clock, their friend and colleague was dying before their eyes, and it just breaks my heart to imagine what that was like! I'm welling up as I write this! And the more I read about Freddie Mercury towards the end, the more brave and selfless a man I find. Forced to retreat from his headier days of parties and high living into the seclusion and tranquillity of Montreux, where Queen would record their last albums, he endured the extreme pain of his condition in order that he would be able to make as much music as he could. And that music remains so accessible, so listenable, watchable, so much to read about, so many people to talk about it with but always just out of reach, all recorded in the period just before I awoke to music. 1970–1991. Burnished by time.

* * * * *

---

271 See 'Rain Must Fall' from *The Miracle*.

Freddie Mercury was a cat. He is the most cat-like man I've ever come across. He could be as barbed and demanding as he could be soft and shy. He was a short-tempered diva who would cover his teeth in interviews because they made him self-conscious. He threw enormous parties, but trusted only a small group of close friends. He stood on stage in front of crowds, the size of which no one had ever played before, and held them in the palm of his hand, but offstage he often preferred to hide away.[272] He taught me that it was OK to be outgoing and extroverted, while also feeling self-conscious and shy. I love him. And as a role model, I don't think I could have made a better choice.

---

272 If you need a reason not to buy the tabloid press, read some of the articles written about Freddie Mercury in 1991, how the journalists hounded him in his final months, how they climbed the trees outside the house in which he was dying, how they crowded outside his front door so that he couldn't leave and people couldn't visit, and what they wrote, a lot of which nowadays would be classed as hate speech.

potato.

R:

Ronnie! C'mon

'The man's an absolute genius' **Peter Ebdon**
'Unbelievable! Have you *ever* seen *anything* like that on a snooker table?!' **John Virgo**
'Well, well, well, well, would you have a look at that!' **Dennis Taylor**
'He's not going to make a 147 left-handed, surely?!' **Willie Thorne**
'Snooker from the Gods' **Clive Everton**

It's 10.33am on Saturday 24th March 2018, and I'm sitting with a coffee after spending two hours browsing YouTube. For about the last 45 minutes of that session I really, really needed the toilet. My toilet is fully functional, and a mere eight feet from where I'm sitting in bed,[273] so why didn't I just go? Well, dear friend, because the subject of that YouTube session was Mr Ronald Antonio O'Sullivan, AKA Ronnie, AKA The Rocket, AKA The Greatest Snooker Player of All Time, and, I think, a contender for The Greatest Sportsperson of All Time.

Last night, I watched Ronnie beat Judd Trump in the

---

273 A genuine nightmare for the old love life.

semi-final of the Players Championship in Llandudno (Wales?).[274] He won 6–5 after being behind twice, and won a place in his sixth ranking-event final of the season. I've seen all those finals, and watched him win four of them. If he wins a fifth, he will equal the all-time record for most ranking-event wins in a season. And though a relatively small event on the snooker calendar, as I watched I was as captivated, amazed, frustrated, enchanted and exhausted as I have been now for some 25 years of watching Ronnie O'Sullivan play snooker.

I've just reread BBC Sport journalist Ben Dirs's wonderful article 'Ronnie O'Sullivan: The Da Vinci of the Baize'. In it, he makes the long-overdue case for placing Ronnie among the very best sportspeople of modern times, and compares him to Roger Federer, in whose hands 'a tennis racquet is a paint brush and a tennis court a canvas'. The same is true of Ronnie. When he plays snooker it's like watching someone who is not playing snooker at all. It's like watching someone paint. And whereas with a Van Gogh or a Monet you see none of the planning, the sketches, the torn first drafts, the ones where the sunflowers weren't quite sunflowery enough, with snooker you see every stroke, every break[275] is a final piece drawn live. And when Ronnie has the cue in his hand the beauty of these breaks transcends the sport itself. Not always, of course; there are mistakes, transgressions, tussles with commitment, temptation and self-control. There is self-flagellation, redemption and often miracles. For 25 years, watching Ronnie O'Sullivan play snooker has been a religious experience.[276]

---

274 [EJ] Not only is it in Wales, John, Catfish and the Bottlemen are from there.

275 A 'break' is the score a snooker player makes by potting consecutive balls. All breaks must start with a red ball being potted and then a coloured ball, then back to a red, then a colour, and so on until you miss a pot or clear the table.

276 [EJ] A lovely turn of phrase. Classic Robins.

Snooker, as anyone who has played it will understand, is a phenomenally difficult game. In my teens, I was a decent American pool player, even playing in a few tournaments, and I once cleared up from the break in a game of English pool. However, my highest-ever break in snooker is, I think, a paltry 21. I may have played one nice shot, then fluked a colour, then an easy red, before missing the next ball completely. When you watch Ronnie, it is easy to forget just how difficult a game it is. It inspires a confidence that fills the snooker halls for a couple of weeks after every tournament, only for people to wander home dejected thinking, 'How on earth does he do it?!'

Ronnie is exceptional for a number of reasons: through a series of small nudges he uses the white ball to move other balls after potting the object ball. This is his great skill – it means you have to play less difficult shots as you're constantly improving the lay of the balls. He is fantastic into the middle pockets, the best in the world, and this massively increases your options when playing around the black. His cue power is outrageous, but not only that, his judgement of that power is superb. He could land a bullet on a sixpence. He sees shots so quickly that, even now, he has the shortest average shot time in the world, meaning he can bully players simply by how quickly he racks up points. His safety play is ever improving, and is now one of the best ever. He is phenomenal with the rest. Oh, and did I mention

HE CAN PLAY LEFT-HANDED TOO

And then, there's that certain something, that mood, that atmosphere when he's in full flow. It's an electricity that just hums, opponents become spectators, commentators run out of superlatives. And I marvel.

Watch a compilation of Ronnie on YouTube, watch his clearance of 92 against Ali Carter in the 2012 World Championship final, his record 556 unanswered points in his 6–0 whitewash of Ricky Walden in the 2014 Masters, then watch my favourite moment in all sport, his 147 against Mark King in the 2010 World Open.

When he approaches the table not a ball has been potted, and he asks the referee what the prize is for a 147 break.[277] The commentators laugh. 'Oh Ronnie, behave yourself!', the crowd mutter. The referee has to ask someone to find out. Word comes that there is no extra prize for a 147,[278] Ronnie cringes, screws up his face, then makes a 147. He tries to leave the final black, which would leave him on 140 and send out a very strong message about how he felt about there being no bonus prize. The referee persuades him, saying, 'Come on Ronnie, for the fans'. He pots it. It is *beyond audacious*. If a single pot had gone wrong he would have looked an arrogant, spoiled millionaire. Like Muhammad Ali, he has to do the impossible, or he will embarrass himself. And he does the impossible. And he has been doing it for 25 years.

Twenty-five years. Twenty-five years! I'm not talking about a fairytale run at the British Open (golf) for an old-timer making a comeback. I'm not talking about a boxer who comes out of retirement for another shot in their 40s. I am talking about a sportsperson who has been consistently winning the most competitive titles in their sport for a quarter of a century. And not

---

277 A 147 is snooker's answer to a nine-dart finish or perfect game in bowling. It's every ball potted in order, fifteen reds, each followed by a black, then the colours in sequence. It's far harder than the nine-darter or perfect game, as there are just so many variables. There were eight made in total in the 1980s, but they are becoming more common – the same number were made in 2017. Ronnie holds the record for most made, with 14.

278 This is a direct result of Ronnie making so many. You used to get £147,000quid for making one at the World Championships, but figures like that are now unsustainable.

only that, but someone who in their 26th year as a professional has won more than they've ever won before.

Have a look at this chart:

	Titles won	Winning span
Stephen Hendry	(18)	1989–1999
Ronnie O'Sullivan	(18)	1993–2017
Steve Davis	(15)	1980–1997

This is my favourite statistic in snooker, probably in sport. It's the winning span of triple-crown events for the three major forces in modern snooker, with the total number of titles won in brackets. Let me explain. The snooker calendar is made up of multiple ranking events (where players earn their money and points earned help you break into the top 16) and a few invitational events (where those top 16 players compete for prestige and also more money). This list of tournaments changes year to year, events get added, lose or gain ranking status, or disappear altogether. But three events stay the same, snooker's equivalent of the treble in football: they are the UK Championship, the Masters and the World Championship. They have an elevated status due to the history, the length and the coverage of the event. If you have seen snooker on the BBC, you'll probably have been watching one of these three events. And though Ronnie and Stephen share the record for the most won (seen in brackets above), the winning span, for me, confirms Ronnie's status as the greatest snooker player of all time. Even Steve Davis's record is misleading; his first 14 triple-crown titles came between 1980 and 1989, and his 1997 Masters title (annoyingly beating Ronnie in the final) is an anomaly that extended his span by eight years. So you can see, even though Davis and Hendry dominated snooker for a decade each, Ronnie blows them out of the water for longevity, and I never, ever thought I'd say that.

In past conversations about the greatest snooker player of all time, there was a dull inevitability about the eventual conclusion: Stephen Hendry. No he wasn't flash, no he wasn't the crowd's favourite, but you just couldn't argue with the numbers. He was head and shoulders above the rest. He was Michael Schumacher, Pete Sampras, Celtic and Rangers combined. He. Was. Boring. But, as of today, he's no longer the dominant force stats-wise. Over the past five years Ronnie O' Sullivan has become what no one thought possible, a mercurial talent who dominates. A Jimmy White with five world titles as opposed to six lost finals, an Alex Higgins without the wasted talent and sad demise.

As a lifelong fan of Ronnie, for so many years statistics worked against me, they were pulled up by commentators to paint a picture of a temperamental genius who underachieved. Well, not any more.

Let me take you back to the early days of my Ronnie fandom. As a kid I was a Steve Davis fan; I was a little bit young for Alex Higgins, and I think I would have found it too crushingly sad to have followed him. His story is one of breathtaking talent that just couldn't be contained. The game was very different in the 1980s – most players were amateurs at heart, but Steve Davis was the first person to take the game seriously, really seriously. A bit like when Arsène Wenger started at Arsenal and he found the players all hungover and eating chips. Of course, the first person to knock the booze on the head and stop eating chips is going to dominate. Since then the margins have got smaller and smaller. Hendry came in and was mostly playing dinosaurs when he started, and revolutionised a sport by showing just how good it was possible to be at it. The reason a 147 was so rare back then is not necessarily because people couldn't make them, but more that it didn't occur to them to try. My youth was spent watching aging men make 40 or 50-point breaks then going back to their seats, and people would *applaud*, seriously *applaud* a break of 40! So you can imagine the impact it had on my young mind when Ronnie O'Sullivan made a 147 in five minutes 20 seconds at the 1993 World Championship.[279] It wasn't a shockwave, it was a meteor that hit snooker and wiped out an entire species. The only way I can really give you some comparison is to imagine a batsman making a thousand runs in a day, or a footballer scoring ten goals in ten minutes, or someone running 100m in five seconds. It just doesn't happen.

Following that moment, Ronnie's career went through three phases: child prodigy to genius underachiever to mature dominance. And it's the transition from underachiever to mature dominance that interests me the most and makes me his most passionate advocate.

In the late 1990s to the late 2000s, life as a supporter of Ronnie O'Sullivan was a genuine rollercoaster; the child prodigy was now a man and was just not winning as much as Stephen Hendry did. The comparisons were endless, infuriating and always ended in mentions of 'underachievement', 'wasted talent', 'battling demons' and the dreaded 'two Ronnie's' comment. People would call him 'the most naturally gifted player to ever pick up a cue', which basically meant he could do things no one else could do, but just didn't do them often enough. Here was a man with clinical depression, whose father was in prison for murder, whose mother had been in prison for tax evasion, who

---

279 This time is actually inaccurate. An investigation by deadspin.com found the actual time to be five minutes and five seconds, as technically the break should start from when Ronnie strikes the white, and not when the white of his opponent stops prior to the break.

was being constantly hauled over the coals for being inconsistent. He would threaten retirement on an almost weekly basis, make the most insane breaks, win a tournament and then throw in the towel against someone because he was bored. Well, stop the presses, guys, SNOOKER CAN BE VERY BORING. I commend you to watch a video on YouTube of a split screen where Ronnie makes a break of 147 in the same time it takes Peter Ebdon to make a break of 12. Ebdon was the worst, just the absolute worst person you could dream of being forced to watch. And for years it drove Ronnie mad, like it drove mad every person who had to watch this weirdly angry vegan grind entire tournaments to a halt.[280] Whenever commentators used to criticise Ronnie I would *literally* shout at the screen:

'YOU CANNOT BE AS TALENTED AS HE IS AND BE CONSISTENT! HE IS BEYOND PERFECT! HE'S A MIRACLE WORKER, NOT A ROBOT!'

They just didn't get it. In order to have him at his best we had to accept him at his worst.

And then things got a little tricky. He conceded a match against Stephen Hendry in the quarter-final of the 2006 UK Championship from a position where he could still very much have won (unheard of). His concession also came as he himself was at the table and in a winning position during the frame, which is not only unheard of but not a little unsportsmanlike. Why unsportsmanlike? Well, imagine if your football team were 4–2 down after 70 minutes and just walked off the

---

280 In fairness, Ebdon seems pretty chilled these days and is a very good commentator.

pitch because they couldn't be bothered.

The next three years were not ideal to watch him. Between 2005 and 2010, he averaged only one ranking tournament a year and for a player of his standard, this is pretty poor. This did include two Masters' victories and his third world title, but his temperament, ever-changing coaches, approaches and haircuts, did suggest that the naysayers were right – we would never see this man fulfil his potential. He would go down in history as a crowd favourite, alongside Alex Higgins and Jimmy White, who got all the ooohs and ahhhs while Hendry got all the trophies – fireworks exploding next to a gas fire.

And then something truly amazing happened.

On 6th May 2012, I performed a preview of my soon-to-be 2012 Edinburgh show 'Incredible Scenes' at the Machynlleth Comedy Festival.[281] As soon as I came offstage, I got in my car and drove from Machynlleth to Bristol in record time.[282] I got home to watch Ronnie play Ali Carter in the final of the World Championship. It was Ronnie's fourth final, and he had three wins under his belt. It was very important to me, because it would put him third on the all-time list of winners, and, while not proving him to be the best, I felt very strongly that it meant people could no longer say he'd underachieved. And, when he came through 18–8 that is exactly what I shouted at the screen, hoping beyond hope that Parrott, Davis, Taylor et al could hear me:

'YOU CAN NEVER, *EVER* SAY HE'S UNDERACHIEVED *EVER* AGAIN!'

---

281 This is not the amazing thing, by the way. The show itself was only my sixth-best Edinburgh Show, or second worst, depending on how you look at it.

282 Again, not the amazing thing, though I did balance speed and safety with breath-taking aplomb, if, indeed, aplomb can be breathtaking.

It was one of the best days of my life, sitting in my living room with a crate of Sainsbury's Biere Des Moulins, watching him win his fourth world title.[283] But this is still not the amazing thing. The amazing thing is that following that victory Ronnie took a year off. A complete year off from all snooker. He didn't play a match. He didn't practise. He went running and worked, briefly, in a community-run pig farm.

And then, in May 2013, he returned to the world championship.

And won.

Again.

No one had won back-to-back world championships since Stephen Hendry in 1995/6, a phenomenon that became known as the 'Crucible Curse'. And Ronnie did it. He did it after a year off. That year I watched his contemporaries and various bright young things – Neil Robertson, Mark Selby, Ali Carter, Stuart Bingham and Judd Trump – pick up the spoils, all players that would have blown Hendry's 1990s competitors off the table. Then Ronnie rocked up and absolutely destroyed them. Personally I think it is the greatest achievement in sport. The audacity, the narrative, the talent and sudden dedication all play a part, but I think, even objectively, it has to be up there with the Rumble in the Jungle, Tiger Woods winning the 2008 US Open on one leg and Leicester winning the Premier League.

Since that final, Ronnie has played in fewer events, picking and choosing the tournaments he wants to compete in. As a result, he has won more frequently and probably extended his career by 10 or 15 years. Older players such as Mark Williams are following his example and coming back to form, younger players are being embarrassed by the old guard and Ronnie has, once

---

283 See picture section.

again, shaken up the snooker world. You may think that playing snooker to a high standard in your 40s is no miracle. After all, it's not a particularly physical game. But no one has done it before, and it's no coincidence that the fittest player on the tour is also the most successful.

It's now Monday 26th March 2018, and during my tour show in Southampton last night Ronnie won in Llandudno (Wales?).[284] He beat Shaun Murphy 10–4 in the final. I watched on 4G on the way. I watched on the wifi in the dressing room. And I checked on the TV during the interval. But my private joy was in rechecking the updated stats sites, seeing Ronnie move his way up the lists, increase his percentages, add another green W box to his career timeline on Wikipedia. Because I am lucky enough to witness someone change their reputation and I can revisit all of those interviews where he was criticised, where I, as a kid, wanted to just jump through the screen to defend my hero. 'You can't be that talented and be consistent!' Most remarkably, it is I who have been proved wrong. Ronnie has shown, and is still showing, that you can.

---

284 [EJ] Not only is it in Wales, John, Neville Southall, the ex-Wales international goalkeeper and LGBT-rights activist, is from there.

potato!

S:

Spice, Project

I love curry so much that I regularly dream about it, and the adrenaline I get from a Madras will put me in a good mood for two days.

New converts are often the most irritating kind of people – we've all been annoyed by a new disciple to wild camping/Zumba/learning foreign languages with Duolingo. 'But the lack of facilities when you're wild camping is the point!' they might say, as you sigh and check your phone. 'You don't need a toilet, just a trowel, and then you keep the wipes in a clearly marked plastic bag. Believe me, once you've defecated on the side of a road in Scotland, you start to realise how unnatural having a toilet in the house is.'

Hmmm, sounds to me like someone has never completed a bushcraft course! The practice of defecating by the 'side of a road' is not endorsed by any approved bushcraft instructor. Toilets must be away from water sources, lakes, ponds, people, dwellings and roads. Dig a small hole, or a trench for longer stays, burn paper with a lighter when the job is done and cover with the removed earth. As ever in bushcraft, the motto is: 'Leave No Trace'. For an insight into the effects of

JR

> shitting next to the side of the road, see the fantastic documentary about the M25 called *Britain's Busiest Motorway*. The scene with the layby cleaning squad is genuinely chilling.

As tiresome as you may find being preached at, I have a new tolerance for these people. I too have had my life-changing, Damascene conversion – at the age of 34 I embarked on a year-long endeavour to improve meal times forever: Project Spice.

Until a few years ago, spicy food played as big a part in my life as Orthodox Catholicism or zorbing. I had been in Indian restaurants, of course, but never ventured further than the korma or tikka masala options.[285] I have been teased for my unsophisticated palate since I started university. At 18 I thought all cheese tasted the same (caveat: it was either 'strong' or 'weak'), and I once had to spit out a ginger biscuit because it made my mouth burn. I feel no shame at this. We're all products of our upbringings, and as a money-saving exercise (and to prevent food waste), my mother cooked the same seven meals as part of a rota that went unchanged for 25 years:

Monday: Sausage casserole
Tuesday: Chicken Kiev and spaghetti hoops
Wednesday: Pork chops (with boiled vegetables and gravy)
Thursday: Pizza (my mum had aerobics on a Thursday so pizza was nice and quick)
Friday: Fish (obviously)
Saturday: Curry (a slight misnomer, as it was about as spicy as Hubba Bubba. It was basically chicken on a bed of rice with a few raisins)
Sunday: Sunday dinner (obviously)

Welcome to Wales. This rota wasn't entirely unchanged for 25 years

---

285 I didn't like spicy food, but always thought opting for omelette and chips from the 'English section' of the menu was 'a bit UKIP'.

– chicken Kievs were replaced by 'the Kwik Fit meal'[286] for a period in the early 90s, after Mam saw a recipe she thought would delight in a magazine that had been left in the Carmarthen branch of Kwik Fit. Adorably, rather than tear out the recipe from a magazine that had clearly been there since 1987 (that, of course, would have been theft and criminal damage), she simply read the recipe over and over again while the car tyre was being changed, thus committing it to memory. Like all pretenders to the Kiev throne, however, the Kwik Fit meal only lasted about six months before normal service was resumed.

One thing you may notice from my mum's menu is the lack of Eastern influence. This left me with a tolerance for spicy food you might find slightly feeble in a toddler. Deciding to 'own' what some of my friends (Robins included) saw as a physical impairment, I would defend my unsophisticated tastebuds: 'Why would I want to eat food that hurts? Why are you bringing pain into mealtimes? To satisfy some hard-man need to impress? That's pathetic. I'm actually a feminist.'[287] However, as I reached my early 30s, hanging out with John caused me to suspect that I was probably missing out.

As listeners to the show will realise, John likes chilli more than Charlton Heston liked guns.

> **Amazingly, I'm actually eating a hot curry while reading the first draft of this chapter. It's 1.35pm in the afternoon.**
>
> *JR*

I initially saw this as a wilful eccentricity and oddly macho behaviour for someone who regularly bursts into tears on public transport because he likes T. S. Eliot so much.

---

286 The best way to describe the Kwik Fit meal was a lasagna, but where the pasta was replaced with potatoes. It was a kind of entry-level lasagna for reticent farmers who are scared of trying new things.

287 I was actually saying this in the mid-2000s before all the other lads were saying it, apart from Kurt Cobain and the Manics.

Guilty!

But, as I lived with John in Edinburgh, and realised that him putting Tabasco sauce on toast first thing in the morning wasn't an affectation, I became intrigued. Captivated, even. This process was also hastened by Isy, another lover of spicy food, and so I began the journey[288] to improve my tolerance.

From my base level, it was important to take things slowly, as I had over 30 years of Welshman's Inclination to get over. The entire project was almost derailed forever in 2009 when I was staying at John's house. I had a semi-residency at one of England's best gigs, The Comedy Box in Bristol. John lived round the corner, so I would stay with him after the shows and we would drink wine and listen to music, and by around 1am John would be drunk enough to sing along and do all the harmonies as he smoked fags out of the window. Those nights are the best nights I had doing comedy, and I have nothing but golden memories of that time in my life. The only moment I would rather forget is when John made me try the hot sauce '100% Pain' so he could video my reaction for his personal archives. I watched the video back quite recently, and in the run-up to the sauce being put on my spoon, I list my favourite foodstuffs as Coco Pops, microwaveable lasagne and Birds Eye[289] Potato Waffles (who could have predicted the impact Birds Eye would have on my career?). To give a man used to eating that kind of food '100% Pain' is like dropping a Cub Scout into a warzone. The look of confusion on my face as my tongue becomes coated in this fire juice is harrowing, as John slurs his commentary (at one point he tells me to 'bow down in front of the Lord', before laughing at his own joke). The video is six minutes long and ends before I have fully recovered (although I have

---

288 Modern TV documentary-makers are obsessed with people's 'journeys', and so this sentence is a transparent 'come and get me' plea to the commissioners at BBC Four.
289 [JR] Far too early!

The first time I travelled with
Elis on a train I thought he
was performing some kind of
skit, perhaps an impression of
Toulouse-Lautrec. It turns out
he has a unique seating position
that terrifies osteopaths nationwide. The enigmatic Producer
Vin provides scale.

With Brian Harold May CBE, guitarist, activist, scientist, b.1947.

With Roger Meddows Taylor, drummer, lover of cars, b.1949.

Lee Trundle looks frightened because seconds before this photo was taken, I'd told him he'd given me the most intense experience of my life (his time at Swansea City, 2003–2007).

The One Show insisted I wear full kit to interview Gareth Bale, so meeting him like an anxiety dream.

Elis picked out in the BBC's coverage of Wales at Euro 2016, (pre tops-off).

A selection of Queen paraphernalia, some bought, some home made. In the background is my secondary school DT Folder, which served not only as a lasting tribute to the band, but also helped keep girls at a safe distance, something I credit for having kept me free of glandular fever to this day.

A master at work. World Snooker Championship Final, 2013.

The original
Oxford Day
pub crawl plan.

OXFORD DAY 2015
8th January

2.48pm   Arrival
3.15pm   Pizza Express
4pm   Check in
5pm   The Star
5.50pm   The Half Moon
6.45pm   The Grapes
7.15pm   The Eagle And Child
7.45pm   The Lamb And Flag
PENCILLED SLUMP / FOOD BREAK
9.15pm   The Jude The Obscure
10pm   The Harcourt Arms
10.45pm   The Bookbinders

John shares a birth-
day pint with seven of
his eight friends. The
Mayflower, Rotherhithe,
May 2015.

Jericho works its magic, blend-
ing time present and time past.
With The Lovely Robin and Mike
The Barman, Oxford Day I, The
Harcourt Arms, 2015.

After some cajoling from I, Robins, Isy proposes to Elis, under a Welsh flag. Elis' face is superb.

After recording our episode of 'Drunk History', I, having imbibed more alcohol than Elis, stand behind the camera eruditely discussing the political matters of the day while completing *The Times* Crossword. Elis is attended by a medic.

My answer to
The Lovely Robin,
The Lovely Rhodri.

A very, very hungover show.

The dream team: winners of The Chortle Award for Radio, 2017. Presented by Radio X's Dan O'Connell.

160,000 miles and still going strong. Though even the beloved Fabia is not immune from the menace/crime of anti-social behaviour, aka graffiti.

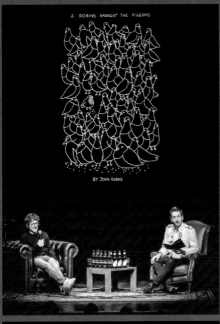

A Robins Amongst the Pigeons live 2015. Fun Fact: this gig holds the record for largest ever bar take for a seated gig at The Shepherd's Bush Empire.

I flick the Vs while Elis plays ball at a live recording of Stuart Goldsmith's The Comedian's Comedian Podcast, 2017.

Far too many Potato Potatoes at The Machynlleth Comedy Festival, 2018.

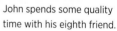

John spends some quality time with his eighth friend.

The picture that launched a thousand memes: I arrive an hour and seventeen minutes late to provide Welsh support for The Darkness Of Robins at The Hammersmith Apollo. The text Robins sent said, 'Are you f**king kidding me?! ON TODAY OF ALL DAYS!'

suitably recovered to berate him for 'ruining my night' as I drink milk straight from the carton). I can only describe the next day's toilet as like sitting on a Catherine wheel. With this in mind, if the project was to be a success I knew I had to start slowly.

Step one was putting English mustard on ham sandwiches, until this became pleasant. I then moved on to eating ginger with sushi,[290] before taking the plunge and giving wasabi a go. After beginning hesitantly, experimenting with amounts most people would be comfortable spreading on a newborn baby's dummy, within weeks I was having Robins-sized portions on tuna and salmon. This was an important step. By now my tolerance had definitely increased (which was hugely encouraging), but excitingly I really liked these new tastes. At this stage I began to sprinkle red chillies on salads, etc. After a tentative few steps, this quickly became addictive, and I was well on my way.

Friends and family found Project Spice curious, and I occasionally detected mild disapproval (those closest to you often fear you changing the most). By now, I was adding red chillies (available at any supermarket) to risotto, soup, spaghetti Bolognese, anything other than breakfast cereal. Going up a spice level happens in three stages:

Stage 1: The new level is pleasantly challenging.

Stage 2: The new level becomes tolerable, and you start to notice the taste as opposed to the heat, so you start showing off about it, and dropping it into conversations where this information is irrelevant.[291]

Stage 3: A bird's eye chilli tastes about as spicy as Special K, at which point John sends a congratulatory text.

---

290 I am a huge fan of sushi, but learning to love it is easier than getting to grips with spicy food. The thing that took a while was getting over the counterintuitive idea that eating raw fish wouldn't give me horrific food poisoning.

291 E.g: 'Hasn't Homebase been taken over by an Australian company? Isn't it called something else now?' 'Yes it has. I like curry.'

E.g. 23.03.17 10.43pm. Hey El, Isy told me about the three bird's eye chilli stir fry! Big moment man, big moment. I knew you could do it, we were all rooting for you! Love you babe xxx p.s Can I borrow £300quid? Cash ASAP if poss?

I was now researching the health benefits of spicy food. Chillies aid digestion, they help lower cholesterol and can apparently help prevent certain kinds of cancers.[292]

They also make toilet time a varied and exciting rollercoaster, a trial for those who work in offices with inadequately cubicled toilets, but a welcome distraction for the solitudinous comedian. I see it as the equivalent of a fag break or chat at the water cooler.

I was falling in love with the new me. Around six months in I attempted a chicken Madras – my objective at the beginning, and inconceivable at the outset of Project Spice. Not only was it tolerable, *it was one of the most delicious things I had ever eaten*. I punched the air and wept for all of the years I had wasted, until Isy asked me to stop. It had a slight kick, of course (offset by the sweetness of a Peshwari naan, a combination to rival a good book and a train journey, or being late and then realising everyone else is going to be later than you), but the taste made my heart sing. I felt like a lovesick teenager. The notebook I had once used for stand-up was now covered in drawings of curry.

'Tikka Pad'? . . . As in Pukka Pad? . . . BAD JOKE! . . . Sorry . . . sorry I take it back! I take it back!

---

292 Source: 'the internet'.

I read reviews of Indian restaurants and memorised their exotic names – Balham's Chatkara, Clapham's Maharani or Cardiff's Standard Balti.

> Pukkadom? No, not quite there yet. Give me a sec . . .   *JR*

Having conquered the Madras, I was now driven by a desire to push myself with varieties such as Scotch bonnets, habaneros, the komodo dragon. I quickly became bored with the over-the-counter stuff. I tried a vindaloo, and although not as tasty as a Madras, I stared it in the eyes and finished it. Phall notwithstanding (I'm not a lunatic[293]), I had gone as far as the British high street could take me.

> PilauFax! . . . Knew I'd get there . . . You're absolutely welcome.   *JR*

A few notes:

1. If you are new to spicy food, it is difficult to imagine it could ever be pleasant, as you'll be used to it hurting your mouth – this is why it's important to take things slowly. Once you build up a tolerance for chilli, eating it will release endorphins (similar to those released by exercise), which will make you feel great. This is why people become addicted to it. Running five miles if you have never trained before is painful. If you are used to running five miles, it is exhilarating (for more on this, see **B: Body, Shock Your**).

---

293 There is a very funny YouTube video of John eating a phall in a curry house in Bristol called Oh Calcutta! for a dare in 2011. It's well worth a watch – he makes repeated trips to the toilet to rinse his mouth with hot water and the whole venture is almost derailed by the sheer volume of cloves in the curry. It's edited with tense music and features a brief interview with the owner of Oh Calcutta! Fun fact: it was the night before he flew to Australia to do the Adelaide Comedy Festival – one can only imagine the digestive challenges he faced at 30,000 feet.

2. The toilet. Having heard people make reference to this all my life, I was initially hugely wary of what hot curry would do to my toilets. In a sentence: I was pleasantly surprised – maybe it's because I increased my tolerance so slowly. I think the side-effects people make jokes about are more to do with everything else that going for a curry in the UK entails (seven pints of strong lager after work). Don't eat too much and, if you are moving up a level for the first time, maybe wash down your curry with a nice glass of squash.

I have to agree with Elis here. That phall I had was actually not too bad the next day. I mean, I knew I'd had it, but it wasn't troublesome. On the other hand, if I have Tabasco *and* jalapenos on a pizza . . . well . . . it will Cut. Me. In. Half. Where's the logic in that?! Maybe it's the vinegar?

3. A tolerance for spicy food will not 'kill your tastebuds'. This is an extremely common misconception. It is true that your tastebuds change with age, and from my experience, introducing a new sensation into your evening meal will probably make fish fingers and peas appear boring. But you are not irreparably damaging your tongue.

I would add, and the video I took of Elis trying 100% Pain in 2009 bears this out, if you do ever find yourself with your mouth absolutely on fire, the best and only cure is to rinse your mouth out with hot water. Ideally as hot as a drinkable cup of tea. Swill, gargle and repeat. It will sting but take most of the heat out. Ice cream, and to a lesser extent, milk, also help but will curdle with the spice in your stomach. OK if you've had a teaspoon of Dave's Insanity Sauce, but not suitable to wash down a full curry.

To the naysayers, the cautious, the Doubting Thomases and plain eaters – I cannot recommend Project Spice enough. You're opening up a whole new world of taste, and it's exceptionally liberating. It's like learning to ride a bike, but with your mouth. Best of luck, everyone. I believe in you!

The Cut-Out-and-Keep Project Spice Planner

This is a general guide for someone beginning from the base camp of a classic WWP (West Walian Palate). In 2018, spicy food is as readily available in Carmarthen, Haverfordwest or Llanelli as crisps or bed-sheets, but it was a different story when I was growing up. If you have tastebuds like I had until a few years ago, follow this plan very care-fully. This planner is designed to be cut out and pinned to the kitchen wall, like a World Cup wall chart but for your mouth.

Stage 1: Try to add English mustard to your lunchtime sandwich. It will initially be a shock, but you might find the endorphins make you more productive and bypass the post-prandial afternoon slump your unspiced colleagues will get. After two weeks of this, talk to your boss about a pay rise but be careful not to give your secret away.

Treat day: Your tastebuds will still be very unsophisticated at this point, so after a week of this punishing regime, treat yourself to a plate of boiled potatoes and a glass of lukewarm water in front of *Call the Midwife*.

Stage 2: You should now feel as comfortable with English mustard as Holly Willoughby is with an autocue. It's time to introduce other low-level spicy sensations to your palate. Black pepper should make an appearance at mealtimes – say hello to peppery Findus Crispy Pancakes. Swap your mid-morning chocolate digestive for a ginger biscuit, although the first time you do this make sure you're supervised by a person you're comfortable blowing your nose in front of. Before moving to Stage 3, you should be applying amounts of English mustard to your sandwiches that civilians regard as 'insane'.

Treat day: Your tastebuds will now be maturing in other ways, so treat yourself to a Cheddar cheese sandwich (3+ on the maturity scale) in front of the 2012 Olympic Ceremony on YouTube.

Stage 3: Personally, I found this one of the most satisfying stages. Buy a low-level red chilli from a supermarket (they will be in the fruit and veg section, near the garlic), chop and start sprinkling it (sparingly) onto otherwise bland food (something like a shepherd's pie). There might be a slight kick but your training has prepared you for this. Exercise caution, but once you are comfortable with the heat, add in abundance. You are setting a marker. You are telling the world that you are changing. You are embracing spice. By now you should be seeing an improvement in your sex life, and groups of teenagers on bikes will be more likely to respect you.

Treat day: The caution of **Stage 1** will feel like a very, very long time ago. Celebrate this by eating a ham and mustard sandwich and some ginger biscuits on a treadmill. It's time to showboat!

Stage 4: It's time to make soup. I personally like butternut squash soup, so make plenty of it (enough to freeze), but add lots of the weak chilli you can buy from any supermarket. This is purely a confidence-building exercise. Once you have finished that soup, make another one, but this time add a bird's eye chilli (alongside the normal ones). The bird's eye is a significant step up from your average supermarket chilli, but the sheer quantity of soup will make it manageable, despite leaving a detectable heat. You are now making genuine progress, and if you are that kind of person – it's time for an insta story.

Treat day: By now you will be craving spice, so chuck a bit of chilli into your morning Ready Brek and bask in the admiring glances of your colleagues. Ask your boss for another pay rise – you are leadership material. It's now time to update your wardrobe – have the confidence to dress like Michael Hutchence in his INXS heyday.

Stage 5: It's Madras time. Madras is a medium-hot curry as far as the high street is concerned, but it was a psychological barrier for me. For that crucial first time I would get mango chutney and maybe have a yoghurt to hand, and the counteractive sweetness of a Peshwari naan is also advised. If you want to properly assess your tolerance for Madras-level spice you could let the curry go cold, so as not to confuse spice heat with temperature heat. But fear not – you are capable of this. Wash it down with a cooling glass of orange squash and try not to overeat. You are top of the table, but no one has ever won the league by Christmas.

Treat day: Madras is addictive, and if your training has gone to plan you will be perfectly placed to enjoy it. So have another! Why not eat it in the bath? But never the shower.

Stage 6: Spice should now be a part of your everyday life. You should be adding bird's eye chilli to almost every meal (it's particularly nice in a risotto), and your coat pocket should have emergency Tabasco in it. You might be boring your old friends by constantly discussing the Scoville scale, but don't worry – you can get new, better friends. The internet is full of forums where chilli heads can discuss everything from Nagas to the golden cayenne. You have been dismantled and rebuilt. This is your new life now. Enjoy the experience of your parents describing you as 'unrecognisable' as they wipe tears from their eyes.

Treat day: Feign illness to get out of a social event where you know the food will be bland, in favour of staying in to eat Madras in your dressing gown.

Stage 7: It is now difficult for you to remember your old, drab existence. Even music sounds different. The world has become sepia, apart from occasional bursts of technicolour at mealtimes. If Madras was a psychological barrier, you are ready for the next one – vindaloo. Vindaloo is the byword for a hot curry, despite being usurped in recent years by the phall and tindaloo. But vindaloo is the one everyone has heard of. It's a punchline. It might not pack the punch of a phall or tindaloo but the time for those curries will come. The principles are the same as the first time you tried a Madras, all those months ago. Mango chutney, yoghurt, Peshwari naan, orange squash, and try not to overeat. I personally don't think it's as tasty as a Madras, but the sense of achievement will be unbeatable. Once you have finished, take a moment to stare at yourself in the mirror, in awe at what you have accomplished. If you are an American citizen, consider running for President. If you are a Catholic, E-Mail the Vatican about a sainthood. You deserve it.

Treat day: Eat a ham and mustard sandwich, and laugh and laugh and laugh. To think you once saw this as a challenge! End with a flourish by throwing the jar of mustard against the wall. You won't be needing that anymore!

potato!

T:

Top Threes
(Quickfire)[294]

Right then, Elis, want to explain to readers what's going on here?

Well . . . 'T' was the last chapter of the book left to be written, and we're writing it together. Here at the offices of Orion Publishing.

Is that as much detail as you want to go into?

Yes, I think so . . .

I mean, for example, where are we at deadline-wise?

We are four days past the deadline for handing in the book.

Ah, I see. And who was responsible for chapter 'T'?

I was.

Interesting, very interesting. Yes, and you were supposed to write a chapter about fandom called 'Teenage Fan Club', weren't you?

---

294 The original recording of this conversation is featured in the audiobook, which is available for download now.

Yes, yes I was . . .

. . . and what happened?

It was absolute dogshit.

Correct, it was absolute dogshit. So, very much like the feature of the same name, it promised much, and delivered so little.

Yes.

So, in a last gasp attempt to drag ourselves over the line, what are we doing?

Well, very much like in 'I: It's Just a Body', we're going to riff a chapter reminiscent of the 'Quick-Fire Quizzes' we used to do on the show.

Indeed, necessity is the mother of invention, so we're going to surprise each other with topics to choose a 'top three' of, and I am going to transcribe the conversation, an act of selflessness on my part that will push my word count even further beyond yours.

Thanks, mate.

[Transcription commences]

Here we go, quick-fire top threes. I'll start. Crisps.

Er . . . Doritos

Number one?!

Er, no, roast beef Monster Munch, generic plain/ready salted and Doritos Cool Original.

Oh my God. So boring. I'm tempted to not even write that down. OK, what have you got for me?

Top three things you would do if a meteor was going to strike.

How long have I got?

Oh, an hour.

Where's it striking?

It's wiping out the planet.

It's wiping out the whole planet?

Oh, OK then, Europe. It's wiping out Europe.

So I'm going to die.

Yes.

Top three things? That I'm going to do?

Yeah, before you die instantly.

And nothing I can do will stop that?

Yeah.

OK, I'd buy fags, then drink and smoke fags.

What's your third thing?

Smoking the fags.

OK.

OK, back to you. Top three sports.

Football, boxing, cricket.

But you don't really like cricket.

I like the idea of it. I like reading about it and watching documentaries

The Holy Vible

about it. So I don't have the patience for a five-day Test match, but *Cricket's Greatest* on Sky Sports . . . Dennis Lillee . . . Yes please! Um . . . Your top three non-top-shelf memories.

[Laughter] Oh God . . . Oh God . . . Oh Man . . . but that's gonna take me into dangerous emotional territory.

OK then, would you like to write this up later?

No.

OK then, top three top-shelf memories.

[Laughter]

Maybe, names redacted, in radio-friendly language.

Oh man, top three memories. What about three good memories that are neither top shelf nor overly emotional

Yeah, that's nice.

Going on the first-ever Oxford Day pub crawl with The Lovely Robin, going to see Lou Reed twice on the *Ecstasy* tour in 2000, and the first time you and I did a gig together, not as stand-ups but at The Phoenix to fans of the podcast.

And now your top-shelf memories . . .

[Laughs] Your turn: football teams other than Swansea.

Liverpool, Carmarthen Town . . . And I have a soft spot . . .

[Elis now whispers under his breath for a good two minutes]

HIBS!

Why Hibs?

Because they're exceptionally unlucky and in my experience their fans are cool. Liverpool for their history. Carmarthen for obvious reasons. And Hibs, they're Irvine Welsh's team and I've always thought their fans were really cool. OK, pieces of advice you would have given 16-year-old Robins?

Very gooooooood question! Um . . . One: chill out.

[Laughter] Ah, good grief . . .

Two: if you ever write anyone a poem or a letter, sleep on it . . .

. . . Yeah . . .

then don't show it to them.

[Laughter]

and Three: Um . . . really enjoy every cigarette you ever have cos one day you'll have to stop and you'll really miss them . . . [Mimes shooting self in the head] Your turn. Decades in the history of the world.

Oh, 1980s.

Feel free to give a location . . .

Of course, of course. London in the 1960s, absolutely. London in the 1990s.

HAHAHAHAH. So, like, Britpop era. And where else? London in the 80s?!

The 70s feels quite hard done by in this.

This is the whole history of the entire world.

But you're always saying this. Go too far back, you wouldn't be able to eat the food!

Yeah, but for the sight of it, like I would go like 1460s, 1680, then 1960s.

But why? The healthcare! The standard of living!

This is just to visit! Not to live there!

OK, well, I'd like to visit these places.

OK, London 60s, London 90s . . .

And, if I'm just visiting . . . South Wales 80s.

Great.

Pieces of advice you'd give 36-year-old Robins.

I think I've perfected everything.

[Big, big laughs]

I've had enough time on my own to perfect everything. I dropped two capers on the floor yesterday because I hadn't properly prepped where the jar was and how I was getting them out. And I put the jar down and said, 'Come on, John, this isn't you. They went on the floor but you're better than this.' I think broadly, in the kitchen, prep your ingredients and give yourself enough space, but apart from that I've absolutely perfected myself.

Wow, OK, an answer I could never have predicted there. 'There is no advice because I'm perfect except from when I dropped capers.'

Er, smell, top three all-time.

Sweat and garlic frying, the smell of football, which is fags, urine, lager and onions. Er and, I don't know what it is, but the fabric conditioner my auntie uses. Her house smells absolutely lovely. A very simple one: top three spicy sauces?

OOOOOOOHHHHH! Lovely! So, as an all-rounder, the Crystal hot sauce – it comes in big bottles and is like a more vinegary Tabasco. Then in second place, Rectum Ripper.

You're not selling it to me, John . . .

Which, as the guy selling it at the Bristol hot sauce shop said [affects Birmingham accent], 'All joking aside, it is a lovely sauce.' It's quite garlicky. And there is a third. I mean, I don't want to do Tabasco down as it is a good all-rounder. Hmmmm . . . cos I've kind of covered the Tabasco base, I'm gonna go for the Frank's Buffalo Wings Sauce.

How spicy is that, out of interest?

I put too much of it on a corn on the cob and regretted it, but I ate the whole thing.

HAHAHA . . . that is a very good summary of your personality, I think.

OK, top three parts of your own body?

My bum.

Why?

Cos I like the power it can achieve.

In what arena?

Cycling sprints over ten yards. Um . . . my calves and my thighs.

Nice.

Nothing from above the waist.

The engine room.

Yeah. Certainly not the brain. Top three Van Morrison songs?

SONGS?!

I thought this might be slightly unfair.

Oh man! I'll give it a go off the T of my H.[295] Can I access my iTunes to check? Mmmm, interesting . . . I don't mind it, mate . . . oh wow . . .

You could go iTunes playcount, couldn't you?

That's exactly what I've done Elis . . . [vapes] Oh God! This is so hard! So I'm gonna go . . .
[Two minutes elapse]
   This is really tricky. I'm gonna go for . . . AAAAAAAARGH . . . I'm gonna . . . top me s'en! . . . errr . . . I'm gonna go for erm . . . oh . . . oh my God . . . I'm just gonna have to really vibe this . . .

OK.

I'm gonna go for . . . hang on . . . but then there won't be one off *Astral Weeks* if I do it that way!

But I think you can have amazing albums without having stand-out tracks.

OHHHHHHHYEEEEEEEEEEAHTHOOOOOOOOOOUGH I'm gonna go for. 'Linden Arden Stole the Highlights' . . . 'Saint Dominic's Preview' . . . 'Avalon of the Heart' . . . OH MY GOD . . .

OK.

No one saw that coming. OK, films.

Number one is *Taxi Driver*, number two *Raging Bull*, number three is either Francis Ford Coppola's *The Conversation*, which I absolutely loved, or Jonny Owen's *Don't Take Me Home*, because of the memories

---

295 Cool shorthand for 'top of my head'.

it brings back. So I'm gonna say Jonny's film, actually, cos it takes me back to a very special place, but special mention to *The Conversation*, which was recommended to me by Stephen Merchant.

Lovely stuff.

Meat substitutes?

GREAT QUESTION, MATE . . . Great question, mate . . . as in the base thing?

Completely up to you. I mean you were a meat eater until five years ago.

Quorn chicken dippers/nuggets are indistinguishable. Why you would ever eat a chicken nugget when those are available is beyond me . . . Deep-fried/Chinese-style tofu in general has been a revelation to me. When I ate meat I thought tofu was a joke and I was in contempt of people who ate it, but now I actually crave it. And when it's done well, oh Holy Eff . . . Hang on a sec, I'm gonna go for tempeh and seitan when done well. Though I have no idea what it is or how to cook it.

What is it?

Tempeh? So I had these tempeh ribs in a place called The Tipsy Vegan in Norwich. It's like a harder version of tofu, I guess. And seitan is made from wheat, I think. There's a place called Temple of Seitan in London – there's two of them – and it's a fried-chicken shop but it's all vegan. And it's amazing. I would say, bizarrely, and I think this is often overlooked, that the meat substitutes that are substituting the shittest meats are the best, because there's so little meat in those things.

A Quorn sausage and mustard is one of the great combinations.

Exactly, because a sausage is mostly starch, what's it called . . . rusk! It's mostly non-meat. So, to replicate a McDonald's burger is so easy, because it doesn't really taste of anything.

I once ate a sausage at a farmers' market that was 99 per cent meat and it actually tasted very weird, cos there were none of the things in it that made it taste like a sausage.

And people assume vegan or veggie food is kind of holier than thou or super-healthy, but where it really excels is in creating the crappiest comfort food that, ironically, when it's made from meat, causes the most harm to animals and the environment because it's made so cheaply. So why not get your nuggets and burgers from Holland and Barrett and your steak from a local butcher's? Great question! OK, top three hashtag Fringe[296] memories.

What a superb question. Top shelf or non-top shelf?

Any, but make it radio-friendly.

Getting heckled by Jim Rosenthal at the 2008 Comedy Zone, which I wish I had footage of cos I remember it as one of the defining Fringe moments of that decade. That thing we discussed on RHLSTP when you were drunk and you spotted that PR lady.

Mel.

Mel, who said that you weren't her cup of tea and you followed her round saying you weren't her cup of tea.

Haha!

Trying to manage that, is one of my top three Fringe memories. Umm . . . I think being, it's not really a Fringe memory, but being asked to do

---

296 Edinburgh Fringe Comedy Festival.

the Comedy Zone is one of the best moments of my life, cos it was like being asked to sign for United.

Yeah.

I thought it was this hugely important thing, and you'd done it the year before.

Yeah, I agree.

Bearing in mind they used to be very London-centric in their choices, and I'd only done one or two gigs in London, one of which was in front of Maria Hemming, who booked the show, and her boss, to sign it off. It felt like I was kicking the door down or something.

Mmmm, I absolutely agree with you.

I remember where I was. I was in James Dowdeswell's flat in Clapham.

I remember where I was when I got the call. I was in that shared house on Coldharbour Road in the daytime, and everyone else in the flat was out and I went for a fag.

I found it in one of my gig diaries.

OK, my go.

Why you like poetry?

Top three reasons why I like poetry?

Only cos I never really got into it. I was always a novels man. I don't think I've ever read a poem for pleasure.

OK. The best words in the best order.

Nice.

This is going to sound super-pretentious but . . . the spaces after the lines that you fill yourself.

AAAAAAAW! Why aren't you a teacher?

Cos of the pay.

[Laughter]

Cos it doesn't pay well enough.

[Laughter]

The imagined lifestyle I think, of a poet, smoking a fag . . .[297]

[Long, rather boring discussion about how much poets earn omitted here. Needless to say it's not much at all, and the Poet Laureate only gets £5,750quid plus a barrel of sherry a year.]

English towns and cities?

York, definitely York, Liverpool and Manchester.

Good, very good.

Top three Oxford memories?

Sitting on my own in a pub smoking a pipe reading medieval poetry.

Great stuff. Classic Robins.

Walking towards an English lecture at a reasonable hour cos they were never before midday.

LOOOOOOOOOVELY!!

As the mist rises above the University Parks . . .

---

297 Transcribing this, I realise how often I'm mentioning smoking. As discussed in **I: It's Just a Body,** I'd been trying to ween myself off electronic cigarettes that I have used in some form for seven years. By the time we recorded this I'd been without nicotine for nearly two weeks for the first time since 1997, so it's clearly occupying an unusually large room in my mind palace.

There was always gonna be mist in there . . .

Just being in your room at about 6.30.

Pm?

Pm. Getting ready for a night out, whether it's darts, putting on your shirt, sharpening your darts. Or just drinking a bottle of orange WKD in your room . . .

Loooovely.

Frank Zappa on . . .

Yeeeees!

Going down to the college bar, everybody there.

Great answers to a great question.

Injuries you'd least like to sustain?

Cock and balls shot off in a war.

[Massive laugh] 'in a war', OK, great.

Anything to do with my eyes. I'd hate to be made blind. I'd hate to jam something and then to lose it. Whenever I pass a big red London double-decker bus I imagine it driving over my foot and it makes me feel sick.

Yeah, OK, but something driving over your foot would be fleeting. You probably wouldn't actually be that injured.

What, a bus?

Yeah.

Over your foot?

Yeah, if you think about it.

No, I actually can't think about it so . . .

But that wouldn't be as bad as a boulder landing on your foot. Have you seen *127 Hours*, that film where the guy cuts his arm off?

No I haven't but I have read the BuzzFeed article.

From what I gather the guy was a bit of a tool.

HAHAHAHA!

OK, good questions.

Top three pubs in Bristol?

Highbury Vaults.

Knew that would be in there.

It's difficult cos some of my favourite ones are not actually the best pubs.

But you can qualify this.

Well, hmm, God . . . kind of need Robin here. I think for . . . OOOOOOOOOOOOH GOD!

[Three minutes of silence]

Oh God. I'll have to say for less beer reasons and more nostalgia reasons, The Hare on the Hill and . . .

Which is the one up the hill, and we once went there in the snow?

These are the two I'm talking about. The Hare on the Hill and The Hillgrove Porter Stores. OK, historical figures you'd like to have met?

Lloyd George. Nye Bevan. Although I don't think he'd like me; I think he'd think I was a bit of a tit. What a superb question. Andrew Marr, who's now written so much history I think of him as a historical figure. Thomas Jefferson was a Welsh speaker – I'd quite like to have met him. Muhammad Ali.

So which one is three?

Muhammad Ali. Top three things you'd change about yourself?

Oh God. Um. Er. Like fantasy things, like make myself invisible, or regular day-to-day stuff?

Both.

OK, face and scalp skin. It's not that noticeable, but it just takes a lot of effort. Also, if you look closely I've got the beginnings of a boozer's nose, a few thread veins.

Have you?!

Oh you wouldn't notice. You'd think I had great skin from a distance.

Yeah, a hundred, hundred and fifty feet away.

Um I, I wish I didn't have the . . .

Oh this can be personality too . . . not that I'm saying any of it *needs* changing.

Oh bowels! Just wish they would chill out. You're not rushing to a deadline . . . You really have got all the time in the world . . .

HAHAHA, there was a bowel heyday, though?

Oh I don't think it's really a problem, not until you meet some-one you like and then you start to become conscious of it. I wish, er ... I've been quite lucky in lots of respects with my body. Personality-wise, I dunno, it's been a bit of a mixed bag. I wish I didn't have the gene for nicotine and booze.

Great answer, great answer.

I wish I just enjoyed it. I wish I could have smoked socially in my teens and 20s, and wish I could drink two or three nights a week.

A social drinker.

And not to have to really put an effort into not drinking.

Yeah.

Eurgh. Uh. Oh God. Got there. Top three insults?

Div. Cunt.

Great.

Div, cunt and whopper.

Lovely. Something for everyone.

Good question that. Top three reasons why silence is nice?

Oh, lack of agitation.

That's a good answer.

When you say silence, do you mean absolute pin-drop?

Well, you crave it, so I often wonder if you're getting more out of it than me.

Well, are you including the ability to hear birdsong?

Yeah yeah, though that would annoy me.

Or the natural world, the rush of wind through the trees that makes me think of the Philip Larkin poem 'The Trees'.

I was writing yesterday with the window open, and the rush of wind through the trees got on my nerves.

Oh. Um. It just feels like when there's lots of noise around me it's like every muscle in my body is tensed, and some of those muscles are in my brain, whereas when there's silence it's like I can swim without fear of bashing into another swimmer in my own mind.

Yoooooou thoughtful little man.

Top three rivers?

Tawe, Cleddau, Thames. Top three reasons to like Queen?

Melody, balance, bravado.

It's almost like you spend a huge amount of your day thinking. I've only got two left, but I've completely lost faith in both of them.

I've got one left.

So you can ask me one more.

If you could only travel on three motorways, what would they be?

M4.

Of course.

Of course . . . it wouldn't be very useful, but I do like the M5 going down to the south-west.

Beautiful.

The M32 reminds me of staying at your house.

But it's one of the shortest motorways in the country! Just take a different route to Bristol! Take the A38! Or M5 then A4!

Good, good point. M50, cos it feels like a cheat code.

OK, so M4, M5 and M50?

Yeah, cos I've only ever had bad times on the M1, the M6, the M62.

A1M . . . tricky . . . I mean practically for me it would have to be M4, M40, M25.

Yeah, it's just the M25 is such a B ache.

But, OK, let's say, I would probably go M40, M4, M6.

Oh, I don't know. Practically it would be a different answer.

Oh, who knows . . . this is going to take a long time to transcribe.

Let's leave it there . . .

U:

Up Games, Made (Made-up Games)

In a commercial digital indie radio station tense music plays. Over the top of it the sound of a clock can be heard ticking. At one desk a man sits relaxed, an air of total peace and contentment on his face, reclining in a faded Queen hoodie. He looks for all the world like the crown prince of some bountiful land, gazing from his veranda over luscious plantations and rolling hills. He sips lemonade, he snoozes, he vapes. To his left, Elis James has his head in his hands.

'A: . . . ummmm . . . .A . . . .A . . . Apple! B . . . B . . . Oh sugar my halloumi[298] . . . Oh come on, Dave!. . .B . . . B . . . Banana . . . C . . . Ca . . . Co . . . ChiLLLLL . . . I DON'T KNOW, DAVE!'

'Time's running out, El'.

---

298 See **Appendix i: Glossary of Terms**.

'Chips in a binbag!'

The tense music has reached its conclusion, the clock has ceased ticking. Elis James has lost at Betabet™. Again.

'AAAAAAARRRRRRGH! I hate this game! I hate this game! Kiss me and kill me!'

In truth, Elis does not hate this game. Were Freud[299] here, he might suggest that what Elis actually hates is himself, or his mum, maybe even his twig and/or berries. In truth, Elis is devoted to his mother, and his berries – though colossal – are fighting fit, and his twig has been certified 'classic medium' by two separate GPs.[300] No, Elis has a run-of-the mill case of Quiz-Induced Self-Loathing.

We all suffer from this from time to time, maybe in a Tuesday night pub quiz, maybe over Christmas in a tense game of Trivial Pursuit, maybe on national TV after Tim Farron gets asked questions on Blackburn Rovers IN THE NINETIES that a child of any decade could answer while you get asked questions on the rock band Queen (EVERY DECADE) that even an experienced Queen Quizzer would categorise as moderate/hard, some of which are quite oddly worded so as to confuse you into trying to think of 'Irish' bands as opposed to just remembering that it was THIN LIZZY WHO SUPPORTED QUEEN ON THEIR AMERICAN TOUR AND YOU KNEW THIS A) ANYWAY AND B) COS YOU READ IT THE NIGHT BEFORE IN YOUR PREP. Anyway, I'm cool with that, I'm fine with it, fine, cool, relaxed.

---

299 Sigmund, not Emma.
300 [EJ] And a district nurse.

I guarantee this will be John's last thought on earth.   *EJ*

I think you're probably right.

And, while for me, Quiz-Induced Self-Loathing forms a small part of a larger range of life-induced self-loathings, this is pretty much the only part of the week where Elis genuinely hates himself, and given that, I'm quite happy to enjoy every single second of it.

Ever since our show started, Elis and I have played a made-up game in order to play a song of our choice. Initially we played Winner Plays On™, a game where we would ask each other five questions on a specialist topic we chose for ourselves. The loser would have to change topic for the following week. Eventually, as is the case with even the most remarkable polymaths, we ran out of topics.[301] Winner Plays On™ gave birth to Betabet™, a simple game in which players had 30 seconds to name examples of a thing in alphabetical order. Depending on how hard the topic was, there could be as many as five passes allowed in order to stop players 'Passing to Paris'.[302] So, if, for example, the topic was Airlines, you might go American Airlines, British Airways, Cathay Pacific, Delta and so on. While one player played, the other would enter a soundproof booth in order to stop them hearing the answers of the other. It's that simple.

Alas, there was a flaw in the plan. Elis was absolutely

---

301 [EJ] I think a particular low point was when John chose the topic 'Cats, ' which as I'm sure you can agree, is too broad.

302 [EJ] During a game of Betabet™ where we had to name capital cities, John did uncharacteristically badly during the early letters. This was in the days of unlimited passes, and in a display of gamesmanship even José Mourinho would be disgusted by, he passed to P because he could remember Paris, and then passed onto R because he could remember Rome, winning that week's game of Betabet™ with a score of four points to three. In a low point for John-and-Elis relations, this was agreed to be unsporting and the three-pass rule was introduced.

terrible at this game,[303] and, as a man not familiar with high-level self-loathing, it had to be shelved. Luckily, however, our listeners provided the solution.

Made-Up Games

We've all made up games in our lives, maybe in childhood (e.g. Collect the Farthing), maybe at university (e.g. Ebay the Farthing), maybe on a rained-out holiday in the mid-2000s (e.g. Remember the Farthing). And for the last year or so Elis and I have been playing the games that listeners made up and sent in. The beauty of a made-up game is that the rules evolve, loopholes are ironed out, unfair advantages are rebalanced through tweaking, and these games can often rival the very best that the boffins at Waddingtons, Hasbro and Mattel can come up with. They can be answer-based, skill-based, even vibe-based. Playing the games our listeners have made up has been a genuine pleasure; I would liken it to entering the Crystal Maze every Saturday, unsure what will lie behind each door, just without access to O'Brien/Tudor-Pole.[304]

The secret to a good made-up game is either complete simplicity or baffling complexity. You shouldn't need many props or anything that is difficult to source. Also, it's nice to have rules that speak of a complex evolution, perhaps 'No Keithing' to correct a way Keith found of cheating on the minibus in 2008, that sort of thing. Below are a few of our favourites. We hope they give you many happy hours.

---

303 See appendices for in-depth statistics of just how bad he was.
304 Or Merchant/Ayoade, if you are a member of 'Generation Snapchat'

POPULATION SPECULATION

Submitted by: Brendan Woulfe and friends

Number of players: As many bored people as you can fit in a caravan

Rules: The quizmaster chooses a country, and the players have to guess the population (according to Wikipedia). Closest person wins.

Difficulty level: 3/5. Sounds easier than it is, because the other day I played with John and got Canada's population wrong by more than 150m

Winner: Elis

Notes: If the game becomes hugely popular among its players you can move on to cities, towns, etc., although for some unknown reason this isn't as much fun. Brendan (who submitted the game) told us that his friend Matthew Pinfield loved playing this game so much he went to the trouble of composing a theme tune, and this can be found on YouTube. The video has lots of photos of Jim Davidson for some reason, but if anything that made me enjoy it even more.

POTTER OR NOTTER

Submitted by: Ffion Burke and Jamie Allen

Number of players: 2

Rules: This can only be played under certain circumstances – one player must know lots about Harry Potter, and the other player must know absolutely nothing. Perfect for us, as John is obsessed with Harry Potter and I am an adult. The Harry Potter Devotee (HPD) offers ten names that might be characters in the Harry Potter series of books (preferably from the backbenches of the wizarding world to make it more challenging), and the adult must try to guess whether they are real or fake. E.g.: Sylvanus Kettleburn is a genuine character, Elandus Splattermold was made up by John.

Difficulty level: 3/5 – Very much dependent on the inventiveness of the HPD

Winner: Elis

Notes: If the person who likes Harry Potter is a fan of other books in the fantasy genre, they can use names from other books to wrongfoot the cool, Elis-style person who only likes current affairs and sport and is a 37-year-old father of one.

GESTATION!

Submitted by: Nick Austwick

Number of players: Two or more

Rules: The 'dealer' names a mammal and the players have to guess the gestation period of the named creature. Points are awarded to the player who guesses closest to the gestation period listed by Google/Wikipedia. E.g., the gestation period for a domestic cat is 9–10 weeks, for a short-beaked common dolphin it's 10–11 months.

Difficulty level: 4/5

Winner: Elis

Notes: Gestation! (with the exclamation mark) is a great name for this game, although John did suggest 'Womb Warriors'.

TEACHER/SUBJECT

Submitted by: Owen Hathway

Number of players: 2–5 (although you cannot play with people who went to the same school as you)

Rules: One person (or a group) have to guess what subject one of your school teachers taught from a few clues and a name. Round one, you simply say the teacher's name, e.g. Miss Williams. For five points the players have a single guess at her subject. As long as no one gets it first time you move onto round two. Here you offer a very general clue, maybe a nickname. Three points are awarded if you guess correctly. If not, you move on to round three. Another vague clue is offered, (e.g. 'this teacher was allergic to chalk and had to wear surgeon's gloves in class'), and one point is awarded if the correct answer is given.

Winner: It was a draw.
Difficulty level: 5/5

HOW OLD IS THIS COIN?

Submitted by: Paul Salisbury
Number of players: Perfect in a pub situation. Minimum of three
Rules: One person pulls out loose change and presents a coin to the group (date facing down), asking the group, 'How old is this coin?' The winner is the person with the closest guess.
Difficulty rating: 3/5
Winner: John (who as an ex-coin collector was at a distinct advantage)

IRRELEVANT MALLETT'S MALLET

Submitted by: Andy Hill
Number of players: Two players and an adjudicator
Rules: In a twist on the popular game you might remember from Wacaday and the Wide Awake Club, the aim of Irrelevant Mallett's Mallet is to take it in turns naming words that have nothing to do with the preceding word. The adjudicator decides if the words are linked or not, this can be challenged by the players and you must make your case accordingly, e.g. John very sportingly argued on my behalf that the word 'green' has nothing to do with 'mascara'. Irrelevant Mallett's Mallet is surprisingly difficult, as you are punished for hesitation and repetition.
Difficulty level: 4/5
Winner: John

2P OR NOT 2P

Submitted by: Matt Thomas
Number of players: 2
Rules: Player 1 is a guesser and player 2 a dropper. The dropper has

two coins – a 2p and any other coin that's legal tender in the country you're playing in. The guesser must close their eyes (blindfold optional) and the dropper drops a coin onto a hard surface. We changed the rules slightly to make it easier – the dropper dropped two coins in each round, one of which was always a 2p piece. You'd think this 50 per cent chance of getting it right would make the game easy, but John in particular found it very difficult. The game works on a best-of-three basis.

Difficulty level: 3/5

Winner: Elis

Notes: The coins were dropped by intern Lawrence from a distance of about 12 inches, or as John described it (based on a top-shelf E-Mail we once had to the show), 'a full Ronnie'. If you play more than one round it's fun to mix things up by choosing different coins. This game will be the first of our Made-up Games to disappear, as Britain hurtles towards the reality of a cashless society.

MINCE OR MINTS

Submitted by: Vic Thompson

Number of players: 2

Rules: Player 1 says out loud either 'MINCE' or 'MINTS'. .Player 2 guesses which one they are saying by shouting 'BEEF' or 'POLOS'.

Winner: Elis

Difficulty level: 3/5

Notes: John tried to throw me off the scent by saying 'mince' or 'mints' in a variety of different accents and got himself in a right tizz. I personally think a one-syllable word like 'mints' (or 'mince') is too short to start saying it like you're from Cape Town or Moscow when you're actually from Thornbury. I found closing my eyes and actually visualising a plate of mince or a Trebor Extra Strong Mint helped my enunciation and concentration in this game.

SLANG OFF!
Submitted by: Joe Nicholson
Number of players: 2
Rules: One person chooses a word that has lots of slang terms, e.g. money. Players take turns to say slang terms for that thing, e.g. spondoolicks, greenbacks, wonga. The loser is the person who can't carry on. Players may interject and challenge a person's slang term if they deem it incorrect or if there is repetition. Challenging the person's slang term can make this a lot of fun; during a game at the Machynlleth Comedy Festival, the subject was 'food' and John successfully challenged my claim that people refer to food as 'a little bit of mouth-mouth'.
Difficulty level: 2/5
Winner: John

LOWEST POPULATION DARTS
Submitted by: Adapted by John from a game sent in by Tim Price
Number of players: 2–4
Rules: You need three darts and a large map of the world. Players take it in turns to throw three darts at the map. You count the total populations of the countries you hit. The person with the lowest total population wins. Oceans count for 200 million.
Difficulty level: Dependent on the standard of darts you played at university
Winner: Unknown (never played)

It is impossible to end this chapter, however, without explaining the rules to the game Potato Potato, the only game we have played every week since the Made-up Games feature began. Although derided by some guest presenters on the show (James Acaster, in particular), it provides the perfect antidote to turbo-capitalist pastimes such as Monopoly and the murder-endorsing Cluedo.

POTATO POTATO

Submitted by: Katie and James Collins (not the ex-West Ham Utd and Wales footballer)

Number of players: 3 – two contestants and an umpire is the ideal, although it can be played by two or more players who are on the same wavelength and are willing to be sporting about it.

Difficulty rating: 1–5/5

Rules: The rules to Potato Potato are very simple. The only thing you need to play the game is an acute feeling for the vibe of your playing partner – it's perfect for two members of the rhythm section of a band, a strike partnership in a successful football team or, in our case, two digital DJs who are in complete synergy with each other. As seasoned players, John and I have experimented with inflection, intonation and a series of different accents – we have taken Potato Potato to the next level. The game was inspired by an advert for potato waffles, and in praising Potato Potato's inherent simplicity, James, the game's deviser, wrote, 'I do accept, however, that it may be limited in terms of radio content for more than a few weeks.' He had no idea how wrong he was.

V:

Vintern/Vin, Producer

Part 1, being a partly declassified MI6 file made available after a freedom of information request

Name: VINAY ███████████████████ JOSHI

D.O.B: ██/██/91

Aliases: Vin, Vintern, Vinigma, Prod V, ████

Profession: Commercial Digital Indie Radio Producer

Previous Jobs: Commercial Digital Indie Radio Intern, Official Maccabees Fan Club (treasurer), World of Denim (part-time), Good Jeans (receptionist), The Human Jean Gnome Project (founder), Trainee Assistant to Head of Research at Levi's UK

VINAY ███████████████████ JOSHI first came onto our radar when a restraining order was sought by ▇▇▇ guitarist ▇▇▇▇▇▇▇▇▇▇▇ in 2013. Following a chance meeting by the stage door at the Brixton Academy, Joshi pursued communications beyond a level ▇▇▇▇ was comfortable with. Joshi's communications included over one hundred letters, some accompanied by ▇▇▇ , ▇▇▇ and once a lifesize ▇▇▇▇▇▇▇▇▇ ▇▇▇▇▇ from his own hair, hand drawn ▇▇▇ ▇▇▇▇▇ and a ▇▇▇▇▇▇▇▇▇ 34m² and using seventeen different types of denim. Police were made aware when Joshi ▇▇▇▇▇▇▇▇▇▇▇▇ twelve live oxen to the guitarist's house. At the same time, he dumped 50kg of Kellogg's All-Bran on the driveway of frontman ▇▇▇▇▇▇▇ 1000 packets of Fruit Pastilles to the offices of drummer ▇▇▇▇▇▇▇ . Nothing was found on or near property or land belonging to bassist ▇▇▇▇▇▇ , who most likely wasn't a target of Joshi's affections. He said later in police interview '▇▇▇ , ▇▇▇▇ and ▇▇▇ were the main ones. I was never that bothered about ▇▇▇ , in fact, he always struck me as a bit of a ▇▇▇ '

Joshi was born on the ▇▇▇ of ▇▇▇▇▇ 1991. The son of ▇▇▇ ▇▇▇ and ▇▇▇▇▇▇ , rumours that his birth mother was in fact ▇▇▇ Parton were never substantiated. Her movements in the UK to promote her 1991 album *Eagle When She Flies* do not tie up with the birth date, and ▇▇ rumours ▇▇▇ ▇▇▇ ▇▇▇ ▇▇▇▇▇ explain Joshi's intense love of denim.

Joshi attended ▇▇▇▇▇▇▇ secondary school, and ▇▇▇▇ ▇▇▇▇▇▇ Croydon Denim Society, after which little is known. ▇▇▇▇▇▇▇▇▇▇▇▇▇▇ . No record of him exists between the years 2005–10. ▇▇▇▇▇▇ TED Talk in 2011 entitled 'Denim 2.0' but the recording is lost. He then ▇▇▇▇▇ again 2012–13. He was a keen ▇▇▇▇▇▇ ▇ , jazz enthusiast and bass guitarist. Perhaps his talents on

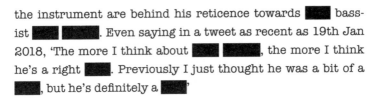

the instrument are behind his reticence towards ████ bassist ████ ████. Even saying in a tweet as recent as 19th Jan 2018, 'The more I think about ████ ████, the more I think he's a right ████. Previously I just thought he was a bit of a ████, but he's definitely a ████'

Our interest in Joshi ended after ████abees frontman ████ndo ████eks brokered a truce between Joshi and ████. Joshi admitted his actions had amounted to harassment, the result of a denim-induced mania, and after chatting to ████ about his solo albums, ████ ████ ████ and ████ ████, the two bonded.

END OF FILE

I immediately considered Producer Vin a close personal friend, despite his being totally silent for the first 18 months I knew him. He would ghost in with impeccable cups of tea[305] at the perfect moment, and we knew that he was happy because he would stroke the nearest item of denim to hand, for example the cuff of his shirt, the tip of his tie, but never, following a course we were all sent on, the tight denim of a colleague's behind.[306] Vin initially began as the intern, and his rise to Radio X producer is one of the feel-good, rags-to-riches stories of the decade. Imagine Dickens, but soundtracked by Tom Grennan.

---

305 The colour of a Clarks Desert Boot for me, a combination of Earl Grey and normal for John, with one sugar and no milk.

[JR] For reference, Elis's ideal colour of tea is RAL 8007 Fawn Brown. The most disappointed I have ever seen him was when he asked a producer at Channel 5 for 'a very strong cup of tea', only to receive a cup of tea the colour of melted Milkybars.

306 According to the tribunal, Toby Tarrant's habit of tickling members of staff represented nothing more than a 'genuine childlike love of tickling' and was 'conducted without malice or any sexual overtones whatsoever'. That said, he has agreed it was inappropriate and 'Toby Tickle' has not been active since December 2017.

But his first shift as producer didn't pass without incident. Vin was, and always will be, a punctual man. Not Robins-level, but close. Most days Robins is only in 45 minutes to an hour before Vin, and Vin's still there a good half an hour before either of us need to be there. Classic Robins.

However, on his first ever day as sole producer of the Elis James and John Robins show, Vin experienced the kind of train-based nightmare that Elis imagines to give his lies authenticity. After watching a documentary about lie detectors and US interrogation techniques, Elis has learned to imagine the fictional delays he recounts while giving his excuse, so that, to polygraph or state-sanctioned torturer, they seem legitimate. Vin, on the other hand, was clearly telling the truth. Rushing in with 16 minutes to go, he had sweated through four separate layers of denim. Regulation sweat would usually permeate the base-layer of thermal denim, maybe even the second layer of his loose denim T-shirt, but to make it through his denim jumper and jacket, I could tell his commute had been a nightmare. When I saw that his denim socks and hat were also affected, he had my immediate sympathy.

I had read the E-Mails, humblebrags, shame wells and made-up games, and Elis had read one page of *The Times* in preparation for The Lighthearted Paper Review, so his lateness would not be catastrophic. But, alas, ever the perfectionist, Vin couldn't let it go. Though on the outside the sweat relented, silently and unnoticed by Elis or me, Vin's mind began to sweat. Though you wouldn't know it from his kind, chilled-out exterior, Vin sets himself very high standards. Commercial digital indie radio isn't awash with Punjabi-Croydonians, and doubtless he feels the weight of expectation from a large part of the northern subcontinent of India/small pocket of south London on his shoulders. He is their Golden Boy of radio, their wunderkind, their Bruno Brookes.

Unfortunately, this interior mind sweat led Vin, on his first shift, to broadcast three minutes of silence to the nation. Amazingly, we were alerted by a security guard who had heard an alarm going off in reception that he couldn't find the source of. On taking the call, Vin's face went ashen, and he threw his denim scarf and gloves to the floor in silent rage. Having set the mixing desk right, I genuinely believe we could have read *Mein Kampf* out loud for the rest of the show and he wouldn't have noticed.

It was the last mistake Vin has ever, or will ever make. His penance was such that for two months he restricted himself to one item of denim clothing a day. And you have to truly know the man to understand what punishment that was.

Blur to Dave's Oasis, Maccabees to John's Meat Loaf, threnim to my more mainstream approach to clothing, Producer Vin has been the still point in our turning world since Producer Dave left Radio X to sell timber to millionaire footballers in Cheshire with his dad. After three years at the station we were a more polished prospect than when we began, although Vin still needs to lay down the law from time to time, and he does this in his own understated way. Reiterating, adapting, and adding to Producer Dave's list of sayings with his own fresh takes:

'Please try.'
'You've been getting that wrong for four years, Elis. You don't introduce adverts like they're a song.'
'Why don't you try writing your login details down, El?'
'Stop showing off that you've written down your login details, John.'
'No, it's not anger, it's dismay.'
'It's probably best if you get here more than three minutes before the show starts, El.'

'Four years. It's been four years. That's a presidential term. We
can't do a text-in feature on farthings because we just can't.'
'John, you know it's not OK to call him a racist on air.'
'John, you know it's not OK to call them racists on air.'
'John, you know full well you can't call it a racist publication on air.'
'I'm not sure what's in it for the listeners.'
'If the boss has heard that we'll all get sacked.'
'I don't think there's a feature in ISAs, John. How many times?'

If Producer Dave was our cool dad, Vin is our talented, savant
nephew who's showing his two increasingly doddering uncles how
the Sky box works. After four years at the station, John's confidence
in his own convictions as a commercial digital indie DJ occasionally
causes arguments, but some truly great radio comes from these creative tensions:

John: I think we should devote the whole second hour of the
show to a thought experiment where international relations are
seen through the prism of Queen lyrics. So we'd start off with
Trump tweeting the lyrics to 'Tenement Funster', and then El
has to guess which Queen lyrics Putin tweets back. I'd help him
obviously, because El doesn't like Queen.

Vin: I'm not sure what's in it for the listeners?

John: International relations are very fragile Vin, haven't you seen
the news?

Elis: Viiiin . . . I can't log in.

Vin: [exasperated] Why don't you try writing your login details
down, El?

John: I wrote mine down when we had to change our passwords
in February. They're on my phone just in case but, I've also
remembered them.

Vin: Stop showing off that you've written down your login details,

John. As El's still eating mango, I'll play double Foo Fighters.

And so on.

Producer Vin is the bass-playing, jazz-loving, AFC Wimbledon-supporting quiet man of Radio X, but he is an indispensable, crucial part of our show. Like Dave he is a pleasure to work with, and both John and I hope this relationship continues for a very long time indeed.

That was a chapter on Producer Vin – you're reading *The Holy Vible* by Elis James and John Robins, we've got plenty of great features to get through but now it's time for some adverts.

Shit. Sorry.

Birds Eye

W:

Welsh Language, The

I feel a sense of relief whenever anybody tells me they speak Welsh. 'Great,' I think, 'we can switch from *yr iaith fain* ('the thin language'/ English) to '*iaith y nefoedd*' ('the language of heaven'/Welsh).' At its most basic, a language is merely a tool for communication, so why does it mean so much to people?

You can't change your first language. It's the language a parent might have said 'there there' to you when you were poorly as a kid ('*dere di*' in Welsh); it's the language you instinctively swear in when you stub your toe;[307] it's the language you might slip into by mistake when you're tired or if you've been woken at 2am by the secret police who are shining torches in your face. I've lived in England for eight years and, as you can imagine, the occasions I meet a Welsh speaker in London cause my heart to skip a beat and put an immediate spring in my step. I can slip back into who I really am. If this person happens to speak with one of my four favourite Welsh accents (1. Carmarthenshire

---

307 I once had a girlfriend whose radiator had broken and was turned on permanently. The bed was pushed up against it and, as the brave boyfriend, it was my job to sleep next to it. I would wake up and exclaim '*IESU MAWR!*' ('Big Jesus!') every couple of hours during the night as I burned my back on it.

[rural]; 2. Carmarthenshire [urban]; 3. North Pembrokeshire; 4. Swansea Valley), then I may as well have taken Prozac.

If I meet someone and they speak Welsh, I instinctively assume, 'Oh, they'll be alright.' It is paramount that in this chapter I don't make Welsh sound like a secret handshake or the entry requirement to an exclusive club; it's a modern European language that people use to swear at traffic, write passive-aggressive notes to pin to the fridge and talk about the telly, like any other. I have also been proven wrong by all of the Welsh speakers I know who aren't 'all right'.[308] But that feeling of bonding with other Welsh speakers I described comes from being a small minority within a small minority. If I meet a Welsh person on holiday, I know there are hundreds of things we can talk about – how BBC Wales go on about Dylan Thomas a bit too much, the lack of toilets on the A470, the way Port Talbot smells better than it used to – but if that person is a Welsh speaker we can double those things and do it in a language that is part of our soul.

> I now have an image of you meeting a Welsh speaker on a beach in Lanzarote and immediately getting off with them for ages. *JR*

Welsh is spoken by about 560,000 people in Wales. That's just under 20 per cent of the population, although proportionally most of these speakers live in the north and west of the country where it's likely you'll hear Welsh spoken in the street. If you count people like me and other friends of mine who have moved away, it's estimated to be around 700,000 people worldwide. Bearing in mind that around 2,000 of the world's 6,500 languages are

---

308 Having gone to a Welsh school, I can admit to having had wedgies through the medium of Welsh, and had my trousers and pants pulled down on a minibus on the way to play another school at cricket through the medium of Welsh. Although I'm over it now, at the time I did not think the perpetrators were 'all right'. I thought they were complete coins.

spoken by fewer than a thousand speakers, and about half have fewer than 3,000 speakers, in global terms we're actually a major player (Sheffield Utd to Mandarin's Real Madrid). This was recognised by NASA, because in 1977 Welsh was one of the 55 languages included on the Voyager Golden Record, part of the NASA *Voyager* programme launched that year and chosen to be representative of earth. The greetings were unique to each language, and NASA wisely included Welsh on the off chance that alien life forms originated in Llanfihangel-ar-Arth.

I was educated in Welsh, and spoke Welsh at home. It is a huge part of my identity. Like Russian, French, Spanish or Arabic, Welsh has masculine and feminine words, and so I instinctively think of cats and spoons as feminine, and doors and maps as masculine. However, the majority of my career has been in English, and as long as you ignore my performance at Betabet™ I am perfectly happy and comfortable in both languages.[309] It is a happy accident of birth that I grew up in a family where Welsh was the language of the household, in an area where this was very common. However, if this wasn't the case for you I would encourage anyone and everyone to learn it. If chatting to me, Rhys Ifans, Ioan Gruffydd, the Super Furry Animals, Lloyd George,[310] Richard Burton,[311] Cerys Matthews, Russell Grant, *The One Show*'s Alex

---

309 Just a quick, slightly serious word on bilingualism. Multi-lingualism is the global norm – more than half of the world's population speak more than one language (I've seen figures claiming it's as high as 65 per cent). It's very difficult to learn a language, of course it is, but Switzerland has four national languages, and Man Utd striker Romelu Lukaku can speak six. My dad grew up on the same street as a man who had severe learning difficulties, and yet he was bilingual in both Welsh and English. Bilingualism is shown to stave off dementia and help with your cognitive abilities. (Again, my performance on Betabet™ is not the best advert for this. Imagine how I would have done if I were monolingual.) As I said above, you can't change your first language, but you can learn other ones, and in the same way I have never met any multi-instrumentalists who regret learning one of their instruments, I have never met any multilinguists who don't see the value in learning more than one language.

[JR] Oui oui! Très bien!

310 RIP.

311 RIP.

Jones and Thomas Jefferson[312] wasn't enough of an encouragement, hopefully by the end of this chapter you'll be watching *Pobl Y Cwm* with subtitles as part of your immersion-learning techniques.

My grandmother couldn't speak a huge amount of English, and as she got older and her world became inevitably smaller, she forgot most of the English she knew. I only mention this because when Welsh is criticised (frustratingly it's a hugely emotive subject in Wales, and sadly a large proportion of the criticism comes from non-Welsh-speaking Welsh people), it is either criticised for being an odd hobby or an affectation, or looked down upon as an inferior language to English. But my grandmother lived a fulfilling life in Welsh: she worked in Welsh, loved in Welsh and grieved in Welsh. She wasn't making a political point about British imperialism or rule from Westminster or the outlawing of the use of Welsh in Court after the 1536 Act of Union, which is what some critics of Welsh assume. Put simply, it was as natural to her as turning the video off at the plug every night or boiling carrots for 55 minutes on a Sunday. I am occasionally jealous of how simple her life must have been, until I remember that she had never seen *The Wire* or listened to The Smiths and I am glad that I am fully bilingual. I also feel sorry for people who don't understand the Super Furry Animals or the Gorky's when they sing in Welsh. Because that's the best bit. Two cultures for the price of one.

Right, I'm going to learn Welsh!   JR

Seeing it as 'two for the price of one' is essential to the language's future. If you have ever spent any time in Wales, you will have noticed that the shops aimed at tourists are full of tea towels that say things

---

312 It's thought that the third President of the United States and principal author of the Declaration of American Independence had some understanding of Welsh because his family apparently originated from Snowdonia in North Wales, and Welsh books were found in his library after he died. Jefferson was a linguaphile who once claimed that he'd learned Spanish on the course of a 19-day voyage to France using a dictionary and a copy of *Don Quixote*, although his friend John Quincy Adams expressed scepticism at this.

like 'Welsh: Europe's Oldest Language'. It's not really true (all languages develop; it's like saying, 'My family is older than yours') and, in my opinion, it's not very helpful. Surely you should be emphasising some of the great modern Welsh-language music that's being made, rather than making it sound like a subject you'd study at Oxbridge as part of an archaeology degree?[313]

> OK, I gave it a bloody good go, but it looks genuinely impossible and there's a documentary on Channel 4 about how HMRC catch tax dodgers.

There are great Welsh-language bands, there are great Welsh rap groups, just like there are French rap groups and heavy metal bands from Finland. That said, as you can imagine, there's some utter, hideous doggerel, but this is a question of proportion. There is some terrible television made in England, but you have 100+ channels and Netflix to choose from, so you will always find something you like. When you only have 500,000 people making television or comedy or music and there is only one TV station and one radio station (that has to please ALL of the people ALL of the time), the proportion of good stuff is going to be similar but in real terms there will be less of it – this is why bands like the Super Furry Animals mean so much to Welsh people. If John had to switch languages to enjoy anything that hadn't been made in Bristol, I'm sure he'd have very strong feelings towards Massive Attack, Portishead and Tony Robinson.

> That's a very good way of putting it. I'd be obsessed with Charlie from *Casualty*; he'd be some kind of trailblazer, part of who I am . . . more so . . . I'd probably even go easier on Banksy, and Bristol City fans. But I'd still *hate* slavery.

---

313 Not that there's anything wrong with an archaeology degree – some of my best friends are archaeologists.

With this in mind I would like to talk about the band Datblygu. Datblygu, one of my favourite bands of all time, sang entirely in Welsh and are one of the best reasons I can think of to learn the language. They split up in 1995, meaning I never got to see them live (until they reformed in 2012), but they are second only to the Gorky's in my affections. To use a lazy comparison, the music sounds a bit like The Fall, but lyrically the band's lead singer David R. Edwards changed my life – a combination of The Smiths'-period Morrissey, Leonard Cohen, Ian Curtis, Bob Dylan and Gil Scott Heron, but with a few bottles of wine clinking in a Co-op carrier bag and 120 fags stuffed into his coat pockets.

YES PLEASE! *JR*

When a language is only spoken by half a million people, you very quickly get to know everyone, and this can often feel claustrophobic. As a generally nice bunch who will bump into each other at some point,[314] this makes genuine radicals like Dave (he is known by all Welsh music fans simply as 'Dave') even braver than their English or American counterparts. Dave had one radio station to play his records, and one music programme on S4C to show his videos.[315] This didn't stop him from criticising the shows, the producers, the people who ran gigs for being narrow-minded, the record labels for being unimaginative, and the punters who turned up at the gigs for treating the shows as an excuse to try to get off with someone rather than listen to the music. I absolutely loved it, and lapped it up because he was saying things I agreed with but was too frightened or inarticulate to say myself. He ranted about how boring pop culture was, how interesting

---

314 For example, the Eisteddfod is the largest poetry festival in Europe, and everyone goes. My friend Esyllt Sears described walking round the Eisteddfod as 'ex-boyfriend bingo'.
315 Which he got banned from after he used a live show to express his disdain at the privatisation of British Telecom.

Karl Marx was, unambitious bands, teachers he'd hated, being unemployed, Margaret Thatcher, the terrible items on a thrice-weekly S4C magazine show called *Hel Straeon*, his mental health; he gave both barrels to Plaid Cymru, harpists, and untrustworthy people whose jeans are too tidy. He was Charles Bukowski with a cheap guitar, he was William Burroughs with an Aberteifi accent.

> He was Fugazi in a Florist, Rage Against the Machine in a Rotary Club, Public Enemy in a Public Library...

To illustrate my point about bumping into people, my dad was very ill a few years ago and ended up on the same hospital ward as Dave, whom I got to know. Looking back, I should really have spent more time feeding Dad grapes but this was too good an opportunity to miss, and I used these hospital visits to essentially conduct long interviews with one of my favourite musicians. Looking back, it's a candidate for John's Shame Well. I was in my 30s and should have known better – Dave was poorly himself, but he was very gracious as I asked him to discuss the recording process behind every one of his songs and then tell me his life story, which I already knew because I had read his autobiography. During Datblygu's heyday my dad was a quantity surveyor with three young children, and was understandably out of touch with the Welsh-language post-punk scene. That said, Dad became as impressed with Dave as I was, one of the things he was most taken with was the DIY punk ethic. I have very fond memories of Dad marvelling at Dave providing guest vocals for another band by singing them from the hospital ward's communal payphone.

Datblygu's music was uncompromising, and Dave's lyrics were funny, wise, sarcastic, political and challenging. Groupthink (when a group of people have their principles unchallenged and thus make poor decisions) is a danger with any small scene that has limited gigs and a limited audience, but he stood alone and his records sound as good today as they did in 1988. He drank too much and he was sad a lot of the time and he was frustrated at living in a small country with all of Wales's failings, but he wrote in Welsh because he thought in Welsh. I loved him for having international ambitions but staying true to his roots. They were one of the first Welsh-language bands to perform regularly in other parts of the UK and Europe, and because of the patronage John Peel gave them (they recorded five Peel sessions between 1987 and 1993, and appeared on Channel 4's *The Tube*) they tended to go down better in Essex than in Aberystwyth. They used to get bottled at gigs in Wales for saying things that no one wanted to hear,[316] but without the size of a big country like America or England to absorb you, disciples like myself applauded them for being so courageous. Fifty thousand people bought albums by The Fall, and Manchester is a big enough place to hide in. When you are a Welsh-language post-punk band and you live in Aberteifi, eventually you are going to bump into some of the people you've written lyrics about in Tesco. I would like everyone to have Dave's imagination, wit and principles, but that is impossible. It would go some way if you listened to a track, though, because it is my Welsh-language experience in a nutshell. People who seek to place Welsh as a traditional hobby on a tea towel forget that a language is a living thing. You can do anything you want with language, and Welsh is a language that is capable of great things. There's not a huge number of us who speak it, but if you master it, I will love you forever.

A SIMPLE GUIDE FOR BEGINNERS

Welsh is a phonetic language, so the spelling is pretty easy. It has 29 letters to English's 26, and two extra vowels, not that you'd believe it

---

316 His song '*Can I Gymry*' ('Song for the Welsh') about the hypocrisy of the nepotistic Welsh middle classes is one of my favourite songs ever, and I must have listened to it every week for 20 years.

from reading articles by Rod Liddle and Jeremy Clarkson, who find it hilarious to claim we don't have any. To put this to bed, Ch, Dd, Ff, Ng, Ll, Ph, Rh and Th are letters in their own right with their own sounds, but I accept that as an English speaker all those double Ls and Ds can look a bit weird. If you'd like to learn, I would recommend the Say Something in Welsh app, which Isy loves, and the Welsh version of Duolingo, which has been downloaded over a million times. I'm not a Welsh teacher so I won't get into the mechanics of the language, but below I have included a few of my favourite words, sayings and phrases.

WORDS

The cliché is that the Inuit have lots of words for 'snow'. Well, in Welsh there are 27 words for 'rain', including the incredible *'mae hi'n bwrw hen wragedd a ffyn'* ('it's raining old women and sticks'), which means 'absolutely pissing it down'. Honourable mentions go to some of our words for 'drizzle' – *'glaw man'* ('small rain') and *'gwlithlaw'* ('dewrain' – I suppose 'rain that feels a bit like dew'.)

Man a man a mwnci: It means 'may as well' – it directly translates as 'may as well, monkey'. I don't know why.

Pili pala: It means 'butterfly', and it reminds me of the way a butterfly's wings might sound. It was the word I used growing up, but if the slightly onomatopoeic *'pili pala'* doesn't float your boat, you could always use the slightly weirder *'iar fach yr haf'* ('little chicken of the summer').

Cwtsh: I have a slightly uneasy relationship with this word, because it's used on an awful lot of tourist tat. It's one of those words that non-Welsh-speaking Welsh people use as much as the Welsh speakers,[317]

---

317 [JR] I have a very similar relationship to the Bristolian term 'gurt lush'. A phrase I have seen on T-shirts, mugs, Babygros, appropriated by sandwich shops, hairdressers and pubs, and yet a phrase I've never heard spoken without knowing irony by anyone, ever.

and can mean a variety of things. It means 'to hug or cuddle' ('give me a cwtch'), it means to shift up or to sit closely to someone ('cwtch up a bit and I'll sit next to you'), and it's also the word I'd use for that cupboard under the stairs where you keep the hoover and mop – '*cwtsh dan staer*' ('cuddle under the stairs'). It was a perfectly normal word I never thought about until it became the Welsh version of those 'Keep Calm and Carry On' posters, and ended up on horrendous mugs that say things like 'English People Cuddle, But Only the Welsh Cwtch!'. As you can see, it doesn't have a codified spelling, which is quite fitting for a word that can mean recess, cupboard, kennel and cuddle.[318] Welsh doesn't have homonyms (two or more words that have exactly the same spelling or pronunciation but different meanings and origins) like English does, apart from this one.

Cont-y-mor: Jellyfish, and literally translates as 'sea cunt', or 'cunt that lives in the sea'. It has recently been changed to '*sgelfren for*' (sea skater), which is slightly more radio-friendly.

Sgrech y coed: A jay; literally translates as 'scream of the trees'.

Mochyn daear: Badger; literal translation: 'earth pig'.

Eirin gwlanog: Peach; literally translates as 'woolly plum'.

Moron: Carrot.

Sianiflewog: A caterpillar; literal translation: 'furry Jane'.

There are some people who delight in trying to make Welsh sound silly, but they don't understand how language works. When I see the word '*mochyn daear*', I don't think of 'an earth pig', I think of a badger, in the same way French people don't think of potatoes as 'apples from the earth' (*pommes de terre*), but as potatoes. When I see a caterpillar,

---

318 In Welsh it would be spelled 'cwtsh', but in English it tends to be spelled 'cwtch', which if you're following the Welsh rules of pronunciation, makes it sound totally different.

I think of a '*sianiflewog*', not a 'furry Jane'. Although when an English person is referred to as a 'moron', I, without fail, think: 'Why is that person being called a carrot?'

BORROWED WORDS

One of the great strengths of English is that it's the ultimate mongrel language and will borrow from everyone. There are the obvious examples that anyone could name ('déjà vu' or 'rendezvous' from French, for instance), but if you dig a little deeper the origin of some English words might surprise you. 'Mosquito' is Spanish for 'little fly', the Greeks gave us the term 'hoi polloi' and 'tattoo' is a Polynesian word.

The reason I mention this is that Welsh is often criticised by pillocks on Twitter for 'stealing' words from English. (I'll hold my hand up. We don't have a good word for 'fibreglass', I'm sorry.) 'Tacsi' is the obvious one that winds up a lot of idiots.[319] For the good of my mental health, I have stopped searching for the word 'tacsi' on Twitter so that I can point out it's 'taxi' in Spanish and Italian, 'táxi' in Portuguese, 'taksi' in Turkish, 'такси' in Russian, which I feel is letting down the Welsh language but shows growth for me as an individual. Having met many of the potential readers of this book at gigs John and I have done, I am certain the people who find 'tacsi' so offensive haven't picked up this

---

319 Having grown up in Wales and lived in anglicised Cardiff for ten years, I am aware that some people think Welsh speakers have a chip on our shoulder. In 1847, there was a government report into the state of education in Wales which concluded that Welsh was a 'vast drawback to Wales, and a manifold barrier to the moral progress and commercial prosperity of the country', and that the Welsh people were ignorant, lazy and immoral. Welsh was blamed for this. For hundreds of years Welsh was banned from courts of law, you couldn't be educated in Welsh, and English was the only language of public office. Try as I might I cannot blame John or any modern person for this, but its effect was pernicious. It meant that generations of native Welsh speakers in areas that are now heavily anglicised (particularly industrial south Wales) didn't pass on the language, for fear of holding their children back. These attitudes can take years, sometimes generations, to change. I have decided to include this as a footnote because my remit when writing this book was to keep it light. But it's the reason I can occasionally be touchy when I tweet in Welsh and get the inevitable response, 'I think the cat has stepped on your keyboard, Elis.'

book in Waterstones. But on the off chance, here are a few examples to show that 'word stealing' works both ways. The following are Welsh words that have been adopted by English:

Bard: From the Welsh word 'bardd', which means 'poet'.

Dad: From 'tad', the Welsh word for 'father'. In terms of Welsh words that have been borrowed by English, this is our 'Wonderwall', our 'Bohemian Rhapsody'.

Corgi: In Welsh it basically means 'little dog'.

Apparently 'penguin' comes from Welsh. Difficult to find proof for this, but it makes sense as 'pen gwyn' (pronounced the same) means 'white head'.

IDIOMS AND SAYINGS

This, in my opinion, is where Welsh really shines. It often doesn't occur to native Welsh speakers that these idioms are strange until they are translated – I remember a lesson in primary school where this was pointed out to us and it blew my mind. That's one of the joys of bilingualism – it imparts a different way of thinking without you realising it and allows you to frame the world in a different way. Welsh idioms reflect our agricultural past, and also our sense of humour:

Rhuthro gyda'i wynt yn ei ddwrn: This means 'to rush', though it literally translates as 'rushing with his breath in his fist'.

See picture section. YOU KNOW WHAT I'M TALKING ABOUT! *JR*

Mae'n draed moch arna fi: 'I've made a mess', or 'I'm in a mess because of something I've done'. Literal translation: 'There are pigs feet on me.'

A ddwg ŵy a ddwy fwy: A leopard never changes his spots. Literal translation: 'He who steals an egg will steal more.'

Rhoi'r ffidil yn y tô: To throw in the towel. Literal translation: 'Put the fiddle in the roof.'

Ar y gweill: In progress. Literal translation: 'On the knitting needles.'

Perth hyd fogel, perth ddiogel: 'A hedge up to the navel is a safe hedge.' If this is a maxim, I don't understand it. As far as I'm aware it's just a snappy way to discuss hedge construction.

Paid a chodi pais ar ol piso: It means 'no use crying over spilt milk'; its literal translation is 'don't lift your petticoat after you've had a piss.'

Ma croen fy nhin ar fy nhalcen: This means 'I am annoyed'; it literally translates as 'I've got my bum skin on my face.'

Since writing this chapter I have started to learn French. It's been a few months now, so I am under no illusion as to how difficult learning a new language is. As I said above, if you stick at it, Welsh speakers will *love* you. We LOVE it. It's the people who attack the language who are the ones who put our bum skin on our face. So give learning Welsh a go. You having nothing to lose! Diolch am ddarllen![320]

Not only did I adore this chapter, but it made me feel a very deep sense of pride for Elis and what he himself has done for the Welsh language. What he's far too modest to mention is that the Welsh language stand-up shows he wrote and recorded, which he agonised over, took round the country, performed in countless backrooms, pubs and community centres to write and perfect, which he didn't have to do and which I tease him about, well, those shows

---

320 Thank you for reading!

now place him right among the heroes he talks about here. In the same way the Gorky's or Datblygu gave him a sense of pride, purpose and connection to his language and culture, one that some idiots dismiss as dead, or cute, or irrelevant, well, he's rejuvenated it for the next generation of Welsh speakers. I know from speaking to Welsh comics just how much the work Elis has done has reinvigorated, if not created, an entire scene. I'm incredibly proud of him, and I would encourage everyone to root out the recordings of the two shows he's done and watch them with the subtitles on, because you get to see a language alive and evolving and made available to a totally new audience by someone who I'm sure will be an inspiration cited by the next generation of Welsh-speaking artists.

X:

~~XFM~~ Radio X

London's Leicester Square is one of the world's most popular tourist destinations, and, taking time for a walk around, it's easy to understand why. Where else can visiting groups from Europe, America and the Far East witness the majesty of four cinemas, an All Bar One and not one, but three Bella Italias? Gazing onto the uninterrupted run of Burger King, Pizza Hut and Chiquito, one is treated to a view of some of the UK's best examples of mid-2010s architecture. No surprise, then, that Leicester Square saw off bids from Chicago, Milan and Cape Town to host its jewel in the crown, a brand new TGI Fridays, one of only 900 of its kind.

If you choose your spot carefully, the nearby Charing Cross Road provides a view of three separate Pret a Mangers: a small one, a medium-sized one and another medium-sized one. Arrive early and you might be lucky enough to spot David Mellor rushing between them in an attempt to secure a bulk discount. If he spots a member of staff who doesn't know him, he will pose as a wealthy catering mogul looking to source two dozen almond croissants at cost price. He will then move to the next outlet in an attempt to play them off against each other before driving down the quantities for which the discount applies. He's yet to have any success, but I don't think that's what it's about for Mellor. He misses the cut and thrust of frontline politics, and this bartering for baked goods gives him the adrenaline rush once provided by top-level meetings with Hurd, Currie, Lamont, et al.

But where is this foul-mouthed fare heading with his sweet treats and four-pack of lattes? He's heading to none other than Global Radio HQ. And were we to follow him through reception, up the stairs and into the offices of Classic FM, not only would we receive one of the verbal bollockings he's renowned for, but we'd come face to face, or should I say, face to office, with the world centre of commercial digital indie radio: for there, dear friend, you will find the offices of Radio X.[321] The office is separated from Classic FM by a matter of feet and a small hub of desks used for a branch of the company I don't understand, emblazoned with posters saying things like 'Brandalism', 'Visualogy' and 'Personackaging'.

Aspiring indie musicians dream of one day coming here, but only a selected few have ever gained access. One half of Dodgy tried to tunnel in prior to their 2007 reunion and, in 2005, a Stroke was found hiding in the kitchen cupboard next to the dishwasher tablets and herbal teas. All were escorted from the building. That said, some indie legends are allowed special treatment. The Gallagher brothers keep two small en suite studio flats here that they can access 24/5, 313.[322] Though compact, these rooms are more than sufficient should Noel or Liam decide to drop by, equipped as they are with a Beck's beer branded fridge

321 Specific address for gifts, freebies and PizzaExpress Soho 69 cards:

Elis James and John Robins, Radio X, 30 Leicester Square, London, WC2H 7LA.

322 Wednesdays the rooms must be vacated for cleaning between 11am and 3pm, and sometimes Liam can be seen killing time in the nearby Costa as he waits to be let back in. Access on the weekend is possible but cannot be guaranteed without prior arrangement and a special fob.

full of Beck's, a state-of-the-art combined cagoule rack and steam cleaner and themed editions of Monopoly[323] and Cluedo.[324]

If you've ever been to an office before, you'd better be prepared to throw your expectations of Radio X HQ in the bin. It is a far cry from the row upon row of tired desks and drab filing cabinets that a friend and former colleague reliably informs me create a 'soul-destroying and monotonous atmosphere' in Absolute Radio HQ.[325] No, this is Radio X and we do things the Radio X way. Desks? OUT! Cupboards? HI-YA![326] I'm talking vibe hubs, listening pods, virtual foosball and, as of November 2017, 32 USB charging ports per employee. The walls are adorned with signed guitars,[327] commemorative three-quarter-length shorts and ten framed copies of *(What's the Story) Morning Glory?* Sat on beanbags, space hoppers and a throne,[328] a crack team of indie aficionados track the latest trends, uncover the newest bands and create click-worthy memes about topics such as Fridays, Ten Times Greenday Totally Nailed It and Mondays.

During weekdays the offices are a hub of activity: who's that legend hunched over his iPod? It's none other than Chris Moyles, listening to his archive of American Radio Jingles 1972–4 and scouring MySpace's top-rated band pages to hunt out fresh angles for his breakfast show. Who's that Scottish man on the phone to an A-list celeb? Why, it's the equally handsome and threatening Gordon Smart, as comfortable schmoozing with 'It Girls' at the Brit Awards as he is dispensing street justice in a Glasgow alleyway. And who's that beautiful blonde woman playing with her nephew? That's the lovely Pippa with boyfriend

323 *Despicable Me*, Liam.

324 *Game Of Thrones*, Noel.

325 Note to self: remember to thank Dave in the Acknowledgements.

326 As in the karate-chop sound effect. I'm not saying 'Hello' to a cupboard.

327 4 x Kelly Jones, 2 x Noel Gallagher, 1 x unreadable (perhaps Lenny Kravitz).

328 Johnny Vaughan.

Toby Tarrant. I, for one, wish them well. If it works out, great! And if it doesn't, well, though high-profile break-ups with people in your industry can be a fucking nightmare, they do have their upsides.[329]

At one end of the room you'll find the head honcho Matt Deverson. He's known as 'Devvo' around the office. I, however, christened him 'Devvers'; it was a canny power play to both set me apart from the pack and make sure I stood out when it came to contract renegotiations. He splits his time between manoeuvring the latest indie exclusives over the phone and gazing out of the window onto Leicester Square and the statue that stands in the middle of his hero, William Shakespeare. From an early age, Devvers dreamed of being a playwright, and after finishing university he spent four years writing his masterpiece *Hard Luck Inc*, set in the heady world of American real estate. However, towards completion of the project a friend showed him a DVD of *Glengarry Glen Ross*. Realising the plot was almost identical to his play, Devvers threw the script into a stream and never wrote again. But Broadway's loss is very much radio's gain. And the role of indie kingmaker is one he was born to play. Visitors to Radio X can often hear him on the phone giving both barrels to wannabes and has-beens alike: 'If Alien Ant Farm want a comeback they'll have to come to me on their knees! THEIR KNEES!'; 'I don't care if it's two f**king thirty in the f**king morning, tell them to open the f**king Leon. Why?! Because if Noel f**king Gallagher wants baked f**king fries then Noel f**king Gallagher gets baked f**king fries!'

At the other end from Devvers's desk there is a kitchen equipped with instant boiling and chilled water taps. It's a luxury only afforded to the most elite radio stations – I'm reliably

---

329 See picture section.

informed that the offices at Absolute Radio suffer constant damp from the endless boiling of Tesco Value kettles. And if you listen closely to Dave Berry or later Christian O'Connell shows, the initial stages of respiratory problems are all too plain to hear.

Next to the kitchen, you will find a soft play area installed as per Vernon Kay's contract. Vernon used to like nothing more than thrashing around the 8ft × 10ft cushioned zone when the frustrations of modern life got too much. He would even come down during advert breaks to vent. An added bonus to the padded walls was a decent level of soundproofing, so Vernon was free to shout and scream to his heart's content, though older members of staff were careful never to teach him adult swear words lest they come out on air. Vernon was an innocent soul, and I remember him fondly, bouncing around bawling 'Bums! Willies! Big bums!' after Tess had to cancel their trip to Chessington World of Adventures.

However, sit with me a while, here among the hubbub. Let us watch as Friday afternoon rolls around. Complimentary cakes and doughnuts become crumbs and empty boxes, coats are grabbed, earphones put in, and plans to meet in All Bar One come to fruition. As Devvers (ever the last to leave, patrolling the corridors to ward off infiltration by down-on-their-luck 90s indie bands) picks up his briefcase and knuckledusters, the hub of UK commercial digital indie will fall silent. In less than five minutes the automatic lights will dim, then turn off.[330] Silence. Those lights won't flicker into action again until some 14 hours later. That is, unless Classic FM's John Suchet has fallen asleep among the shredded remains of confidential waste paper kept in a big bin and has roused, as happens at least once a month, to

---

330 How's life in the dark ages (literally) of the light switch treating you, Dave?!

find himself disorientated.[331] And who is it that will cause those automated movement sensors to fire on the state-of-the-art LED strip lights? Why, it's none other than I, John Robins.

Arriving between 11am and 11.14am, I will have built up a healthy glow from 'Pounding the P' between Marylebone and Leicester Square[332] or Oxford Circus and Leicester Square.[333] This intense period of exposure to the rest of the human race, many of whom are not sure of what direction they are going, basic pavement etiquette or, at times, even how to walk, means my first few minutes will be used to simply breathe, close my eyes and bathe in the silence of a deserted office. I might imagine how ideal a hideaway Radio X HQ would be if some kind of deadly virus or *The Day of the Triffids*-style attack threatened humankind,[334] or simply enjoy the knowledge that it provides key holders with a central London toilet/crying nook 24/7, 365.[335] I will then arrange my brunch, a vegan spread put together from usually no fewer than two of the nearby Prets[336] and coffee from

---

331 Initially, Global Radio top brass suspected that Suchet's night-time sessions among the shreds were a smokescreen for him to attempt to piece together copies of Myleene Klass's contract to find out how much she was being paid. But after a meeting behind closed doors, executives were satisfied that he was merely attracted to the warm atmosphere that allowed him to imagine he was hibernating.

332 Personal best 31:13.

333 Personal best 10:21.

334 That said, its central location would mean it was NOT an ideal place to hide out during a nuclear attack. Quite the opposite. Were a nuclear power to want to attack the West, odds on their first target would be to destroy Britain's most recognisable symbol of freedom and democracy: commercial digital indie radio.

335 Suck it, Gallaghers! No need to call ahead for this legend!

336 The refusal of Pret to house all vegan options in any one store is a constant annoyance. Even a detour to Veggie Pret once left me unable to source an Acai & Almond Butter Breakfast Bowl, which I eventually found in the 39 Coventry Street branch, the smallest Pret London has. It's a frustratingly inconsistent policy, the equivalent of being able to source a double duvet in a Sainsbury's Local but not in their Crayford Megastore (a supermarket that never fails to captivate me with its range and size).

Nero.[337] As I chomp on my breakfast bowl and kale crisps[338] I will read through the week's communications, diligently prepared for me by Intern Joe or Producer Vin. Vin will arrive around 11.45am, giving him plenty of time to prepare any last-minute clips, stings or quick-fire quizzes. Then, between 12.14pm and 12.34pm the unmistakable sound of hurried Adidas Sambas can be heard, accompanied by panting and the opening strains of 'Sorry I'm late,' all delivered in the breathless Carmarthen drawl you've come to know and love. Yes, it's none other than Elis James, arriving at Elis o'clock, EST.[339]

In any partnership, it's important to spread the load evenly so that no one person feels they're taking on more than their fair share of work. The death knell of any duo is when the rot of passive–aggression sets in, with scores being settled publicly in inappropriate ways. And so it is that I prepare humblebrags, shame wells, select made-up games, open our post, read 40 pages of E-Mails, select which are suitable for the live show, the podcast intro, brainstorm potential text-ins/features and discuss notes with Vin, while Elis settles down to eat sushi, browse the papers and tell anecdotes about YouTube videos. It just works.

Come 12:56pm we are both sat in the studio and ready to begin the weekly tussle of logging in to various software programmes, the security of which would rival Fort Knox. Rumour has it that in 2001 Shirley Manson of Garbage gained access to the playlist, enabling her to sneak excerpts from comeback album *Beautiful Garbage* into news reports and adverts for Dell computers. Ever since, access to Radio X systems has only been possible via a

---

337 Though I lose precious minutes to extra queuing, my boycott of Pret a Manger coffee will remain in place until they introduce a stampable loyalty card.

338 At £1.50quid for 12.5g, one of the earth's most expensive products.

339 Elis Standard Time (BST+1).

series of passwords and usernames that are updated, erased and reset on a bi-weekly basis, thus ensuring that each DJ is thoroughly on their toes in the seconds before broadcasting. Once access is gained, we prepare to broadcast. Each of us has our own routine. I will perform brief vocal warm-ups, tongue twisters and sip water whereas Elis will open a pot of mango, slip a segment in his mouth and spill some coffee before finding time to pop in another slice of mango five seconds before the mics go live. And then . . . well, that side of things you know. To my left, Port Talbot's sixth-highest-grossing comedian of 2012, Mr Elis James, and, to *your* left, commercial digital indie radio of the highest calibre.

Y:

Year, Geordie Financial

Occasionally, a lost piece of music or art will enter the public consciousness in a way it never would have had it been released in a proper, orthodox way. The Beach Boys' great lost album, *Smile*, has tantalised critics and fans for half a century, and one can only imagine how Stanley Kubrick would have changed cinema if he'd finished his biopic of Napoleon. In a surprise to both its creator and all those who were forced to hear it, Geordie Financial Year, the opening line I used at all my comedy gigs from 2005–7, has now entered this pantheon. As a feature on the Radio X show I read extracts from the gig diaries I kept faithfully between 2005–8, and the Geordie Financial Year routine became an enigma among our listeners, as it featured so heavily during those early years. In this chapter, I would like to explain the process behind writing it.

2005 was a year in flux. Whether you were a tech pioneer taking 'selfies' of yourself in the queue to see *The 40-Year-Old Virgin* or were still recovering from Janet Jackson's wardrobe malfunction during the previous year's Superbowl, it was a tumultuous time to be taking your first, tentative steps into the world of comedy. Most comedians agree that your opening line can be one of the most difficult things to write – it needs to introduce the comedian to a potentially hostile crowd, assert the comedian's status, reassure the naysayers that the comedian knows what they're doing, and be funny, all in the space of a sentence. With this as my brief, I began writing Geordie Financial Year (GFY).

Early stand-up gigs can be hugely unpredictable for the performer, so I felt it was imperative to attempt broad humour. New comedians are looking to make as many people as they can laugh as much as possible, and so finding a comedic subject that was accessible but untapped was my ambition. Unfortunately, the only things I really know about are football (too laddy), the Gorky's (too niche) and pre-war Welsh Communists (too irrelevant). Thankfully, I had one thing up my sleeve – as someone who worked in admin at the time, I knew the financial year began in April. Even if it doesn't really apply to you (people on PAYE, babies) . . .

And, it would seem, the overwhelming majority of the self-employed. I received fewer RSVPs for my 2017–18 end-of-tax-year party than ever before. It's a sad state of affairs when people know so little about their tax affairs that they're not even tempted by an invite to watch the countdown on a big screen with a few beers and Martin Lewis's Twitter feed on refresh.

JR

almost everyone has heard of the financial year, filling me with confidence that jokes about such a relatable topic could be a hit. But now

I was presented with a new problem[340] – how would I frame my reference to the financial year beginning in April? Naturally of course, by using a regional accent.

I am unable to do impressions of specific people, but being able to effortlessly impersonate all the regional accents of Great Britain is one of my great gifts.[341] It's the comedic equivalent of an eye for goal, or if you're a soap actor, the ability to cry on cue 30 times as you travel behind the hearse containing the coffin of your criminal son on Christmas Day. So I wrote a routine about the financial year but decided to use it as a showcase for my regional-accent abilities. I weighed up my options. After immediately dismissing Northern Irish (having read about the Good Friday Agreement, I didn't want to become bogged down in Sectarianism), another Welsh one (too confusing as I reverted back to my own voice), Cockney (too menacing) and Glaswegian (see Cockney), I settled on Geordie, or to be more accurate, South Shields. As I tried it round the house, it felt as comfortable as wearing old slippers. It was decided. The only thing left to do was write some killer lines.

At this point in my career, the vast majority of my gigs were in Cardiff or Bristol. I had ventured as far north as Gloucester and as far south as Plymouth but I was still a complete unknown, and thus I had no opportunity to work much further afield. I decided I would write a routine known in the trade as a 'gig story' – put simply, I would recount something that had happened to me at a previous gig, in a charming,

---

340 The inherent, unavoidable topicality of using the beginning of the financial year as a comedic reference may interest some of you. There's no sugarcoating this – as a joke it worked best in April. It was fine during May, but quite odd by June or July (in the way making jokes about Christmas would be odd in February). By the autumn, I was able to frame it as a 'slightly odd thing that had happened to me in Newcastle once', and by January I would use my admin background to imply it was the highlight of my year, enabling me to perform the routine with added vigour (by March, near hysteria). Unable to find a better opening line during my three years as an open-mic comedian, I got round the problem of the joke not working in June and July by taking those months off.

341 Apart from (south) Pembrokeshire, curiously, the county in which I was born.

personable way that suggested I was a normal bloke holding court at the bar. Oddly, this story needed to be entirely fabricated, because at this point nothing interesting had happened to me at a gig apart from getting a parking ticket in Torquay. After giving it some thought, chewing on a pen for ages and even borrowing a friend's thesaurus to aid the writing process, I felt I had written a solid routine. This is how GFY played out when I performed it regularly at the Chapter Arts Centre in Cardiff in 2005:

1. I would walk on, shake hands with the compere, and then thank the crowd for being nice; this was an attempt to quell heckling with charm, and to persuade the audience to be pleasant with a little bit of positive affirmation.
2. I would ask if anyone worked in admin; this asserted my low status and humility. At amateur open-mic nights comics routinely talk about their day jobs, and I was keen for the audience to know I wasn't a millionaire banker having an early midlife crisis or a *Made in Chelsea*-type living off a trust fund.
3. I would point out the start of the financial year began in April. I would sell this fact as if it were something really exciting and interesting, when of course it isn't. Looking back at my diary entries from the time, I felt I was on a one-man mission to bring irony to Wales.

It was at this point the routine became intriguing. Having piqued the interest of the audience, I felt they were in the palm of my hand.

4. I would say, 'It wasn't like this in Newcastle!' (the first lie of the routine; it was almost ten years into my career before I gigged in Newcastle). But it was a performative device, and this falsehood had a purpose. Newcastle was geographically far enough from where I did most of my performing in 2005 that I thought it

implied an impressive demand for my talents. After all, if bookers from as far afield as the north-east were eager I played their gigs, I must have something to offer. Even though I was only performing at open-mic nights, it suggested a healthy balance of amateur shows and paid work, and reassured the audience they were in the safe hands of a semi-pro. These are the margins you are working with as an open-mic comedian. Small percentages count.

This was the point in the routine when my regional-accent showcase began, which was designed especially for any Hollywood producers who might be keeping it real at an open-mic stand-up night in Cardiff. I would play the role of 'aggrieved Geordie who doesn't know that April is the start of the financial year'. The aggrieved Geordie is angry I have told him this, and thus embarrassed him in front of his wife, who naturally expects him to know such things. I would play both 'aggrieved Geordie' and 'his passive wife who was trying to placate him', and I must admit this section was never formally written down.

> I have to say the beginnings of Geordie Financial Year are far more duplicitous than I could have dreamed. There was no Geordie! There was no financial year![342] It's the greatest conspiracy since Watergate!

I would enter a frame of mind I referred to as 'Space Riff', when – emboldened by the crowd – I would improvise as a Geordie. It was different every night, and although I had certain comedic beats to hit (the phrase 'Aaah didnea coom heeear to heeeear aboot fiiinaaaance'

---

342 [EJ] Yes there was, the one in question was 2005/6. *You* should have known this, of all people. It was the year of your first ever tax return!

[JR] I can even remember, ballpark, how much I made. I think it was a net profit from stand-up of £1,200quid. Imagine that! My £1200quid-a-year dream job! I'd have made a loss if it hadn't been for the four times I did warm-up for *Deal or No Deal*, which were some of the least pleasant gigs of my career.

always a particular strongpoint), I would let the ebb and flow of the crowd's reaction dictate the direction in which I took this imaginary Geordie and his wife. The 'Space Riff' state of mind that I could call upon was one of the things that set me apart from the other open-mic acts on the Cardiff scene, although I fear this ability has been lost. At the age of 25 I was able to enter Space Riff for periods of ten minutes at a time, but my blunted sword was brought to the nation's attention when John asked me to riff on the radio as he looked for a note he'd written and I just said the word 'pipes' over and over again.

5. Having now withdrawn from this self-imposed period of improvised Geordie reverie, I would hit them with the punchline. I would say, 'So naturally, I asked this Geordie what he did for a living as he didn't want to hear about finance,' making sure to soak up the incredible levels of expectation I had created in the room. When I felt the timing was right I would go back into character and say, 'I wooooark in huuuuman resources . . . and so does she,' in an exaggerated Geordie voice. I then used the inevitable round of applause as an opportunity to put the mic stand in the corner of the stage in that way I'd seen professional comedians do. Fin. I had made my mark. The audience was laughing. The gig was begun.

I am aware this routine might not make a huge amount of sense, 13 years on. In reality, I was keen to imply that I had performed in Newcastle because I thought it sounded impressive and it allowed me to showcase one of my stronger regional accents. I had never been to the city in my life – my entire knowledge of Newcastle came from watching *Byker Grove* as a child, Ant and Dec's performances on Saturday-night television and reading an unauthorised biography of Alan Shearer. John might have written an award-winning show[343] about the break-

---

343 [JR] See picture section.

up of a relationship, but as an inexperienced comic mind I felt unable to take on such big challenges. I felt comfortable pretending to be a Geordie who doesn't know the financial year begins in April. I stayed in this comfort zone for a very long time.

I performed GFY for over two years, and it was the only part of my initial set that lasted that long. When John and I went on tour, in 2016, we began the second half of the show with it, and time has not been kind. I remember GFY as one of my strongest routines, but in the way that Tamagotchis, *Fifty Shades of Grey*, George-W.-Bush-being-thick and Gollum impressions no longer work as comedic references, I can only assume that GFY was of its time. It burned very brightly, before fading away. I mourn its passing.

potato!

Z:

Zappa, Where to Start with

One of the questions I get asked more than anything else is 'Where do I start with Zappa?' – and, folks, it's a great question. His back catalogue can be very imposing; at the time of writing there are 110 albums available (including 58 posthumous releases). I once found a website that categorised them into all the different genres of music he released, and from memory there were eight categories (eg. Classical, Satirical, Guitar Solos, Sex Humour, Instrumental, etc., etc.) and an album could be any mixture of all eight. And though that is RIGHT UP MY STREET, posting a link to that here would defeat the object of this exercise, which is to give you a small base to get going with. This isn't a list of my all-time top Zappa albums, but some options to give you a grounding in his work. I've also limited myself to albums released in his lifetime, just to stop us all going mad. If you get on with any of these albums, I've included recommendations of similar stuff from his oeuvre at the end of each entry.

My introduction to Zappa began in the blissful last few years before internet shopping. As a result my choices were determined by what was available in the record shops/what I could afford, and not because a speaker with a brain told me I might like it.[344] I would thumb through, see a front cover I'd not seen before and buy it then and there. This meant the whole experience was full of surprise, excitement, a little confusion and more than once complete bewilderment. But it certainly beat being handed a USB of 5GB of music, or realising I could just have everything all at once online. I have real reservations about music-streaming sites, some just because it's new and scary, but also because it's like deciding you want to get into wine and someone gives you 200 bottles. Not that I would ever turn down 200 bottles of wine. But I might find myself hammered after the third one thinking, 'I've had too much wine' and that I didn't want any more wine ever again, then weeks later someone is wearing a really cool wine T-shirt and I'm like: 'Oh, wine is rubbish; I had some once and it wasn't for me.'[345]

To characterise him very briefly, I would say Frank Zappa is a musical raised eyebrow. He wrote no love songs, nothing bordering on sentiment,[346] and mocked politicians, other musicians, hippies, groupies, capitalists, the record industry, drugs, men, women, gay people, straight people, all with equal scorn. This does make a small minority of his lyrics quite problematic to listen to in 2018 (if you want to listen to them all in one chunk then get the compilation *Have I Offended Someone?*). But, in many instances, beneath what may seem offensive language, he's calling people up on hypocrisy, or making a point about

---

344 Seriously, what is Alexa for?! Just google it!

345 In retrospect, this is more about Zappa than wine.

346 Save one song, 'Watermelon in Easter Hay', a guitar solo about the end of guitar solos, which I will come to later.

sexual repression, sexual freedom, or just someone being an ass-hole. That said, I can only defend him up to a point in this area, and there are certain songs I could understand someone taking a strong disliking to.

With that as a caveat, the vast majority of his songs are just plain silly or scornful and probably around half his work is instrumental, and you can't offend someone with a guitar solo! But what you *can* do, and I didn't know this was possible before listening to Zappa, is make them laugh with a time signature, titter with a trumpet or guffaw with a glockenspiel.

Whether you like him or not, Zappa is a bona fide musical genius. He picked only the very best musicians to work with, and he worked them very, very hard. His albums, regardless of their individual genre, never fail to surprise, impress and challenge.

Oh, and he's a better guitarist than Jimi Hendrix.[347]

So here we go:

1. *Cheap Thrills/Son of Cheap Thrills*

My first ever introduction to Frank Zappa was from a friend at school called Joe. I'd mentioned I was into Beefheart and he played me a Frank Zappa guitar solo. I just knew it was for me right from the beginning. How often it is that when you experience music, or film, or literature and your first reaction is 'I don't know what this is! What is that?!', it becomes the art that stays with you for your whole life. I went out and bought the two cheapest Frank Zappa CDs, a pair of budget compilations called *Cheap Thrills* and *Son of Cheap Thrills*. Two things immediately struck me: firstly, all the music on it was so different

---

347 TAKE THAT, EVERY GUITARIST POLL I'VE EVER READ!

– how could this all be by the same person?! And there was melody, glorious melody across all of the different genres. Secondly, in some of the live versions on these CDs the band were laughing . . . *laughing*! And some of the other tracks *made me laugh*! I'd honestly never considered that it was possible for music to make you laugh, sometimes with the gleeful insanity of a complex melody, sometimes by in-jokes between the musicians.

There are quite a few other compilation albums, but I wouldn't recommend approaching them before you've got your head round his output. They are either so broad as to be kind of pointless, or so specific (compilations of his experiments with quadraphonic sound, confusing posthumous releases dealing with specific album sessions, officially released bootlegs, etc.) that they will muddy the waters.

2. *Hot Rats*

Save for 'Willie the Pimp' (featuring Captain Beefheart on vocals), this is fully instrumental. If I meet someone who owns a Zappa album, nine times out of ten this is the one they own. The melodies seem to tumble over each other, especially in 'Peaches En Regalia' and 'Son of Mr Green Genes'. A couple of more challenging tracks give a taste of Zappa's more obtuse sound, but Jean-Luc Ponty's violin on 'The Gumbo Variations' is just glorious as it scrapes alongside Zappa's solo. If you like it, then check out *Waka/Jawaka*, *The Grand Wazoo* and *Burnt Weeny Sandwich*.

3. *Roxy & Elsewhere*

This is a live album released in 1974 containing, without doubt, one of the most accomplished groups of live musicians ever assembled. In places it's outrageously complex and so god-damn tight! The percussion alone should have it shelved in a lead-lined bunker to preserve for future generations: Ruth Underwood is mind-blowing. It's also very funny: 'Cheepnis' deals with shoddy monster movie sets and 'Penguin in Bondage' is about, well, let me quote Zappa's words to the crowd before the song begins, which is a great example of 'radio-friendly' language:

> The name of this song is 'Penguin in Bondage', an' it's a song that ah, deals with the possible variations on a basic theme which is . . . well, you understand what a basic theme is. And then the variations include, ah, manoeuvres that might be executed with the aid of, ah, extra-terrestrial gratification and devices which might or might not be supplied in a local department store or perhaps a drugstore but at very least in one of those fancy new shops that they advertise in the back-pages of the free press. This song suggests to the suggestible listener that the ordinary procedure, ah, that I am circumlocuting at this present time in order to get this text on television, is that, ah, if you wanna do something other than what you thought you were gonna do when you first took your clothes off and you just happened to have some DEVICES around . . . Then it's, it's not only OK to get into the PARAPHERNALIA of it all but. . . Hey! What did he say? Ready?

It's about sex toys. And if that's not enough to get you giggling, there's an instrumental called 'Don't You Ever Wash That Thing?' What's not to like?!

If you like this then do check out the footage of the gigs this recording is taken from in the film *Roxy the Movie*, and various clips on YouTube. In terms of other albums, if you like this delve into *You Can't Do That on Stage Anymore* volumes 1–6, *Over-Nite Sensation*, *Apostrophe (')* and *Make a Jazz Noise Here*

4. *Joe's Garage Acts I, II & III*

Though originally released as two separate discs, this is now available as a whole. It's a rock operetta that follows the story of Joe, an adolescent who forms a band in a dystopian society that eventually bans music due to it leading to numerous moral vices. It's very funny and very filthy in exploring issues surrounding censorship, sexual repression, religion, state control and the music industry. Compare the versions of 'Joe's Garage' and 'Catholic Girls' with the live versions on *Cheap Thrills* to hear the band trying to make each other laugh. The penultimate track, 'Watermelon in Easter Hay', is one of my all-time favourite tracks. It's the guitar solo that Joe imagines from his cell when music is finally banned, and I think it's the only time Zappa allowed himself to get a little misty eyed. Telling that his only sad song is an instrumental about a future with no music! Also, this album placed in *Modern Drummer*'s list of the Top 25 Drum Albums of all time, something to do with syncopation, and I have no idea what that means.

If you like *Joe's Garage*, then check out *Sheik Yerbouti*, *Zappa in New York*, *Zoot Allures* and *Thing-Fish* (another operetta about people turned into fish by a contaminated water supply).

5. *We're Only in It for the Money*

This early *Mothers* album was recorded as part of a project called 'No Commercial Potential', which spawned the albums *We're Only in It for the Money*, *Lumpy Gravy*, *Uncle Meat* and

Cruising with Reuben & the Jets. The last of these is a parody of doo-wop so accurate that it is almost indistinguishable from actual doo-wop. *Lumpy Gravy* is an avant-garde, concrete music[348] classical album, and *Uncle Meat* is an experimental jazz rock album that forms the soundtrack to an experimental film that was never finished. During the recordings The Beatles released *Sgt. Pepper's Lonely Hearts Club Band*, and *We're Only in It for the Money* became a direct parody of that album, of hippie culture, drugs, sexual liberation and the commercialisation of underground culture. The front cover is a mock-up of *Sgt. Pepper*, with fruit and vegetables spelling out the title instead of flowers and, fun fact, features a real live Jimi Hendrix standing where a wax sculpture of Sonny Liston stood on The Beatles' cover. At times it's a nightmare version of the California 60s sound, at times a searing indictment of the free-love culture people were in the middle of worshipping, and at others it's a discordant hellhole of overdubs, screeches, electronic noise and maniacal laughter. What's. Not. To. Like?

If it floats your boat then get *Freak Out!, Absolutely Free* and *Weasels Ripped My Flesh*

6. *Jazz from Hell/Francesco Zappa*

I've picked these two together just to try to give an insight into the breadth of Zappa's work. *Jazz from Hell* is an entirely instrumental album, and, save for one guitar track, is entirely composed and recorded on a synclavier (a kind of early synthesiser/ sampling system). Apparently, in some shops it was released with a parental-advisory sticker following Zappa's testimony in

---

348 I have no idea what this means.

opposition to the Parents Music Resource Centre. The PMRC were a political campaign group that sought to censor what they referred to as 'porn-rock' (explicit lyrics/album covers), and from this movement originates the famous parental-advisory sticker. Zappa spoke very eloquently against them in Congress and was extremely vocal at the time defending musicians' rights to depict and describe sex, drug-taking and violence. The whole movement and hearing make for very interesting reading, and Zappa's album *Frank Zappa Meets the Mothers of Prevention* is a direct response to it. Even without all that background, *Jazz from Hell* makes me laugh because it's an instrumental album that came with a warning because one of the songs is called 'G-Spot Tornado'.

Francesco Zappa is the first ever release of music (Opus I and IV) written by 18th-century Italian composer Francesco Zappa. Having stumbled upon a musician with the same name, Zappa took it upon himself to publish his music for the first time in four centuries (when he discovered him, it was only available in the Mormon library), and then record it and release it himself. I've said it before and I'll say it again. What's. Not. To. Like? It's another album entirely recorded on the syn-clavier. The tone here is very different, though; it sounds similar to a harpsichord.

If you like either of these then maybe you won't be put off by some of the more classical Zappa albums. Why not try *The Yellow Shark, Boulez Conducts Zappa: The Perfect Stranger, London Symphony Orchestra Vols I & II* and, if you're feeling particularly adventurous, *Lumpy Gravy*.

So, there you have it. Happy hunting, hungry freaks!

I must admit this chapter has made me grudgingly curious about Zappa's output. I have only listened to *Hot Rats* – but you make it clear that he was hugely prolific and varied, so I would like to pin John down to the three Zappa albums he would take with him to a desert island.

Oh, all right then, *Roxy & Elsewhere*, *Waka/Jawaka*, *Bongo Fury*, *Zoot Allures*, *Burnt Weeny Sandwich*, *Läther*.

[EJ] That's six.

It'll be ten if you're not careful.

Epilogue

And there you have it. An A to Z of Elis and John.

Or, should we say, an E to J of Elis and John.

What did you say?

'An E to J of Elis and John.'

Hang on . . .

What?

WHY DIDN'T WE THINK OF THAT IN THE FIRST PLACE?!

'An E to J of Elis and John'? It does have a ring to it.

Oh how stupid! How stupid! I hate myself!

Steady on.

But E–J makes sense! It sounds better! AND IT'S ONLY SIX CHAPTERS! How did we not think of this at any stage of the process?

Chill out, babe!

But I could have just done it all myself and had it finished with months to spare . . .

Hey, come on, man, it's a good book! We've done well, you're OK!

Is it?! HAVE WE?! AM I?!

Yes!

It's only finished cos I locked you in a glass-walled office at Orion Publishing the day before the deadline.

John, sit down, have a vape, relax. We'd still have had to do the same amount of words and the chapters would just have been impractically long.

Oh yeah . . . You're right . . . Of course . . .

It's OK.

God, I'm an idiot . . .

Hey, relax, man . . .

Sorry . . . It's just . . . It's been a long week . . .

Not a problem. Reader, we do hope you've . . .

Sorry . . .

. . . enjoyed reading this book. There are a few . . .

. . . I'm an awful awful man . . .

. . . appendices to come. But I think really what John . . .

. . . Oh God . . .

. . . and I would like to say, is that genuinely, this book would not have come into existence without every single person who listens to the show, who joins in, who contributes to it. You are all so many thousands of still points in our turning world.

That would make a fixed world; you can't have a thousand still points in a turning world.

Here he is! Back from your self-loathing episode?

Yes, all done!

I was just saying how much every single person is responsible for this book.

Hmmmm . . .

No?

Well, I've got the respective word counts to hand.

Of course, you have.

And I've worked out what percentages was done by each of us.

Are you a laugh?

As unlikely as it sounds, El, though bringing up the rear you have contributed more words than 'The General Public'. There's not even a column for them on the spreadsheet.

I meant in a vibe sense.

Oh! In a vibe sense! Well, for sure! Oh, vibe-wise I'd say it's 40/30/30 Robins/James/public. The PCD vibe contribution has been immeasurable! Despite me having just measured it there . . .

OK, let's settle with that.

Right.

Are you OK, man?

Yeah, I'm struggling a bit with having gone down to 0 per cent nicotine on the ecig.

A problem as old as time.

Indeed.

Is that why you're a bit ratty today?

Possibly...

Shall we go to a pub?

Yes! Which one?

The Whippet?

No! I hate that pub!

OK... The Cross Keys?

Are you high?...

OK, John, what pub would you like to go to?

Great question! Near here? Now, what vibe are we talking? Are we looking for medium-quiet or just quiet? Because in zone 1 there are 18 suitable 'quiet' pubs, but 29 pubs I've identified as suitable 'medium-quiet'. Are we going to talk or sit in silence? Booths might be a factor – are you in the mood for a booth or happy to stand at a bar if it's not too busy? What about nooks? I know six pubs within a ten-minute walk of here that have nooks. I'm thinking minimum three ales on tap. If you had to choose just three ales, I mean dream ales, what would they be? I should download that Untappd app but I can never be arsed. Why do they always want all your bloody details just to find out what beer is on; I don't want a username, I just want to know if they've got Neck Oil, for crying out loud. So, anyway, there's The Harp – I could call ahead to check how busy it is upstairs – and there's always some space in The Admiralty, so we could go to The Harp,

and if that's too busy head to The Admiralty *via* The
Chandos in case they've got booths free. Also they
do Alpine Lager cos it's a Sam Smith's. Or should
we turn to Soho? Because if we head to The
Admiralty we run the risk of running out of
options on this side of the river? Maybe Soho is
a better bet? Though, amazingly, it's never
really impressed for me pub-wise. OK, let's go
to The Harp, and if that's too busy we head
north to The Nellie Dean of Soho via The
French House and with The Ship as a
back-up if The French House is closed
upstairs? Ah, no, The Ship was too
loud last time I was there. Hang on . . .
Let's do this properly . . . Do you
have an OS map of Soho? We
could aim for The Blue Posts?
On Newman Street? Fun fact:
there are four pubs called
The Blue Posts in central
London. Actually, as of
this year it's now
three . . .

Appendix i

Glossary of Terms

#crimes – Short-lived sitcom about a man in his mid-30s going undercover in a young offenders' institution. Also known (by grime artists, convicts and the under-19s) as *Crims*

£quid – British currency, sterling

0.0% Session – The practice of not drinking alcohol, 'keeping it 0.0% session™'

A Robins Amongst the Pigeons – Memoir of award-winning comedian John Robins

Abattoir – An area where overrated bands congregate

Abergwili – A small village on the outskirts of Carmarthen/A large 'gentleman's agreement'

Absolute Radio – Retirement home for disgraced DJs and producers

Absolutement – Absolutely

Ales! Ales! Jägerbombs! Ales! Regret! – A classic night out in list form

All Out Prawn-Wise – Buying solely prawn-based snacks from a WH Smith

Americaaaaaah – Dreamlike wonderland, home of Hollywood, cannoli and 'New Yoyk', as imagined by a cautious Welshman

Anecdote and a Punchline – The format of Welsh storytelling since c.600 AD

ABCC – App Based Cab Comp, slang for UBER

Are You a Laugh? – Retort to anyone not being a laugh

Are You On E-Mail?/You Simply Have to Be These Days – The rallying cry of a generation. The greatest call and response since Wembley '86. A secret code to identify fellow 'Hammer Legends'

Award-Winning – Style of stand-up comedy practised by John Robins

Awards Folder – A once actual, now metaphorical repository for clips of 'good radio'

Badinage – Banter, repartee, back and forth, chat

Benson and Hendrix – See *Billy Bifters*, *Jazz Cigarette*

Betabet™ – Simple quiz in which two competitors have 30 seconds each to get through as much of the alphabet as possible, based on a category chosen by the setter. For example, if it was fruit: Apple, Banana, Clementine, Date, and so on. The amount of passes allowed depends on how easy or difficult it is to get through the alphabet on the given subject, and the Quiz Master's word will be final . . . Not necessarily correct, but final. In the interest of fairness, whoever isn't playing Betabet™ first will enter the 'sound-proof booth'. Elis's Achilles' heel

Billy Bifters – See *Benson and Hendrix*

Birdseye! – The vibe-based end to a game of Potato Potato

Borderline Toolbelt – Someone you suspect might be a 'tube' but haven't quite got the evidence. Potential 'coin'

Borders – Bookshop, now defunct

Breathy Woman, The – A mysterious fantasy lady who haunts dreams and provides commercial digital indie voiceovers. May smoke lots of fags

Brian May's Height – 6'1½". An inordinately hard question for the first round of a quiz on Brian May

Broadly Vegan – Ethical diet specifically phrased to stop idiots 'not being a laugh' on social media

Bumhole Gazette – Yearly mix CD of new music made for John by 'The Lovely Robin'

Chang – Beer/Cocaine (not interchangeable, unless you want to face the wrath of Producer Dave and hear four Stereophonics songs in a row). See also *Phuket*

Chatalytic Converser – Drive-time DJ

Christmas Day! – Exclamation, radio-friendly. Source: Adam & Joe 6Music podcast

CITEH – Abbrv. Manchester City. Reason why the sky is blue

Classic Robins! – Any behaviour befitting of John Robins, including, but not limited to: sudden exclamations of remorse, despair and frustration not usually heard on commercial radio; tales of self-loathing, self-obsession or self-aggrandisement; overly obsessive behaviour related to ISAs, financial markets, the highway code, the price of gold, Queen, Sherlock Holmes, Ronnie O'Sullivan, Frank Zappa, farthings, telling a girl you love her on the first date, walling yourself up in a prison of your own shame, eating Space Raiders on the toilet

C'mon, Ronnie! – Cry of encouragement

Coin/Son of a Coin – Radio-friendly swear word (the worst one)

Coleslaw – Northern delicacy sold by the kilo

Commercial Digital Indie Radio – Digitally broadcasted radio specialising in music such as Liam Gallagher or Noel Gallagher

Coss a Toin – Spoonerism

Couscous – The saddest food

Creme Egg – Object of the perfect weight and size for throwing

Crisps in a Bin! – Radio-friendly exclamation of frustration or despair

Crisps! – Radio-friendly swear word (a mild one)

Crivens – Archaic radio-friendly swear word

CRP – Considerably Richer Partner

Dancing with Dave – Any club or DJ night run by Dave Masterman, ever, regardless of the name he gives it on the flyers

Darkness – The kind of sadness, melancholy or depression we all feel from time to time

Darkness of Robins, The – Form of melancholy specific to John Robins. See *Award-Winning*

Dave Masterman – Heir to a Stockport-based timber magnate

David Mellor – Unpredictable ex-Tory MP who doles out punishment and threat as readily as charm and bonhomie. Fifty-one per cent stakeholder in Pret a Manger. Also known as 'The Cabbies' Bane'

Diabeast – A diabetic heavy metal fan

'Doing It' with Women – Seminal album dating from the mid-2000s

Don't Look at Me, Look at Freddie! – A bizarrely insensitive instruction to a loved one who is paying more attention to you than to the thing you wanted to show them

Dorking Leatherhead Reigate – Rappable Surrey towns

Double Billy – Mythical bookcase that many have lost their minds trying to capture. See also *Unicorn*, *Sasquatch*, *Loch Ness Monster*, *Holy Grail*, *Atlantis*

Double Denim – Vin's raison d'etre

Double Devotee – A 'PCD' who has listened to all available podcasts twice

Double Queening – The practice of wearing two Queen-related items of clothing

Dripping Fridge – Radio-friendly insult

'Dur dur dur dur duh dur dur dur dur duh' – The opening line to 'Jackie Wilson Said' by VAN MORRISON (Not Dexy's Midnight Runners). To be sung in moments of celebration, excitement, drinking

Ear Seed – Extremely rare condition where a seed resides in the cartilage of the ear. Only one known case

Egg Bum Tea – Cup of tea made from water previously used to boil an egg

E-Mail – Electronic Mail, a form of futuristic communication whereby letters can be sent without paper, envelope, ink, stamp, post box or post office. A revolution among the technological elite

Emotionally Thick – Description of the sort of person who tells a girl he's just met that he loves her

Every Cloud – Short-lived radio feature in which devastating events were balanced out by minor victories. Also known as 'Good News About the Chocolate Oranges'. Source: Alan Partridge

Factors, Due to/In Spite of – Life events too painful, explicit or complex to go into on commercial digital indie radio

Farthing Gate – The scandal caused by not adhering to the explicit terms of a quiz. Vague or overly hard questioning. See also *Brian May's Height, John Deacon's A-Level Results*

Fig Rolls at a Funeral – Radio-friendly expression of disappointment or contempt

Fire Me out of a Cannon for Charity – Radio-friendly phrase detailing annoyance or self-loathing

Founding Father/Founding Mother – PCD who has been on the 'vibe train' since episode one

Four Cornerstones of Rock, The – Freddie Mercury, Brian May, Roger Taylor, John Deacon

'Four Euros for a Toast-eh?! Yer Jokin, Eren't Ya?!' – Northern exclamation of disbelief at how much things cost in Europe/outside Manchester

Fridge Magnet That Says Sad on It – Radio-friendly exclamation of regret or despair

Garry Potter – Fictional wizard with a fictional speech impediment

Gentleman's Agreement – The male genitalia. Source: Danny Wallace via Prod D

Georgie Ezra, Little – Well-meaning Cockney born c.1950

Getting It Wrong – Why you should never meet your heroes

Go and Live in a Bin – Sod off

Good Radio Bell – Self-discharged alarm to signal passable broadcasting

Gorky's Zygotic Mynci – Obscure Welsh band

Grief Apples – Any mundane item associated with an ex-partner that gains emotional significance after their departure

Grief Is Living – A moment of self-disgust. The disappointing inevitability of one's own pathetic behaviour. Often involving unhealthy food or snacks. A howl of anguish. A state of mind

Grief Mansion – A house, flat or dwelling where one lives alone due to 'factors'

Hammer Legend – Every single one of you reading this

High Effin' Bees – Noel Gallagher's vanity project

Hubris Dome – *Informal*. The Lyric Theatre at The Salford Lowry/ any regional arts centre with a capacity over 500 booked by an overly optimistic tour manager

'I Don't Mind It, Mate!' – Exclamation of approval

IKEAnicdotes – Any anecdote, normally tragic, depressing or self-lacerating, that takes place in, or relating to, IKEA

Instant Regret – Spicy chocolate. Inevitable side-effect of living

'It's Just a Body' – Expression used to diminish embarrassment about puberty, 'congress', 'twig and berrymanship' or full sex

Jazz Cigarette – See *Mayor Doobie Doobliani*

John Deacon's A-Level Results – Three 'A's

JohnTech – Company renowned for its Christmas parties

Josh/Joshing – Sitcom notorious for having unsuccessfully tried to accommodate a cameo from John Robins

Judge Robins – Half-judge, half-belligerent nudist

'Keep It Light!' – Exclamation used to remind John Robins that he is presenting a mid-afternoon commercial digital indie radio show and not making confession to a priest/compiling his own diary

Keep It Session™ – An imperative to, or the act of, only drinking beer or cider at 4.5% ABV or below

'Kiss Me and Tell Me You Hate Me' – An utterance made by the Welsh when sudden, intense feelings of emotion momentarily confuse them

Larging it – not 'Keeping It Session'. Drinking excessively strong alcohol. See also *Producer Daving It*, *Maximum Shunting*

Life's a Quiz and then You Die – bleak motto

Lighthearted Paper Review – A weekly update on *The Mirror*'s most essential gadgets

Like Ogger Finn and the New Inkton Pairs – 'Like all good things, on you we depend' (misheard song lyric from Queen's 'Radio Gaga')

Live Vibe Taster – Someone who has witnessed the magic of Elis James and/or John Robins performing live

'Live Your Best Life' – An instruction to follow your dreams, change your job, pursue your passion, travel, leave, stay, make changes

'Lovely Stuff!' – Expression of content or approval. Source: Alan Partridge/Shakin' Stevens

Masterman's Faster Vans – Stockport-based delivery service

Maximum Shunting – Source of regret. Fulfilling and exceeding your body's capacity for alcohol above 4.5% abv. Not recommended. See also *Larging It*, *Producer Daving It*, *Shunting*

Mayor Doobie Doobliani – Da 'erb

Meeting the Mayor– The act of smoking 'Benson and Hendrix'

Mince – Ground meat, not to be confused with 'mints'

Mind Palace – The conscious mind/interior monologue

Mints – Type of sweet flavoured with mint oil or mint flavouring, not to be confused with 'mince'

Nap Prison, Trapped in a – Feeling of discomfort when your daily schedule doesn't allow for a nap

Nasty Little Cube – Radio-friendly insult

Nods and Winks – The unspoken understanding between performers that typified the live work of The Jimi Hendrix Experience in the late 1960s/broadcasting of Elis James and John Robins in the mid- to late 2010s

Noise of Life – The inevitable interference of traffic, alarms, people, responsibility, deadlines, work, commuting, bad music, talking, shouting, ravens and once a bee in the wall. Something to be escaped from

O'Sullivan, Ronnie – Greatest snooker player of all time

Oner – Someone who first encountered The Elis James and John Robins Show while listening live to the first show, downloading the first podcast. See also *Double Devotee, Founding Father/Mother, Panini Oner, Regent Oner, Retro Oner, Retro Oner Elect, Widdicombe Defector, Zig-Zag Onderer*

Oxford Brookes – The Seat of Learning

Paddock – Place where musicians deserving of acclaim congregate

Panic Normality – Defence mechanism or form of denial. The instinct to continue with normal tasks in the face of serious injury or crisis, e.g finishing the washing-up with a knife in your foot, unloading the washing machine after your waters have broken

Panini Oner – A PCD who goes back to listen to the podcasts in order while also keeping up with the most recent episodes

Pass to Paris – Loophole in Betabet™ now outlawed

PCD – Podcast Devotee

Phuket – Non-radio-friendly Thai holiday destination

Pintman – A person at one with their pint. Source *Dublin Pub Life & Lore* by Kevin C. Kearns:

> The clock ticks for you and me, but the pintman is on an island in time. He is no longer old or young, rich or poor, married or single. He is beyond the numbing grip of circumstance – a devotee at a solemn rite, a poet with an unfrenzied eye, a man with a pint.[349]

Pointless Middle-Aged Targets – Increasingly spurious tasks or periods of self-denial pursued by people over 30 to pretend they're not having a crisis/ageing. Can range from running marathons to cutting out refined sugar on Wednesdays

Polichips – Feature exploring the relationship between political affiliation and preferred chip accompaniments. E.g. 'Green/Salt and ketchup', 'Remain/Curry sauce'

Potato Potato – Vibe-based game

Pounding the P – Walking at speed to improve health

Producer Dave/Prod D – Former employee of Global Radio sacked for leaving microphones up during a track

Producer Daving It – A Mancunian night out. See also *Larging It*

Prod V – Punjabi-Croydonian Maccabees obsessive. Producer. Loyal. Formerly 'The Vintern'

Producer Joe – Producer hailing from the south-west. Formerly 'Intern Joe'

Project Spice – Any attempt made by the feeble-stomached to increase tolerance for hot food

---

349 Cc. John D. Sheridan, 'Yer Pint-Man', *Irish Licensing World*, December 1952, p. 22. (Quoted verbatim for accuracy but can apply to women just as much as men.)

Proof if Proof Be Need Be – Proof-positive. Source: *The Day Today*, Episode 2

Pub Porn – Erotic literature without the sex but with the pubs

Put Your Mouth in the Bin – Shut up

Quadruple Oner – A PCD who has listened to every episode a mere four times

'Quallo' – Exclamation of endorsement, 'Quality!'

Queens for Queen – Heads

Quenim – Double Denim × Double Denim

Quickfire Quiz – Improvised feature to fill a link where no topic has been planned. Frequently preceded by 'We'll vibe it, Dave!' when only five seconds of 'C'est la Vie' by Stereophonics remain

Rachel Stephens Anecdote – Any anecdote (with or without a punchline) that has been relayed multiple times

Regent Oner – Someone en route to becoming a 'Retro Oner'

Retro Oner – Someone who has retrospectively caught up with every episode of The Elis James and John Robins Show in podcast form. A life event. See also *Bar Mitzva*, *Bat Mitzva*, *Turning 21*, *Sacrament of Confirmation*, *Baptism*, *Sweet Sixteen*, *Upanayana*, *Ritushuddhi*, *Amrit Sanchar*

Retro Oner Elect – 'Regent Oner'

Riffing – Improvisation, jamming, 'vibing it'

Robin, The Lovely – Leading Robins apologist, not to be confused with Robins himself. A real person, contrary to popular belief

Robins Apologist – Someone who still tolerates or even approves of John Robins in spite of 'factors'

Robins Unleashed – Any radio show presented by John Robins *sans* Elis

Sacred Cow – Controversial commercial digital indie radio feature. Any band or musician so highly acclaimed as to be regarded uncriticisable

Scatty Robins – Offensive. A vile slur with little or no basis in fact

Sexy Ghost – Person, or persons, responsible for calling an adult chat line from Elis's home phone c.1994

Shame Spiral – Descent into a 'shame well'. Burgeoning realisation or memory of a shameful situation. A hangover

Shame Well – The place from which stories of shame can be read without fear of repercussion and therefore the sufferer can be absolved. Colloquially, a place one resides when feeling shame

Shivnarine Chanderpaul – Guyanese cricketer and former captain of the West Indies cricket team. Radio-friendly expletive (medium) expressing annoyance or frustration

Shock Your Body – Pointless acts carried out in the name of fitness to disguise the fact we're in our mid-30s, often involving cold water. Rallying cry for new dads/Communist-era sportsmen

Shunting – Drinking

'Shut Up and Kiss Me' – A Welsh exclamation of frustration mixed with desire

Silo of 50-Pence Pieces – Potential alternative to a smaller sum deposited in your bank account

So Low Curry – A curry eaten in a state of despair, not to be confused with 'Solo Curry'

Soho 69 Card – The very real PizzaExpress version of a Nando's Black Card, only known recipient being Amanda Holden. The Holy Grail of PizzaExpressmanship. Andi Peters's bane

Solo Curry – A curry eaten alone, often in a state of despair

Space Marzipan – Traditional Diwali sweet, also known as 'Burfi'

Special Toilet – The more complex of the two toilets

Spider Ghost – The source of any mysterious night-time noise

Statman Ross – Edinburgh resident and whisky expert with far too much time on his hands. See Appendices – *Betabet*™, *Winner Plays On*™

Still Point of My Turning World – A description of anyone who provides a source of calm, reassurance or hope. For example, a life partner, friend or landlady you barely know

Sugar My Halloumi – Radio-friendly expletive (mild–medium) expressing disbelief or annoyance

Surfeit of Meat – Common everyday problem

Tails for Wales, Cynffon i Gymru – The calling of 'Tails' when 'cossing a toin'

Tebay/Gloucester Gate – The Valhalla of UK service stations

Teenage Fanclub – Any short-lived feature that fails to deliver on its excellent premise

The Gift of Shame – Appropriate present for any child aged ten years or above/inappropriate name for a wedding covers band

The Unproduceables – Elis and John

They Kiss You and then Punch You – Fantasy of how a New York barmaid might flirt in 'Americaaaaah'. See also *Americaaaaah*

Thin Idiot – Robins

THIN LIZZY! – Irish rock band that supported Queen in their 1977 tour. Answer to a misleadingly worded question on *Celebrity Mastermind* Series 16, Episode 6. John's last thought on earth

Threnim – One more than 'Double Denim', one less than 'Quenim'

Tick Off a Taste – The act of sampling new foods, drinks or Scandinavian salt liquorice

Tick Tock – Passive–aggressive text to send to a friend running late. Will, repeat, WILL bite you on the arse

Time Checks – The act of telling the time live on radio, devised by Tony Blackburn

Tinyhighmouth – Elis's mouth

Toasteh – Toasted sandwich, often containing cheese, used to calculate RPI in Greater Manchester

Tool belt – Insult, radio-friendly

Top Shelf – An item, subject or anecdote deemed 'too sexy' for commercial digital indie radio

Top Tax Bracket – Elis's tax bracket, a life goal

Tops Off – Welsh celebration

Treble Oner – A PCD who has navigated the vibe space thrice

Triple Queen – A sartorial high-point only once achieved

Turning Right – Northern act of spontaneity involving theft, fraud and trespass

Twig and Berries – A 'gentleman's agreement'

Twigandberrymanship – Sexual prowess

Unsung Onion – Any dish where the humble onion plays a major role but doesn't receive due acclaim

Vibe Taster – Someone who has met Elis or John, having uttered the password: 'Can I taste your vibe?'

Vibe Train – Mode of thought, style, mood or behaviour it is essential to get on board with

Vinigma – Unknown

Vintern, The – *Archaic*. Sweatier, more nervous incarnation of 'Prod V'

Waste Paper Bin – Item suitable for a lounge

WastePaperBinGate – Argument arising from the above statement, which split the nation in half

Welshman's Thigh – A genetic affliction affecting Welshmen, whereby the thigh area is overdeveloped to aid manual labour and other rural activities now made redundant by Thatcher

Whackaging – Technique employed by advertisers whereby products or companies speak directly to you in the infantilising tone of a hip Baptist vicar taking a school assembly. The personification of products and/or services that takes place

on the packaging of said products

Widdicombe Defector – Someone who became a PCD after hearing the bonus episode of Elis and John standing in for Josh Widdicombe sandwiched between Episode 65 and 66

Winner Plays On™ – Quiz where two people set five questions for each other based on specialist subjects they have chosen for themselves. The loser has to change subject

'Yes Please!' – Exclamation of joy or approval

You Tube/Tube – Insult. Radio-friendly. Source: Lee Boardman's voiceovers on *Road Wars*: 'This tube thinks he can outrun a fully marked Impreza!', and Mark Lawrenson: 'Some idiot's banging the advertising hoardings . . . You tube!'

'You're Thick' – Appropriate response to finding out your friend told a girl he loved her on a first date

Zappa, Frank – The greatest innovator, composer, guitarist, musician and bandleader of 20th-century music

Zig-Zag Onederer – A PCD who catches up with podcasts in no logical order

Appendix ii

Winner Plays On™: An Analysis by Ross Middleton

Hello Gentlemen. In honour of your 100th show I wanted to do something to celebrate. As a 'Oner' or 'Founding Father' I have #LargedIt, Kept It Session™, Maximum Shunted, Been on E-Mail, eaten far too much coleslaw at a wedding, paid four Euros for a toast-eh, only listened to Queen and fallen asleep supporting Wales for quite some time now. But I thought I'd pay you back with a little summary of Winner Plays On™. Has John won more than Elis? Does Queens for Queen pop up more than Tails for Wales? Has Elis ever actually won a tiebreaker? I aim to answer these questions and more in this little report.

Let's start with the basics. There have been a total 94 games of WPO over the last two years. Although there have been 99 shows, it was not contested on five occasions. The first game wasn't played until Week 2 of the show. It was missed twice over Christmas, once for John being in Australia and once for Elis becoming be-daughtered. Of the 94 games, only 93 were analysed, one game being omitted. Farthing Gate. After the quality of questions was debated, the game on Week 8 was declared void. This has been taken into consideration and all scores of this week removed from the record.

So over the 93 games John has been the more consistent

competitor, winning 56.4 per cent of the games. Although John is clearly the superior player, Elis can take heart that he has improved over time. After the first 21 games, Elis had a win rate of only 28 per cent. So recovering this to 42.5 per cent has shown real improvement over time. But it's hard to deny John still holds a strong lead.

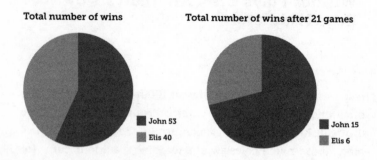

Total number of wins

John 53
Elis 40

Total number of wins after 21 games

John 15
Elis 6

Elis can also take heart that in terms of fairness, Winner Plays On™ is the Radio X equivalent of first past the post. If we were to think of the quiz in more proportional representation terms, it's a lot closer. John has only scored 0.8 per cent more points than Elis, but has won 13 more games.

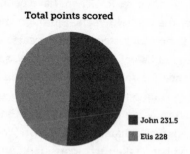

Total points scored

John 231.5
Elis 228

Hero to zero

However, when looking at the times when either player has registered either a full mark of 5 or drawn a blank of 0, it's fairly evident to see that Elis is much more of a flair player. While Elis has only scored one more blank than John, he has been far more adept at scoring full marks. He was the first to achieve this feat in Week 25, answering questions on the 1958 Welsh World Cup team.

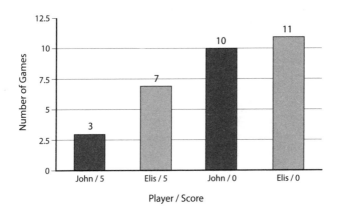

Player / Score

As you can see, he has achieved this feat more than twice as many times as John. The majority of John's full scores were achieved answering questions on music, while for Elis it was sport.

Successful topics

It's clear that Elis has found most success when competing with a sporting topic. Nearly half of his total wins have come when answering something sport-based. Although John has also found success with sport, he has had a better range of winning subjects, demonstrating a wider knowledge.

Number of wins by topic – John

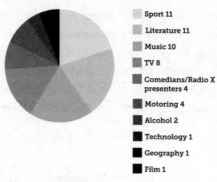

Sport 11
Literature 11
Music 10
TV 8
Comedians/Radio X presenters 4
Motoring 4
Alcohol 2
Technology 1
Geography 1
Film 1

Number of wins by topic – Elis

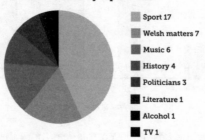

Sport 17
Welsh matters 7
Music 6
History 4
Politicians 3
Literature 1
Alcohol 1
TV 1

Now is a good time to look at individual topics. John is by far and away the master of keeping hold of a topic for a longer period of time. John managed to keep Alan Partridge as a topic for an incredible five-week run. He has also maintained a run of four weeks for a number of topics. The longest Elis has been able to keep a subject running is only three.

JOHN

Number of weeks	Topic
5	Alan Partridge
4	Ayrton Senna
	John Robins at the Edinburgh Fringe, 2005 to present day
	The service stations of England and Wales
	Ronnie O'Sullivan
3	Van Morrison
	Bonnie 'Prince' Billy
	The children's books of Roald Dahl
	The US *Office*
	The pubs of Oxford
	Freddie Mercury
	Philip Larkin
	The Wasteland

ELIS

Number of weeks	Topic
3	Welsh 1958 World Cup campaign
	The Welsh settlement in Patagonia
	Tony Benn
	John Lennon
	The Mod movement of the 1960s
	Joe Calzaghe
	European Cup, 1967–93
	Bob Paisley
	The Welsh language
	Boris Becker

It's also interesting to look at the average scores of the players' more successful topics. Here we see once again that Elis is the master of high scoring. These averages are taken from topics that have lasted at least two weeks. It should also be pointed out that the 4.5 average on Dixie Dean for Elis is somewhat skewed. He was generously awarded seven out of a possible five points by John during his first week on the topic.

Elis	Score	John	Score
Dixie Dean	4.5	John Robins at the Edinburgh Fringe, 2005 to present day	3.5
Mike Tyson	4	Pulp	3.5
European Cup, 1967–93	3.67	Philip Larkin	3.33
The Miners' Strike, 1984–85	3.5	Freddie Mercury	3.33
Tony Benn	3.33	The US *Office*	3.33

Best joint score – Week 53, The Mod movement of the 1960s vs The US *Office*, 5–4.

Worst joint score – Week 29, The Welsh settlement in Patagonia vs Post-War British serial killers, 1–0.

Has Elis ever won a tiebreak?

No.

Number of tiebreaks won

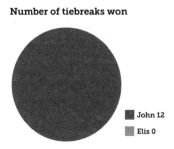

■ John 12
▨ Elis 0

Queen or Wales?

Although there was a period where it seemed like Queens for Queen was unrelenting (nine consecutive weeks at one point), it's actually an awful lot closer than it might seem. The 93 coin tosses have resulted in 49 Queens for Queen and 44 Tails for Wales. Moreover, if you cast your minds back, there were two weeks Elis betrayed his homeland and plumped for Heads, winning both times. That means the winning of the toss is as equal as is mathematically possible, with John winning 47 and Elis winning 46.

So there we have it. I hope you both appreciate this little analysis on what is fast becoming referred to as the 'tensest feature on British commercial indie radio'. I was tempted to try to analyse the number of times John was angry about Elis's level of questioning but didn't want to upset him. It was a lot of fun going back and listening to all the shows again, and I for one can't wait for the next 100.

Thanks, guys!

Appendix iii

Betabet™ Statistics: Compiled by Ross Middleton

As another quiz feature comes to a close, it is now tradition for me to present a few facts and figures based on the exploits of our favourite Queen fancier and Welsh nostalgist. OK, so Betabet™ didn't quite set the world alight in the same way as the tensest feature in commercial digital indie radio, Winner Plays On™, but there are still a number of key stats worth pointing out. It's somewhat trickier to analyse Betabet™, as it's widely considered you need a panel of at least three scorers as well as an independent UN representative to accurately record the results.

Despite this, I have endeavored to examine the results with the highest degree of accuracy possible and present my findings to you now.

We are the champions

Total wins

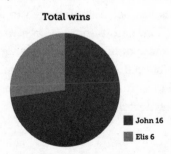

■ John 16
■ Elis 6

So it's hardly surprising to anyone who's actually listened to the podcast since January that John took a dominant win in Betabet™. Although last week Elis was awarded 12 points for his win by Vin, I'm going to be a stickler for the rules and record that as one victory. This takes Elis to 6 wins compared to John's 16. Something of note when looking at these results is that when one compares the numbers to the first 21 games of Winner Plays On™ the pattern is actually incredibly similar.

Number of 'Winner Plays On' wins (after 21 games)

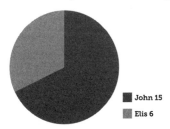

John was just as dominant in the early days of WPO as he has been in Betabet™. We can now only wonder whether or not Elis would eventually settle into the format and peg John back the way he did with WPO. Though I think it's safe to say it's unlikely. No matter how many printouts of the alphabet and discussions about how he reacts under pressure he could have, Elis was never really going to get the better of John. You may remember that when we looked at the actual points scored during WPO, it was actually a lot closer than the number of wins made it seem. I wondered if it might have been the same for Betabet™ . . .

Betabet points scored

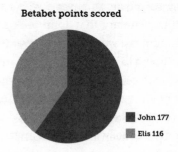

■ John 177
▨ Elis 116

It wasn't.

Me thinks the Queen fan doth protest too much

I think it's fair to say that over both quiz features, John Robins has most vociferously stood up for truth and fairness. As someone who would also consider themselves somewhat competitive I can entirely understand John's attitude and would do the exact same in his position. Only on one of the six occasions that Elis took victory did John accept the result without complaint.

Sports brands and Beatles' song titles were far too geared towards Elis, the existence of the state of East Virginia was up for debate, and of course whether it's India or Indigo in the phonetic alphabet was a bone of contention too.

Furthermore, John has even protested on a number of occasions when he's actually won the game. Despite thrashing Elis 17–4 on English nouns, John still argued Elis shouldn't have even scored his four points. John comfortably scored double that of Elis on car makes but still focused on the validity of Daimler as an answer rather than the win. He even proclaimed his anger at the subject of Premier League players with over 300 appearances despite Elis scoring 0. In the words of the man himself, 'If you need to let something lie, I am not your man,' J. Robins (2017)

The gambler's fallacy

The coin. It can be a radio-friendly swear meaning an unpleasant person. Its age can be up for questioning in a made-up game. However, its key purpose is deciding who answers first in Betabet™. This is even more important than in WPO, as it decides who will sit in the soundproof booth. It will decide who gets to listen to such delights as 'Ignition' by R. Kelly, 'Never Had a Dream Come True' from S Club 7 or Andrea Bocelli's 'Time to Say Goodbye'.

Results of coin toss

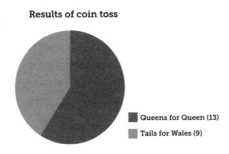

Queens for Queen (13)
Tails for Wales (9)

As with the quiz itself, John continued to dominate the coin toss, with his beloved Queen serving him well once again. Elis's diehard devotion to Wales has seen him travel across France following his nation romp through the Euros. However, when it comes to the coin toss, *'cynffonau cymru'* has been something of a folly. (I don't know if the Welsh is correct,[350] I had to use Google Translate.)

---

350 [EJ] You're very close, Ross. It's actually 'Cynffon i Gymru'

John vs The Guests

There are three Betabets™ I've not taken into consideration thus far – these are the three for which Elis was not present. In his absence, John took the fight to Lloyd Langford, Mike Bubbins and Nish Kumar.

John vs The Guests: points scored

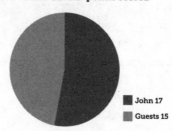

John 17
Guests 15

When up against the three guest hosts, John still managed to reign supreme. Although he was beaten by Nish on BBC sitcoms (to which he, of course, protested), he beat both Mike and Lloyd, making it 2–1. In terms of actual points scored, it was closer still. John took victories over the two replacement Welshman by only two-point margins. This goes to show that with a competitor with slightly more focus than The People's Champion, Elis James, it could have actually been a far more competitive feature.

Betabet™ miscellany

• 14.5 – Elis spends an average 14.5 seconds chatting, stuttering or trying to recall the alphabet, nearly half of the allotted time allowed.

- K – On average John would be able to reach the letter 'K'. Elis would only be able to get as far as 'H'. This stat is slightly askew, given that it includes Pass to Paris Gate and the fact that John's last five answers to 'Kitchen appliances' were 'gardening hose' (kept in the kitchen), 'hat' (kitchen hat), 'ice tray', 'Jack Daniel's' and 'klaxon' (kitchen klaxon).

- 4 – Never has a quiz format been so subtly tweaked quite so many times. The rules with regards to passing during Betabet™ have gone through four incarnations.
    * No passing at all
    * Unlimited passing
    * Unlimited passing but every pass incurs a point deduction
    * No more than three passes (widely acknowledged as the standard)

- 35 – Over the course of Betabet™ John actually gave more incorrect answers to the topics than Elis. John had 35 misses compared to Elis's 24. This was perhaps key to John's success, that rather than hesitate he'd simply give a quick wrong answer, allowing him to move on to the next letter. Elis may have tried to replicate this when giving avocado and abacus as answers to 'Mammals'.

- 11 – John had to use 11 passes to get from Dakar to Paris (the reverse of the famous rally) in the now-infamous Pass to Paris Gate.

- 2 – There were only two tiebreaks during the tenure of Betabet™. Somewhat aptly, the tiebreaks are themselves tied at one apiece.

Appendix iv

The Keep It Session™ Sessions

Just over two years ago, Elis and I decided it would be nice to introduce people to the music we often referenced on the show, but whose genre, length, obscurity or swearing didn't fit into Radio X's cutting-edge playlist of 100 per cent indie bangers. So we began playing small excerpts of songs at the end of the podcast, with a brief explanation of why we liked them and the broader context of their history and release.

Below is a complete list of songs played in the Keep It Session™ Sessions up to the date of publication. It is based on THE KISS REPORT, created and curated by all-round Hammer Legend Moritz Ge, available with additional statistics on the Elis James and John Robins Podcast Devotee Facebook group page.

Suffice to say, were you to purchase every album from which these songs are taken, you would probably be the coolest person on earth. Plus, you'd have lots of Elis's music too!

EJ– Elis James
JR– John Robins
MB – Mike Bubbins
NK – Nish Kumar
LL – Lloyd Langford

JA – James Acaster
EG – Ed Gamble
PV – Producer Vin
JW – Josh Widdicombe

Episode	Host	Artist/Band	Song	Album
98	JR	Frank Zappa	'Peaches en Regalia'	*Hot Rats*
99	EJ	Gorky's Zygotic Mynci	'Patio Song'	*Barafundle*
100	JR	Godspeed You! Black Emperor	'Like Antennas to Heaven . . .'	*Lift Your Skinny Fists Like Antennas To Heaven*
101	EJ	Gang of Four	'Damaged Goods'	*Entertainment!*
102	JR	Neutral Milk Hotel	'Holland, 1945'	*In the Aeroplane Over the Sea*
103	EJ	Can	'Oh Yeah'	*Tago Mago*
104	JR	Syd Matters	'Hi Life'	*Brotherocean*
105	EJ	Kevin Ayers	'Religious Experience'	*Joy of a Toy*
106	JR	Captain Beefheart	'Candle Mambo'	*Shiny Beast*
107	EJ	Bert Jansch	'Strolling Down the Highway'	*Bert Jansch*
108	JR	Lou Reed	'Paranoia Key of E'	*Ecstasy*
109	EJ	Les Fleur de Lys	'Gong with the Luminous Nose'	*Rubble Compilation*
110	JR	Neko Case	'Hold On, Hold On'	*Fox Confessor Brings the Flood*
111	EJ	Wire	'Ex Lion Tamer'	*Pink Flag*
112	JR	Elliott Smith	'Waltz #2'	*XO*
113	EJ	Robert Johnson	'Sweet Home Chicago'	*The Complete Recordings*
114	JR	Bonnie 'Prince' Billy & The Cairo Gang	'Troublesome Houses'	*Wondershow of the World*

Episode	Host	Artist/Band	Song	Album
115	EJ	The Fall	'Theme from Sparta F.C#2'	This is the single version, although a different version exists on the 2004 album *The Real New Fall LP* (formerly *Country on the Click*)
116	JR	Tom Waits	'Christmas Cards from a Hooker in Minneapolis'	*Blue Valentine*
117	EJ	The Delgados	'Pull the Wires from the Wall'	*Peloton*
118	JR	Gillian Welch	'Wrecking Ball'	*Soul Journey*
119	EJ	Public Image Ltd.	'Albatross'	*Metal Box*
120	JR	Papa M	'I of Mine'	*Papa M Sings*
121	JR	Sonic Youth	'Teen Age Riot'	*Daydream Nation*
122	EJ	Warm Sounds	'Nite Is A-Comin''	Warm Sounds were a one-hit wonder who (as far as I can tell) never recorded an album. I discovered this song on *Staircase to Nowhere*, CD 12 of the *Rubble Collection* of first generation British psychedelia.
123	JR	Red House Painters	'Uncle Joe'	*Red House Painters (Bridge)*
124	EJ	NEU!	'Für Immer'	*NEU! 2*
125	JR	Robin Allender	'The Brewery Tap'	*Above the Dreamers Head*

Episode	Host	Artist/Band	Song	Album
126	EJ	60 Ft. Dolls	'Stay'	*The Big 3*
127	JR	Wilco	'Hummingbird'	*A Ghost Is Born*
128	EJ	The Pastels	'Breaking Lines'	*Up for a Bit With The Pastels*
129	JR	Songs: Ohia	'Farewell Transmission'	*Magnolia Electric Co.*
130	JW	John Maus	'Hey Moon'	*We Must Become the Pitiless Censors of Ourselves*
131	JR	Trevor Sensor	'When Tammy Spoke to Martha'	*Starved Nights of Saturday Stars* EP
132	EJ	Right Hand Left Hand	'Tarts and Darts'	*Right Hand Left Hand*
133	JR	Okkervil River	'Westfall'	*Don't Fall in Love with Everyone You See*
134	EJ	Clinic	'If You Could Read Your Mind'	*Visitations*
135	JR	Meat Loaf	'It Just Won't Quit'	*Bat Out of Hell II: Back Into Hell*
136	EJ	The Castaways	'Liar, Liar'	*Nuggets: Original Artyfacts from the First Psychedelic Era, 1965–68*
137	JR	The Band	'King Harvest (Has Surely Come)'	*The Band*
138	EJ	Nick Drake	'Things Behind the Sun'	*Pink Moon*
139	JR	Tim Buckley	'Dolphins'	*Old Grey Whistle Test* version
140	EJ	Sweet Baboo	'The Day I Lost My Voice'	*Girl Under a Tree* EP

Episode	Host	Artist/Band	Song	Album
141	JR	Tortoise	'Glass Museum'	*Millions Now Living Will Never Die*
142	EJ	The Creation	'How Does It Feel to Feel'	*We Are Paintermen*
143	JR	Mogwai	'Yes! I Am a Long Way from Home'	*Young Team*
144	EJ	The Velvelettes	'He Was Really Sayin' Somethin''	*The Very Best of The Velvelettes*
145	JR	Boards of Canada	'Roygbiv'	*Music Has the Right to Children*
146	EJ	Cate Le Bon	'Are You with Me Now?'	*Mug Museum*
147	JR	The Voice Squad	'As I Roved Out'	From YouTube video of them singing in a pub
148	EJ	Lead Belly	'Where Did You Sleep Last Night'	*The Definitive Lead Belly*
149	JR	Dirty Projectors	'Two Doves'	*Bitte Orca*
150	EJ	Genesis	'The Conqueror'	*From Genesis to Revelation*
151	JR	Silver Jews	'Horseleg Swastikas'	*Bright Flight*
152	EJ	Half Man Half Biscuit	'National Shite Day'	*CSI: Ambleside*
153	JR	Jerry Garcia Band	'Rubin and Cherise'	*Cats Under the Stars*
		Richard and Linda Thompson	'I Want to See the Bright Lights Tonight'	*I Want to See the Bright Lights Tonight*
154	EJ	Primal Scream	'Velocity Girl'	C86 Compilation: it was a B-side to their 1986 single 'Crystal Crescent'

Episode	Host	Artist/Band	Song	Album
155	JR	Bonnie 'Prince' Billy	'I See a Darkness'	*Now Here Is My Plan* EP
156	EJ	Nico	'The Fairest of the Seasons'	*Chelsea Girl*
157	JR	The New Pornographers	'Sing Me Spanish Techno'	*Twin Cinema*
158	EJ	Spiritualized	'Come Together'	*Ladies and Gentlemen We Are Floating in Space*
159	JR	Frank Zappa	'Watermelon in Easter Hay'	*Joe's Garage Acts I, II & III*
160	EJ	Love	'Alone Again Or'	*Forever Changes*
161	JR	Massive Attack	'Safe from Harm'	*Blue Lines*
162	EJ	Minnie Riperton	'Les Fleurs'	*Come to My Garden*
163	JR	Car Seat Headrest	'Drunk Drivers/Killer Whales'	*Teens of Denial*
164	EJ	The Flirtations	'Nothing but a Heartache'	*Northern Soul: 20 Original Classics*
165	NK	Fairport Convention	'Who Knows Where the Time Goes?'	*All Our Own Work*
166	JR	Bonnie 'Prince' Billy	'Nomadic Revery'	*I See a Darkness*
167	EJ	Girl Ray	'Trouble'	*Earl Grey*
168	JR	Crosby, Stills, Nash & Young	'Our House'	*Déjà Vu*
169	EJ	Hooton Tennis Club	'P.O.W.E.R.F.U.L. P.I.E.R.R.E.'	*Highest Point in Cliff Town*
170	JR	The Meat Puppets	'Maiden's Milk'	*Up On the Sun*

Episode	Host	Artist/Band	Song	Album
171	JR	The Decemberists	'The Crane Wife 1&2'	*The Crane Wife*
172	LL	Baby Huey & The Baby Sitters	'Hard Times'	*The Baby Huey Story: The Living Legend*
173	MB	David Soul	'Silver Lady'	*Playing to an Audience of One*
174	EJ	Money Mark	'Hand in Your Head'	*Push the Button*
175	JR	Philip Glass	'Symphony No. 3, Movement I'	Stuttgart Chamber Orchestra
176	EJ	Delakota	'The Rock'	*One Love*
177	JR	Trevor Sensor	'High Beams'	*Andy Warhol's Dream*
178	EJ	Alvvays	'Next of Kin'	*Alvvays*
179	JR	Cass McCombs	'That's That'	*Dropping the Writ*
180	EJ	Deerhoof	'+81'	*Friend Opportunity*
181	JR	Red	'My War Is Starting Now'	*Nothing to Celebrate*
182	EJ	Richard James	'My Heart's on Fire'	*The Seven Sleepers Den*
183	JR	Neiked (feat. Dyo)	'Sexual'	Single
184	EJ	Dusty Springfield	'Little by Little'	*You Don't Have to Say You Love Me*
185	JR	The Roches	'Hammond Song'	*The Roches*
186	EJ	The Waitresses	'I Know What Boys Like'	*Wasn't Tomorrow Wonderful?*
187	EG	Clutch	'D.C. Sound Attack!'	*Earth Rocker*
188	JR	Chris de Burgh	'Last Night'	*Into the Light*
189	EJ	The Jesus and Mary Chain	'The Two of Us'	*Damage and Joy*
190	JR	Seamus Fogarty	'Heels Over Head'	*The Curious Hand*

Episode	Host	Artist/Band	Song	Album
191	EJ	Handsome Boy Modeling School	'Holy Calamity (Bear Witness II)'	*So . . . How's Your Girl?*
192	JR	Richard Dawson	'The Vile Stuff'	*Nothing Important*
193	EJ	Meic Stevens	'Y Brawd Houdini'	*Y Brawd Houdini*
194	JR	The Byrds	'Eight Miles High'	*(Untitled)/(Unissued)*
195	EJ	Shack	'Natalie's Party'	*H.M.S. Fable*
196	PV	Villagers	'Becoming a Jackal'	*Becoming a Jackal*
197	EJ	The Sonics	'Have Love Will Travel'	*Here Are The Sonics*
198	EJ	Seazoo	'Dig'	*Trunks*
199	EJ	Shopping	'The Hype'	*The Official Body*
200		NO KISS		
201	JW	Big Thief	'Shark Smile'	*Capacity*
202	JR	William Basinski	'dlp 1.1'	*The Disintegration Loops*
203	EJ	R. Dean Taylor	'There's a Ghost in My House'	*The Essential Collection*
204	JR	Serafina Steer	'Disco Compilation'	*The Moths Are Real*
205	EJ	The Fall	'Cruiser's Creek'	*This Nation's Saving Grace*
206	JR	Baroness	'Rays on Pinon'	*Red Album*
207	EJ	This Is the Kit	'By My Demon Eye'	*Moonshine Freeze*
208	JA	Jim Sullivan	'Jerome'	*U.F.O*
209	EJ	Robin Allender/ The Allender Band	'Riverrun'	*Outer Dark*
210	JR	Kurt Vile	'Shame Chamber'	*Wakin on a Pretty Daze*
211	EJ	Stereolab	'Miss Modular'	*Dots and Loops*
212	JR	Angel Olsen	'Shut Up Kiss Me'	*My Woman*

Episode	Host	Artist/Band	Song	Album
213	EG	Red Fang	'Cut It Short'	*Only Ghosts*
		Black Breath	'Black Sin (Spit on Cross)'	*Heavy Breathing*
214	JR	Gavin Bryars	'Jesus' Blood Never Failed Me Yet'	*Jesus' Blood Never Failed Me Yet*
215	EJ	The Move	'I Can Hear the Grass Grow'	*Great Move! The Best of The Move*
216	JR	Lou Reed	'How Do You Speak to an Angel'	*Growing Up in Public*
217	EJ	The Orielles	'Blue Suitcase (Disco Wrist)'	*Silver Dollar Moment*
218	JR	Cass McCombs	'Laughter Is the Best Medicine'	*Mangy Love*
219	EJ	Stephen Malkmus	'Jenny and the Ess Man'	*Stephen Malkmus*
220	JR	Neko Case	'Curse of the I-5 Corridor'	*Hell-On*
221	EJ	Courtney Barnett	'Need a Little Time'	*Tell Me How You Really Feel*
222	JR	Queen	'Fairy Feller's Masterstroke'	*Queen II*
		(In this episode John realised he'd never done Queen and went mad)	'Save Me'	*The Game*
			'My Melancholy Blues'	*News of the World*
			'I'm in Love with My Car'	*Live Killers*
			'These Are the Days of Our Lives'	*Innuendo*
			'Brighton Rock'	*Sheer Heart Attack*

Episode	Host	Artist/Band	Song	Album
223	EJ	David Holmes	'Sick City'	*Bow Down to the Exit Sign*
224	JR	Azalea City	'I'm Thick'	*Golden Hill*
225	EJ	Buzzcocks	'Everybody's Happy Nowadays'	*Singles Going Steady*
226	JR	Van Morrison	'Listen to the Lion'	*It's Too Late to Stop Now*

Birds Eye

Appendix v

Notes on Non-Dairy Milk

A word on the test: these were all carried out with Alpro-branded versions, save for the hemp milk, which was made by Good Hemp. Now, I'm aware there may be very different taste variations with different brands, and Alpro may not be the best,[351] but the entire range was on offer in Tesco, and combined with a £6quid-off, £40quid-shop offer, made this one of my great savings hauls.

The tea used was regular Sainsbury's own-brand Gold Fairtrade tea.[352] Though I usually go one bag Earl Grey, one bag normal, I went 'civilian' for the sake of the test.

Coffee was Lavazza made in a cafetière,[353] but I have now switched to a Fairtrade alternative.[354]

Are you a laugh?

Hot chocolate was Green & Blacks Organic Fairtrade hot chocolate powder, which, fun fact, is also dairy-free. I have, however,

---

351 Please don't contact me with a message beginning, 'Alpro is actually more damaging to the environment actually than the meat industry actually . . .' I will be far too busy serenading a cow to respond.

352 Remarkably hard-to-find branded Fairtrade tea. But then Fairtrade is probably somehow worse than normal these days. God, I don't know anymore.

353 Unstirred, obviously.

354 Own brand again! What is it with these companies?!

since perfected a hot chocolate preparation that does not feature below. It is three-quarters chocolate soya milk, one-quarter unsweetened almond milk, heated in a pan.

Soya milk does not feature in the test because I never liked it in tea and coffee. It tended to seperate and tasted of dust. However, flavoured soya products such as chocolate milk/vanilla mousse/pear and peach yoghurt are an absolute treat.

Almond and coconut

Hot chocolate: 7/10
Watery and very coconutty but a good chocolate taste. No body, though.

Tea: 9/10
Coconutty, but I didn't mind it! Wouldn't need sugar if you have it, might be too sweet for those who don't have sugar. Almost preferred it to milk!

Coffee: 8/10
Again, worked for me as a one-sugar guy, but might be too sweet for non-sugarists.

On its own: 8/10
Pleasant but very sweet, tastes like the milk from a bowl of Frosties!

Almond – unsweetened

Hot chocolate: 5/10
Very bitter, had to add a lot of sugar, tasted like dark chocolate.

Tea: 8/10
Really good, but probably cos I'm in charge of the sugar. Might suit 'straight-edge' non-sugarists.

Coffee: 8/10
Works well. I think the hint of almond may work slightly better with coffee than tea.

On its own: 6.5/10
It's creamy, but you really notice the lack of sweetness, has an almost plastic/salty aftertaste. But this would be hidden if used on sweet cereal.

Almond – sweetened

Hot chocolate: 8/10
Creamy and not too sweet, still missing a bit of body, but I could live with it.

Tea: 9/10
Country blimmin' mile, that's the one for me!

Coffee: 8.5/10
A good all-rounder this is turning out to be! But might not be suitable for people who don't have sugar in hot drinks. I'd say it's the equivalent of having ⅓ teaspoon of sugar.

On its own: 9/10
Very impressed.

Oat[355]

Tea: 6/10
Tastes OK but separates and looks like it's curdled, so not very appetising.

Coffee: 5/10
No no no no no. Still separating, reminds me of gone-off milk to look at.

Hot chocolate: 3/10
Awful, unuseable. Tastes zero of chocolate and massively of oats.

On its own: 6/10
Without curdling issues it's palatable, but no more.

Rice

Hot chocolate: 6.5/10
Very watery, just like hot chocolate made with water, but a decent chocolate flavour. Leaves no residue in the pan, so easy to clean!

Tea: 6.5/10
The watery nature here means the tea is very tannin-heavy. I think I'd rather have black.

Coffee: 7/10
Better than with tea, but then I'm a black coffee fan, so lack of creaminess less of an issue.

---

355 From speaking to others, apparently oat milk really comes into its own with porridge, which, alas, I do not eat.

On its own: 7.5/10
Milk-like and very refreshing, but a bit too sweet.

Hazelnut

Hot chocolate: 9/10
The best yet! Felt creamy and the hint of hazelnut really works with the chocolate.

Tea: 7/10
Good, but, again, our old friend the tannin is back. Made it taste too strong.

Coffee: 9/10
Excellent! Almost indistinguishable from milk.

On its own: 8/10
Creamy but not like milk. Very hazelnutty, so dependent on how you feel about that flavour. Quite luxurious, I would say.

Cashew

Hot chocolate: 8/10
Almost a little too creamy and the cashew taste is too high in the mix.

Tea: 9.5/10
Wowzers! Was not expecting this. Almost exactly the same as milk.

Coffee: 8/10
Not half bad! Just pipped by hazlenut, though.

On its own: 6.5/10

Good initial taste but the aftertaste is just raw cashews, which I'm really not a fan of.

Hemp[356]

Hot chocolate: 7.5/10

Decent initial taste, but the slightly plant-like aftertaste made the hot chocolate taste like cheap American chocolate. Somewhat plasticy but certainly drinkable.

Tea: 9.5/10

I was not expecting this late entry to score so highly! I think this is the closest to milk. You'd be hard pressed to tell the difference. And the best balance of sweetness to appeal to non-sugar-havers.

Coffee: 8/10

I think maybe my teaspoon of sugar hid the hemp flavour more than the hot chocolate did. Turned out not dissimilar tasting to the Pret Coconut Latte (which is very sweet, and delicious). Had a hint of Bailey's on the palate!

On its own: 7.5/10

Tricky this. It's refreshing and milk-like. Not too sweet and not too plant-like. It has a slight taste of UHT milk, but the aftertaste is of oats. Think boring muesli. Yes, it tastes like boring muesli with no added sugar or raisins.

---

356 Please rest assured, only for the good of animal welfare would I dabble with milk made from illegal drugs. Though I have been assured by three separate outlets that hemp and marijuana (street name 'waster weed') are not the same, I have my suspicions. As they say, the apple doesn't fall far from the tree, and in this case hemp is the tree, so one can only assume the marijuana apple (street name 'dope head's demise') cannot be far behind.

In conclusion

Were I to have all the alternatives to hand at any one time I would have hazelnut for hot chocolate, hemp/cashew for tea, hazelnut/sweetened almond milk for coffee and sweetened almond milk on its own. However, this is not practical space-wise. One great thing about all these alternatives is that they keep longer than milk. But a downside is it's hard to tell when they've gone off. Now that I make hot chocolate from three-quarters chocolate soy and one-third unsweetened almond milk, these are the only two I have in the fridge. I have coffee black and use the unsweetened almond milk in my tea (plus one sugar).

A word on the sugar: semi-skimmed milk has about 5g of sugar per 100ml. Sweetened almond milk has about 2.5g. So it's still much less. Unsweetened almond milk has 0g and is very, very low-calorie, if you're into that kind of thing. But it will make tea and coffee taste even less sweet than with just milk, so might be a bit bitter. If I were a non-sugar-adding enthusiast of all the above drinks, I would pick sweetened almond milk as my one all-rounder.

potato!

Acknowledgements

OK, acknowledgement time . . .

I'd like to start by thanking myself, John Robins . . .

Of course . . .

. . . for completing all my chapters in a timely and organised fashion. And Elis . . .

Here it comes . . .

. . . for putting up with me, a man who is genuinely hard work, for the last thirteen years.

Oh, that's sweet of you to say, don't mention it babe. I love you.

I'd also like to thank Ronnie O'Sullivan, Bonnie 'Prince' Billy, Neko Case . . .

Aren't acknowledgements meant to be personal, friends and family, etc.?

. . . Sherlock Holmes, Inspector Morse, Cracker . . .

Those people aren't *real* John, you need to thank *real people* . . .

OK then, 'Spike', 'Jacko' and all of the team from Police interceptors, Martin Lewis, HMRC . . .

You can't thank HMRC!

Just you watch me!

Right, before you thank Chiltern District Council . . .

Yer jokin', aren't ya?! With those potholes?!

To Isy, your support means the world to me. Thank you for being so relaxed about me working every weekend for four years, and thank you for buying me a house. *Caru ti, does neb tebyg. Ac i Beti fach annwyl – ti werth y byd i gyd. Ma pob dydd gyda ti yn wyrth.*

I mam a dad – diolch am fod y rhieni mwya cefnogol, cariadus ma fe'n bosib i ddychmygu. Gallen ni ddim ofyn am fwy.

I've whacked that into Google Translate and I have to say I'm very moved.

That's the vibe we're looking for.

Fair enough. To my family, Jane, John, Kate, Eleanor, Charlotte and Andy for their endless love, support and encouragement. And for instilling in me a respect for admin, deadlines especially, which, alas, Nesta and Eurfyl singularly failed to do.

There it is . . .

To 'The Lovely' Robin Allender, my best unbeaten brother.

And my darling Coco, for telling me off when I'm hard on myself, for crappucinos, surprise champagne and blue hairs in my washing that make me smile and keep me going.

See, John! It's so easy to be nice!

To everyone at Phil McIntyre management, our tireless agent Chris Lander, tour wunderkinds Ed Smith and Amy Clear. To Kate Watson, Luke Malloy, Lucy Ansbro, Adele Fowler and

Lindsay Jex. And to Phil McIntyre himself, who not only bank-rolled our early careers but provided stories of, anecdotes from, backstage passes to and meetings with, Queen, as in the actual band Queen.

To everyone at XFM and Radio X whose hard work, kindness and belief in us has made all this and so much else possible. Chris Baughen, Matt Deverson, Simon Fowler, Neil Fearne, Simon Williams, Sunta Templeton Jo Goode, Dan O'Connell, 'The Lovely' Pippa, Dan 'The Gasman' Gasser, Mike Walsh, Lea Stonhill, Steph May, Gordon Smart, Maz Tappuni, Chris Moyles, Johnny Vaughan, Christie Evans, Dan Riedo, Deacon Rose, Ferds, Jenny, Martin, Zoe, Abi, Carl and the rest of the online & video teams. To our interns past and present, for all the tea, editing, recording and time you gave: Travis Glossop, Anna Sharp, Emma Terry, Michael Dale, Tom Harrison, Laurence Hall, Rachel Jones, Josh Collins and Michael Lavin.

To the best support group two men could ask for: Josh Widdicombe, Ivo Graham, Nish Kumar, Matt Forde, Tom Craine, James Acaster, Lloyd Langford, Matthew Crosby and Ed Gamble.

And to all the friends of the show: Mike Bubbins, Sarah Millican, Scott Long, Ross Middleton, Lise Richardson, Jenny Greene, Moritz Ge and every single PCD. For all the pictures, memes, humblebrags, whack-aging, links, articles, PhD dedications, tastes, presents, tweets, texts and E-Mails. Your contributions, jokes, honesty, humour, obscure knowledge and niche interests keep us going.

To Claire Vickers, Mark Taylor for design and Photoshop wizardry. Ed and Aemen for lugging our ugly mugs around, literally.

To the team at Orion: Tom Noble, Elizabeth Allen, Marleigh Price, Paul Stark and our editor Anna Valentine . . . a woman who accepts that John and I have 'different approaches'. You are a dream to work with, and I'm sorry if I have shortened your life expectancy with worry. Interestingly, John feels more guilt than me, even though it was my fault. But thank you for being more 'arm round the shoulder' than 'Brian Glover in *Kes*' about it.

And finally, to our producers, Dave, Vin and Joe. You are such special people and we are honoured to work with you. Thank you for making us sound great, for your hard work, inestimable talent and unfailing support. It's all because of you.

ISA Calculator

To Do List

_____
_____
_____
_____
_____
_____
_____
_____
_____
_____
_____
_____
_____
_____
_____
_____
_____
_____
_____
_____
_____
_____

Top 10 Queen Deep Cuts

_____

_____

_____

_____

_____

_____

_____

_____

_____

_____

_____

_____

_____

_____

_____

_____

_____

_____

_____

_____

_____

_____

_____

Snow Cave Survival: 10 Item List

_____

_____

_____

_____

_____

_____

_____

_____

_____

_____

_____

_____

_____

_____

_____

_____

_____

_____

_____

_____

_____

_____

Dream Pub Specifications

If a teleporter by your front door opened on one pub, which would it be?

_____

Which five drinks would it contain?

_____

_____

_____

_____

_____

Sketches of Ronnie O'Sullivan

Email address ideas

 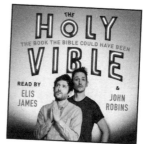

Birds Eye